2/06

Electric Dreams

Electric Dreams

Computers in American Culture

Ted Friedman

NEW YORK UNIVERSITY PRESS

New York and London

NEW YORK UNIVERSITY PRESS
New York and London
www.nyupress.org

Library of Congress Cataloging-in-Publication Data
Friedman, Ted.
Electric dreams : computers in American culture / by Ted Friedman.
p. cm.
Includes bibliographical references and index.
ISBN-13: 978-0-8147-2739-3 (cloth : alk. paper)
ISBN-10: 0-8147-2739-5 (cloth : alk. paper)
ISBN-13: 978-0-8147-2740-9 (pbk. : alk. paper)
ISBN-10: 0-8147-2740-9 (pbk. : alk. paper)
1. Computers and civilization. 2. Computers—Social aspects.
3. Computers—History. I. Title.
QA76.9.C66F745 2005
303.48'33—dc22 2005017512

New York University Press books are printed on acid-free paper,
and their binding materials are chosen for strength and durability.

Manufactured in the United States of America

c 10 9 8 7 6 5 4 3 2 1
p 10 9 8 7 6 5 4 3 2 1

To KT

Contents

Acknowledgments   ix

Introduction: The Dialectic of Technological Determinism   1

PART I **Mainframe Culture**

1   Charles Babbage and the Politics of Computer Memory   23

2   Ideologies of Information Processing:
     From Analog to Digital   35

3   Filming the "Electronic Brain"   47

PART II **The Personal Computer**

4   The Many Creators of the Personal Computer   81

5   Apple's *1984*   102

6   The Rise of the Simulation Game   121

PART III **The Interpersonal Computer**

7   Imagining Cyberspace   161

8   Dot-com Politics   171

9   Beyond Napster   186

10   Linux and Utopia   198

     Conclusion: Cybertopia Today   209

     Notes   221

     Bibliography   235

     Index   257

     About the Author   275

Acknowledgments

This book could not have been written without the guidance and intellectual example of the following people: Janice Radway, Jane Gaines, Lawrence Grossberg, Fredric Jameson, and Barbara Herrnstein Smith. Cathy Davidson, Joseba Gabilondo, and Michael Hardt were also generous with their advice and encouragement. Joan McNay, Sandy Mills, Sandy Swanson, and Pamala Terterian time and again went beyond the call of duty in the face of scheduling crises and paperwork pileups.

The Communication Department at Georgia State University provided the research funding that allowed me to finish this project. My friends and colleagues at GSU have been an inspiration. I've received great feedback from both departmental colloquia and lunchtime conversation. Thanks to Gayle Austin, Kay Beck, Jack Boozer, Michael Bruner, Allaine Cerwonka, David Cheshier, James Darsey, Yuki Fujioka, Mark Gallagher, Cindy Hoffner, Greg Lisby, Marian Meyers, Ray Miller, Jason Mittell, Merrill Morris, Mary Ann Romski, Sheldon Schiffer, Greg Smith, Sujatha Sosale, Mary Stuckey, Leonard Teel, Cal Thomas, Nik Vollmer, David Weberman, and Carol Winkler.

My students at Duke and GSU always taught me as much as I taught them. Special thanks to the subscribers of Tedlog, the listserv that's kept me in touch with so many, and to my graduate research assistants, Mark Cornwell, Heavenly Littleton, Bryce McNeil, Sumitra Srinivasan, Laszlo Strausz, and Keith Tims. Susan and Victor McFarlane-Alvarez contributed their formidable design savvy to the book's look. Elizabeth Strickler of the Digital Arts and Entertainment Lab provided much-needed technical support. Thanks also to the readers of Tedlog, first as a listserv, then a blog.

This work has also benefited in innumerable places from the feedback of Robert Allen, Lynn Appleton, Anders Carlsson, Pat Hemmis, Heather Hicks, Norman Holland, Henry Jenkins, Steven Jones, Henry Lowood,

Jean Mansfield, Midori McKeon, Janet Murray, Howard Segal, Jonathan Sterne, Jaakko Suominen, and Edward J. Valauskas.

Ellen Gartrell of the John W. Hartman Center for Advertising History at Duke University was invaluable, tracking down copies of old television commercials and print ads I'd been afraid I'd never gain access to. I would also like to thank the staffs of the Smithsonian Museum of American History's Division of Information Technology and Society and the Museum of Broadcasting in New York.

At NYU Press, I've been thrilled by the support of Eric Zinner and Emily Park. I'm especially appreciative of the two anonymous reviewers who pushed me to anchor this book historically while taking it all the way into the present and future.

Many friends have lent me their support and advice over the years of writing, including Renu Bora, Gavin Edwards, Wendy Greene, Maude Hines, Charles Lewis, Svetlana Mintcheva, Andrea Moed, Rob Sheffield, Gillian Silverman, Jay Smith, Viv Soni, Mark Sternman, and Ursula Swiney. I couldn't have made it through the last year without the Werewolves, who introduced me to the joy of *Kingdom of Loathing:* Nichole Arnault, Emily Noonan, Stephanie Paulk, Nate Steiner, Jere Recob Tesser, and Louis Tesser. My neighbors, the Horvieths, have shown me what family is all about—thanks Vicki, Richard, Jackie, Jordan, Joe, Jacob, and Joshua. Belinda Dowdy, James Dykes, Mike Greenberg, Frank Meaux, Linda Rayner, Darlene Swain, Shannon Van Wey, Ken West, and Samuel Yanuck helped keep me in one piece along the way. And eight wonderful pets reminded me to stop and smell the cat food: Moby, the Dude, Callie, Cheeto, Halley, Wilson Peanuthead Crybabyface, and two lost along the way, Minnlow, and Morannon.

My parents, Elaine and Joel Friedman, and my sister, Jennifer, have supported me ever since my first TRS-80. I can't wait to see what the world will look like to my niece, Sophie, as she grows up a child of the twenty-first century. Kate Lewis has been my rock through this whole process. I never could have gotten this far without her strength, wisdom, and love.

Finally, I'd like to thank the friends I've lost during this project: Renee Crist, Josephine Friedman, Irwin Greenbaum, and Brian Selsky.

Introduction
The Dialectic of Technological Determinism

Is Resistance Futile?

Why do we think what we think about computers? A computer is just a tool. Or, more specifically, a medium—a means of processing and communicating information. It lets us do so with incredible speed and efficiency, but in principle, the hardware is as open-ended as a blank piece of paper. Just as the tiny wood fibers of a sheet of paper can absorb ink into any pattern a user might create, the binary circuits of a computer can store any input.

But we rarely think of a computer as a "blank slate," and for good reasons. The writer beginning a manuscript with pencil and paper sees only the blank page, two-dimensional and practically weightless. As I sit here at my computer, on the other hand, the means of production making my intellectual work possible are almost overwhelming: a keyboard clacks at every stroke, a mouse sits off to the side, a heavy monitor takes up much of the desk, and the big, rectangular processor makes whirring, chugging noises (and on rare, unpleasant occasions, suddenly stops working altogether). My entire office is oriented around the demands of my computer: the keyboard sits on a pull-out shelf to be at the ergonomically correct height for my hands (I have carpal tunnel syndrome), the monitor is positioned to avoid glare from any window, and behind my desk, nests of wires snake from monitor to processor to printer to speakers to modem to phone line to power supply to . . .

Of course, the seeming transparency of the act of writing with pencil and paper hides its own complex social processes. The chair and desk had to be built, shipped, and bought. That thin strip of paper began long ago as a tree, before being whittled down, processed, packaged, and sold. As design historian Henry Petroski has shown, even our current pencil is the result of centuries of technological refinement.[1]

And I've only been talking about the physical technology. Even more significant is the rich cultural matrix in which any medium is embedded. Learning to use a computer may seem like a daunting task for many; but to use a pen and paper, you need to have learned how to read and write, a far more complex—and still far from universal—skill.

In short, it takes a lot of work to produce any "blank slate," and no two media get there the same way. The difference with computers is that the social processes creating that slate are still visible. Americans don't take computers for granted yet.

This difficulty with computers creates inequity—what's known as "the digital divide."[2] Some people can comfortably use computers, many others can't. Since this uneven distribution of technological expertise corresponds so closely to disparate levels of education, wealth, and social status, the importance of computers in contemporary life in many ways reinforces unequal social relations. Well-off kids from the suburbs grow up around computers; poor children are less likely to get that level of exposure. Boys are more likely than girls to be encouraged to explore computing.

But the fact that computers aren't taken for granted yet also offers an opportunity. Users of almost any communications technology are typically alienated from that technology in contemporary society. We read our books, watch TV, talk on the telephone, with very little awareness of how these processes work, or how they might function differently. Science studies theorists such as Bruno Latour, Wiebe Bijker, and Trevor Pinch refer to this as the "black box effect," through which the choices and conflicts that produce a technological object are hidden in a walled-off machine whose operations are simply taken for granted.[3] While most users are alienated from computers, too, the difference is that they *know* they're alienated. The very clunkiness of computers creates a level of self-consciousness about the computing process; there's no way to pretend it all simply happens "naturally."

Once the use of a technology becomes "natural," the battle to shape the uses and meanings of that technology is to a large degree finished. Specific systems of practices have become essentialized, so that historically contingent processes are now seen as inherent to the medium. Take the example of television. We all think we know what "television" is. But that's not what TV had to be. As scholars such as Raymond Williams and Ithiel de Sola Pool have demonstrated, TV could have been developed, marketed, and regulated as a two-way, open system, like the phone system, in which every viewer is also a broadcaster. Instead, of course, TV (at least in the United States) became a centralized, one-way form of communication.[4] I'd argue that the point at which the battle was lost was when the way that TV was structured—the contingent result of political and economic struggles—became reified into the common-sense notion that that's simply what TV "is."

This is not to say that the cultural meanings of every technology aren't continually being challenged, struggled over, and altered. Current political battles over the regulation of media ownership, for example, show how the meanings of television continue to be contested terrain.[5] But the early stages of flux, when meanings haven't yet stabilized, are the most critical moments in defining the shape of new technologies. These are the moments when strategic interventions have the greatest opportunity to effect real change, before the powerful inertia of naturalization sets in. This is the era we are still in with regards to the personal computer.

It is in the interests of many of the pundits of computer culture to presume that the ultimate meanings of computers are already settled. Preempting the moment when we will simply take those meanings for granted, they suggest the future is already inevitable. Their argument rests on the logic of technological determinism, which presumes that certain supposedly unstoppable technical capabilities of computers will necessarily determine their future use. Thus, MIT Media Lab chief Nicholas Negroponte, author of the surprise bestseller *Being Digital,* insists that the nature of computers as digital storage devices will determine how they are used in the future.[6] Likewise, one of the lab's corporate sponsors, AT&T, produced a series of now-famous *Blade Runner*-esque visions of the future in the mid-1990s—a globetrotting mother tucking her child in via a long-distance TV phone transmission, an executive sending a fax from the beach—all with the insistent tag line, "You will." Notice how even the futurists' favorite verb, "*will,*" so quickly slips from the *future* tense into the *command* tense.

But the future hasn't happened yet. We still aren't sure what we think of computers. It's all still up for grabs. And so the struggles over the way computers are used, regulated, and understood are crucially important.

The Utopian Sphere and the Dialectic
of Technological Determinism

Why are the struggles over the meanings of computers so important? Well, of course, because computers hold an important place in American culture today—to say nothing of the American economy. But beyond this, I believe the debates over computers are particularly significant because they are where we talk about the future. Debates over the meanings of computers are notoriously speculative. This has the disadvantage of encouraging ahistorical, ungrounded hype, but it's also part of what makes cyberculture so compelling and important. The debates over cyberculture take place in what I call the *utopian sphere:* the space in public discourse where, in a society that in so many ways has given up on imagining anything better than multinational capitalism, there's still room to dream of different kinds of futures.

Let me clarify "utopian sphere." My claim is not that cyberspace is a medium where one can transcend the bounds of race, gender, age, and so forth, and discover a kind of utopia on earth. (Although this is exactly what much internet hype still baldly proclaims.) As we shall see, cyberspace is much more grounded in the "real world," in all its inequities and injustices, than this fantasy would admit. Rather, the debate over the uses and meanings of computer technology is one of the few forums within the contemporary public sphere where idealized visions of the future can be elaborated without instant dismissal.

Here's an example: contemporary debates over unemployment. The range of acceptable discourse on this topic in the American public sphere—what Pierre Bourdieu calls "doxa"[7]—is depressingly narrow. Liberals argue for faster economic growth to create more jobs. Conservatives insist this isn't worth the risk of higher inflation. The imaginative scope of possible remedies is astonishingly thin: a decrease in the Federal Reserve interest rate, perhaps a modest government jobs program. What's beyond the scope of debate is the current structure of the economy as a whole. At a time when increases in productivity as the result of new technologies are making more and more workers unnecessary, should we scale back the 40-hour work week? Or perhaps, at a point when many people's labor is simply unwanted and unneeded, should we reconsider the "work ethic" altogether, and try to find other ways in which to define social worth? These ideas can be broached on the fringes of academic discourse,[8] but not in the talk shows, newspapers, and magazines of mainstream America.

However, there is one public space in which these possibilities can be explored: the discourse over future uses of new technologies. While the left has no room in the American public sphere to critique the merits of the 40-hour work week, writers who call themselves "futurists" *do* have an open space to suggest that, some day, many of our needs will be fulfilled by machines, and 40 hours (or more) of labor a week will be unnecessary. Couched in this science-fictional language, there's even room to suggest that capitalism itself might some day be rendered obsolete. In as ubiquitous a dream of the future as *Star Trek*, for example, the replicator, a machine that can produce a copy of any object, appears to have done away with the market. The economy instead seems to work under the principle "from each according to his ability, to each according to his needs."[9]

This form of futurism may seem hopelessly technologically determinist, less about the future we want than the future machines will give us. Capitalism may disappear in *Star Trek*, but only because of a deus ex machina: the replicator. But the presumption of technological determinism actually functions as a cover, authorizing a safe space in which to articulate utopian values. The public religion of technology can momentarily suspend the "pragmatist" doxa that derails utopian projects as impossible and utopian thinking as a foolish waste of time. It opens up a space—a utopian sphere—where we can imagine what we might want the future to look like.

Thus, technological determinism is double-edged. On the one hand, it is in many ways politically disabling because it denies human agency and proclaims specific changes to be inevitable. At the same time, however, the rhetoric of technological determinism is often what opens up room for utopian speculation. This dynamic is what I call *the dialectic of technological determinism*. Again and again in the pages that follow, we will see this tension in the cultural history of computing, as promises of a brighter future through technology both open up and shut down utopian thinking.[10]

My notion of a "utopian sphere" borrows from two strands of theoretical discourse: post-Marxist theorists' examination of the utopian dimensions of mass culture and Jürgen Habermas's conception of the "public sphere."[11]

The German critic Ernst Bloch pioneered the examination of the utopian elements of mass culture in *The Principle of Hope*. Arguing against a model of ideology as simply "false consciousness," Bloch argues that all ideology must contain the seeds of utopian desires—hints of a vision for a better world. Without this vision, it could not win the consent of its subjects. In contemporary capitalist culture, however, this utopian impulse is suppressed and diverted into consumerism, nationalism, and other oppressive ideological formations. This is the dynamic described by Fredric Jameson, influenced by Bloch, in his essay "Reification and Utopia in Mass Culture."[12] For Bloch, the goal of the critic is to bring this utopian longing to the surface, and explore its possibilities. As Douglas Kellner writes, "Critique of ideology, Bloch argues, is not merely unmasking (Entlarvung) or demystification, but is also uncovering and discovery: revelations of unrealized dreams, lost possibilities, abortive hopes—that can be resurrected and enlivened and realized in our current situation."[13]

One might argue that today, the once-radical-seeming gesture of searching for glimpses of utopia in late-capitalist mass culture has been repeated so often in the field of cultural studies that it is in danger of seeming little more than a meaningless cliché. If utopia is everywhere, why does it even matter where we look? This is the redundancy Meaghan Morris identified back in 1990 in her essay "Banality in Cultural Studies."[14] Part of the problem is that rarely do cultural studies critics distinguish the specific properties of the utopias they identify, beyond a vague hope of transcendence or a gesture towards radically egalitarian politics. But all utopias are not identical; different visions embody different values and different political priorities. The notion of a utopian sphere offers room to see utopia not as a fuzzily defined goal, but as a site of debate and conflict, out of which emerge different distinct visions of the future.

Granted, the utopian sphere does not operate the way Habermas's public sphere does.[15] Habermas's model of a public sphere rests on the idea of a civil dialogue conducted in broad daylight, in a transparent language where all questions can be clearly engaged and evaluated. The utopian sphere I'm trying to identify, by contrast, is a shadow sphere. At times, its ideas may be explicitly expressed, as in the manifestoes of the open-source movement described in chapter 9; more often, visions of the future are more vague and obscure, as in *Star Trek*'s fuzzy postcapitalist fantasy. The utopian sphere is at times a utopian unconscious, repressed and barely visible without the work of critical recovery.

My goal is to drag cyberculture's utopian sphere into the light of the public sphere—to draw out the hopes and fears implicit in computer culture's visions of the future, unravel the rhetoric of technological determinism, and evaluate underlying political ideals and assumptions. One purpose of this work, to be sure, is ideological demystification—to puncture hollow promises. But it is also a project of ideological *recuperation*—an attempt to draw ideas and inspiration from one of the few corners of late capitalist culture that hasn't lost the capacity to dream of different futures, and in so doing to rejuvenate a public sphere shriveled by neoliberal cynicism.

Fredric Jameson notes in *The Seeds of Time* that under late capitalism utopia is in some sense unrepresentable.[16] These days, he points out, it seems easier to imagine the end of the world than the end of capitalism. The utopian visions I discuss here are all inevitably partial, conflicted, and compromised. But they're as close as American culture gets to a utopian discourse; working through their promise and limitations can help us to get beyond them. As Henry Jenkins and David Thorburn write in the introduction to their collection *Democracy and New Media,*

> The utopian rhetoric predicting an imminent digital revolution is simplistic and often oblivious to complex historical processes. But its tenacious, diverse history is instructive and significant. For one thing, such pervasive talk about revolutionary change implies some fundamental dissatisfaction with the established order. Even if we believe that the concept of a digital revolution is empty rhetoric, we still must explain why a revolution, even a virtual one, has such appeal. A surprising range of thinkers on the right and the left have used the notion of "the computer revolution" to imagine forms of political change. Examining the rhetoric of digital revolution, we may identify a discourse about politics and culture that appears not only in academic writing or in explicitly ideological exchanges, but also in popular journalism and science fiction. This rhetoric has clear political effects, helping to shape attitudes toward emerging technologies. And even if such discourse is not an accurate measure of the impact of new media, it may nonetheless nourish serious discussion about core values and central institutions, allowing us to envision the possibility of change. Utopian visions help us to imagine a just society and to map strategies for achieving it.[17]

Much contemporary left discourse, as Meaghan Morris elsewhere points out, suffers from "insatiable critique," the knee-jerk impulse to deconstruct without offering any more constructive alternative.[18] The analysis of the utopian sphere suggests how the tools of cultural studies can do more than incessantly demystify (an increasingly superfluous project in an age of cynical reason)[19] or discover forms of "resistance" defined only by their negation of hegemony. They can help identify and cultivate the spaces out of which new movements may emerge.

What's So Special about Cyberculture?

By emphasizing discourse about computers as a utopian sphere, I don't mean to imply that other aspects of American culture don't contain glimpses of utopia. In fact, following Bloch and Jameson, I would argue that just about any mass cultural text must inherently have a utopian aspect, if it is to connect with the desires of its audience. This is why cultural studies' repeated discovery of the utopian (or, in a different framework, the resistant) in specific popular texts can start to feel so redundant. It's shooting fish in a barrel. There's *always* a utopian aspect to popular culture. Mass culture is often categorized as "escapism." This is usually meant as a dismissal, but it actually reveals the power of popular texts to transport audiences momentarily to a different, better world. That moment of escape is a utopian moment, even if the rest of the text circumscribes and undercuts the power of that glimpse of a better way of life.[20]

Cyberculture, then, is not different in kind, but in degree. It is a space with more room for the utopian: a discourse where visions of the future may be more explicitly elaborated, and where different visions of the future may come into conflict. I don't mean to presume that cyberculture is necessarily the only discourse where this kind of utopian thinking takes place. I hope, in fact, that this work will encourage other critics to trace other utopian spheres. But cyberculture, with its emphasis on the future, is a good place to start, and a fertile ground for new political visions.

Cyberculture follows in a long tradition of technological utopianism in American culture. Debunkers of cyberhype often draw this connection. James W. Carey and John J. Quirk in their essay "The Mythos of the Electronic Revolution" wryly trace a history of hollow promises and bad faith back to the development of electricity:

the rhetoric of the electronic revolution . . . attributes intrinsically benign and progressive properties to electricity and its applications. It also displays a faith that electricity will exorcise social disorder and environmental disruption, eliminate political conflict and personal alienation, and restore ecological balance and a communion of humans with nature.[21]

Carey and Quirk aren't wrong to demystify the ideology of technological progress. Indeed, much of this book does similar work.[22] But they don't tell the whole story. It's not surprising that utopians' promises often look foolish in retrospect—their dreams unfulfilled, their hopes exploited, their faith in technology misplaced. But against the inertia of everyday life, theirs are the voices that insist that history isn't yet over, that these are not the best of times, that the world can still be changed. The rhetoric of technological progress has galvanized the progressive movements of modern times, as the following examples demonstrate.

Edward Bellamy's hugely popular 1888 utopian novel *Looking Backward* helped set the agenda for Progressive Era reform. It was the second-best selling book of the nineteenth century in the United States, after *Uncle Tom's Cabin.*[23] Franklin Rosemont writes,

Well into the new century, up to the eve of the First World War, the great majority of those who brought something new and original to the cause of working-class emancipation in the United States [including Eugene Debs, Charlotte Perkins Gilman, Upton Sinclair, and many others] . . . were those whose first steps as radicals had been guided by what Elizabeth Cady Stanton called "Edward Bellamy's beautiful vision of the equal conditions of the human family in the year 2000."[24]

Likewise, the technological futurists of the 1920s and 1930s were not all simply technophilic apologists for capitalism. Andrew Ross's study of early-twentieth-century futurists delineates three groups—technocrats, socialists, and progressives—each of whom offered a critique of business as usual:

At a time when science and technology were becoming the primary rationales for capitalist growth, technocrats, socialists, and progressives each assumed, in a publicly visible way, that they were the historical heirs to a tradition of technological futurism—a tradition not at all adequately described by today's derogatory term "technophilia." For tech-nocrats, it was a tradition in which expertise, rationality, and knowledge challenged the arbitrary diktat of capital; for socialists, it was a tradition in which the technological forces of production undermined the existing social order even as they reinforced it; and for progressives, it was a tra-dition in which technology was the ally of democratization and the enemy of limited production for profit.[25]

Ross contrasts the "critical technocracy" of early science fiction with the dystopianism of the contemporary science fiction genre of cyberpunk. Cyberpunk largely follows the spirit of Carey and Quirk, relentlessly de-mystifying the "naïve" technophilia of its forebears. But Ross argues that this abandonment of utopia simply accedes positive visions of the future to corporate control:

> Cyberpunk literature, film, and television express all too well the current tendency to unhitch the wagon from the star, to disconnect technological development from any notion of a progressive future. In doing so, they leave the future open to those for whom that connection was and still is a very profitable state.[26]

Ross wrote this warning in 1991, before the dawn of the internet age. But it helps explain the corporate takeover of the cyberpunk vision through *Wired* magazine and dot-com hype, as we'll see in chapter 8.

Like much contemporary cybercultural studies, my own work has been greatly inspired by one particularly influential contemporary utopian vision: Donna Haraway's "Cyborg Manifesto." First published in *Socialist Review* in 1985, and subsequently anthologized in many col-lections and college coursepacks, Haraway's essay sounded a call for a new kind of socialist feminist analysis of technology and culture. Reject-ing the nostalgia and technophobia of much of the 1980s left, she called for a forward-thinking perspective that embraces the radical possibilities in the interface of human and machine. She concluded, famously, "I would rather be a cyborg than a goddess."[27]

The Circuit of Culture

Electric Dreams is a genealogy: an attempt to better understand the debates of the present by identifying the traces they carry of the past. I trace the struggles over the meaning of computers by examining key episodes in the cultural history of computers, slicing through a series of carefully chosen texts to reveal cross-sections of cultural conflicts and tensions.

To address what I hope to be a diverse readership, I have tried not to presume specialized knowledge. So, I'll spend some time explaining basic technical concepts in computing. Likewise, while my work concentrates on a series of key moments in the history of computing, I'll try to fill in the spaces in between, to give a sense of how these moments fit into a broader narrative.

I began my work on computer culture in the 1990s by writing about computer games, cyberpunk literature, and other contemporary topics. As I began to survey the state of cyberculture criticism, however, I found a frustrating lack of historical perspective. The thrill of speculating about the future made it easy to ignore the past. I decided I wanted to complement my contemporary critique with a more historical understanding of how computers have come to mean what they mean today. Inspired by works on the cultural history of technology such as David Nye's *Electrifying America* and Lynn Spigel's *Make Room for TV,* I decided to study not only contemporary computer culture, but also the social and cultural roots of computing.

I started my research by surveying a wide range of primary sources. I visited the Smithsonian Museum of American History's Division in Information Technology and Society, whose collections include owners' manuals for early PCs, user group newsletters, and an original Altair. At the Museum of Broadcasting in New York and the John W. Hartman Center for Advertising History at Duke University, I viewed archives of dozens of television commercials and hundreds of magazine ads for computers. I read every article about computers in *Time, Newsweek, Life, Consumer Reports,* and other general interest publications published between 1950 and 1985, as well as coverage of computers in alternative press publications such as *The Whole Earth Review* and *Rolling Stone.* I also studied the personal computing publications that emerged in the 1970s and 1980s, such as *Dr. Dobb's Journal, Byte, Creative Computing,* and *MacWorld.*

I've never been a conventional historian, however. My training is in literary and cultural studies. My goal has not been to craft a master narrative through a comprehensive assemblage of primary source materials, in the manner of such valuable historical works as Martin Campbell-Kelly's and William Aspray's *Computer* or Paul Ceruzzi's *A History of Modern Computing*. Rather, my method is to focus more closely on specific texts, to understand them in greater detail. The close examination of these texts, in turn, may reveal cultural tensions and ideological undercurrents invisible from the heights of a grand narrative.

In *Doing Cultural Studies: The Story of the Sony Walkman*, Paul du Gay outlines "the circuit of culture": the five interlinked processes through which every cultural text or object passes.[28] These processes include:

- **Production:** the economic and labor structures under which the object is created and manufactured.
- **Consumption:** the social context in which consumers purchase the product and integrate it into their lives.
- **Regulation:** the legal and political framework that shapes how the product is distributed and used.
- **Identity:** the ways the product contributes to the formation of subjectivities.
- **Representation:** the discourse through which ideas about and images of the object are expressed and debated.

All of these processes are continually cross-linked and intertwined in feedback loops. There can be no consumption without production. Consumer response, in turn, influences future production. Identity depends on the process of representation, which depends on both the production and consumption of signs. Regulation determines the institutional structures that constrain and define all the processes, while those processes may in turn reshape regulatory practices. Any work of cultural analysis must engage all these processes to understand the full context of its object of study.

Nonetheless, each work of cultural study must choose where to start—where on the circuit of culture to anchor its examination. Different areas of focus lead to different methodologies. Most histories of computers, including *Computer* and *A History of Modern Computing*, have concentrated on the **production** process, tracing the economic and technological

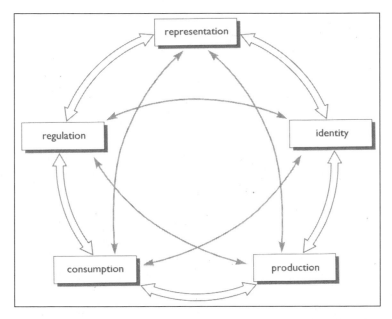

The circuit of culture. From Paul du Gay et al., *Doing Cultural Studies: The Story of the Sony Walkman* (Sage Publications, 1997).

development of the computer industry. Other works of cybercultural studies have focused on the **consumption** process, through ethnographic research (Nancy Baym's *Tune In, Log In*) or psychological study (Sherry Turkle's *Life on the Screen*). Works of legal analysis have examined the system of intellectual property that underlies the **regulatory** process (Laurence Lessig's *Code and Other Laws of Cyberspace;* Siva Vaidhyanathan's *Copyrights and Copywrongs*), while works by feminists (Sadie Plant's *Zeroes and Ones*) and critical race theorists (Lisa Nakamura's *Cybertypes*) have studied the role of computers in the formation of **identity.**

All of these perspectives are valuable, and inform my work greatly. The approach of this book, however, begins in an examination of the fifth process: **representation.** My method is rooted in the close analysis of a range of texts about computers, including books, films, magazine articles, television shows, advertisements, and software itself. The value of this approach is that it can show us details that other perspectives can miss. Individual texts bear the traces of their cultural contexts, in both their surface meanings and their suppressed subtexts. Many of the texts this book will examine will reveal themselves, under close examination, to be rich cross sections of conflicting visions of computing, repositories of American society's hopes and fears about new technologies.

The perspectives of all the other links in the circuit of culture will inform my study of representations of computers. In turn, this angle may provide new insight into all the processes along the circuit of culture. My discussion of the sexual politics of *Desk Set* and *2001: A Space Odyssey* in chapter 3, for example, can help us understand how representations of computers have influenced the construction of gender identity. Likewise, the discussion of the rhetoric of Moore's Law in chapter 4 can elucidate the assumptions and dynamics underlying the production of the personal computer. The analysis of the semiotics of computer games in chapter 6 opens up new ways to think about the experience of gaming for consumers of computer software. And the discussion of the discourse of Napster and Linux in chapters 9 and 10 can help us understand the possible implications of these software systems for the regulation of intellectual property.

Having decided to anchor my study in the analysis of a series of key texts, I have picked my texts carefully, selecting works that stand at crossroads in the cultural history of personal computers, at the emergence of new visions of computing and of the future. In particular, I have chosen texts that seem to have been critically influential in the subsequent cultural history of computers. Let me clarify *influential*. While all of these texts were significant interventions in computer discourse, I don't mean to imply that subsequent developments in the cultural history of computers were *caused* by these texts. This work isn't meant to be an antimaterialist intellectual history. Rather, I mean that these are texts that seemed to speak to large audiences, and whose traces can be seen in subsequent texts. *Why* these texts turned out to be "influential"—why the visions of computing in these texts continued to hold currency—is a more complicated historical question. While I have been anxious to critique the pitfalls of technological determinism, I can't offer as reassuringly coherent an alternative. Still, while insisting on the contingency of history, I have tried to point to some of the broader intersecting factors influencing the cultural history of computers by situating my discussion of these texts in the broader context of the entire circuit of culture.

I have also looked for texts of semiotic richness. Having concluded that almost all the texts I encountered in my research were characterized by tension and contradiction, I looked for paradigmatic texts, texts that best seemed to crystallize surrounding tensions and contradictions. One might think that my interest in semiotic complexity would be at odds with my desire to study texts that reach large audiences—the former pointing to "sophisticated" literary texts, the latter to "simple" popular ones. But, to the contrary, I have found the popular texts I've studied to be deeply complex artifacts. In fact, popular texts by their nature are invariably sites of internal tension and conflict. For one thing, popular media such as film, television, and computer games are collaborative media, demanding the input of multiple contributors with differing viewpoints. In addition, to appeal to a broad and heterogeneous audience, popular texts must be able to encompass diverging perspectives, while speaking to deeply held hopes and fears.

My definition of "text" stretches very widely in the chapters that follow, including novels, essays, films, television shows, advertisements, magazine articles, and computer programs. I have purposely chosen as broad a range of texts as I could, to attempt to capture the range of computer culture. Whatever kind of text I study, my goal remains much the same: to unravel the conflicted visions of the future in computer culture.

Structure

Electric Dreams is composed of three sections. Part I, "Mainframe Culture," examines ideas about computers from Charles Babbage's "invention" of the difference engine in the mid-nineteenth century through the 1960s, when computers were massive, institutionally owned machines run by cadres of trained specialists. Part II, "The Personal Computer," looks at the emergence in the 1970s and 1980s of the personal computer as a widely available consumer product. Part III, "The Interpersonal Computer," turns to the rise of the internet.

Part I, "Mainframe Culture," consists of three chapters. Chapter 1, "Charles Babbage and the Politics of Computer Memory," investigates the historical memory of cyberculture, tracing the contested legacy of Charles Babbage, the so-called "father of computing." Babbage's nineteenth-century inventions, the difference engine and the analytical engine, presaged many of the developments of modern computing. But his machines were considered failures in their day, and nobody followed in his footsteps. Many twentieth-century pioneers of computing were not even aware of Babbage's work. Babbage poses a challenge to cyberculture's reigning historical model of technological determinism, which presumes that if a machine *can* be built, it inevitably *will* be built, with inevitable social and political consequences. To engage contemporary debates over the memory of Babbage, the chapter examines several texts, including William Gibson and Bruce Sterling's *The Difference Engine,* a science fiction novel that explores the contingency of history by positing an alternate version of events in which Babbage was successful, ushering in a steam-driven Information Age in the midst of Victorian England.

Chapter 2, "Ideologies of Information Processing: From Analog to Digital," charts the transition from the "analog" machines of the 1930s, which used continuous measurement devices (akin to the slide rule) to solve complex equations, to the digital machines of the 1940s now widely thought of as the first true computers. These machines processed information as a series of discrete units represented in binary form as a series of 0s and 1s. I argue that underlying this transition rests a set of ideological assumptions in computing culture that value quantifiable, reified "precision" over the fuzziness of the natural world. The chapter then traces the legacy of this transition in contemporary cyberculture, contrasting the technophilic fetishization of digital media such as the compact disc with the nostalgic appeal of vinyl records, hip-hop turntable scratching, and other signifiers of the analog.

Chapter 3, "Filming the Electronic Brain," turns to popular film to chart the utopian hopes and dystopian fears inspired by the emerging computer industry in the 1950s and 1960s. It begins by looking at *Desk Set,* a 1957 Hepburn/Tracy comedy in which the introduction of a computer (then called an "electronic brain") into the research library of a television network provokes widespread job anxiety. While the film's narrative optimistically concludes that the computer will only be a boon to the librarians, this putative happy ending fails to successfully contain the undercurrent of anxiety provoked by the specter of deskilling and technological unemployment. By contrast, the 1968 film *2001* reverses text and subtext. While the narrative places the computer HAL in the role of the villain, the film's prediction of a future of sentient machines inspired a generation of computer science researchers who were undeterred by the narrative's technophobic warning. The chapter also examines the gender anxieties raised by this new, disembodied form of intelligence. *Desk Set* positions its computer as a romantic threat, while *2001* codes HAL as a threat to heteronormativity.

Part II, "The Personal Computer," turns to the rise of the PC as a commodity available for individual purchase. Chapter 4, "The Many Creators of the Personal Computer," examines the range of groups whose competing visions influenced the development of what we now know as the PC. It looks at the early failed attempts by hobbyists and computer manufacturers to introduce computers into the home, the rise of the "time-sharing" model among mainframe programmers, the development of a technotopian vision of the democratization of information by the People's Computer Company and other California-based organizations, the production of the microprocessor by semiconductor companies looking to expand their markets, the coining of the term "Moore's Law" to naturalize the industrial practice of planned obsolescence, and finally the emergence of the first PCs out of the subculture of electronics hobbyists.

Chapter 5, "Apple's *1984*," looks at how the PC moved from being an esoteric hobbyist's device to a fetishized, mass-produced commodity. It examines the approaches used to advertise computers by the early PC manufacturers, centering on a discussion of "1984," the blockbuster ad that introduced the Apple Macintosh. The enormously influential spot, directed by filmmaker Ridley Scott, ran nationally only once, during the 1984 Super Bowl, but remains one of the most well-remembered and influential television commercials ever produced. The commercial succeeded in popularizing the California technotopians' vision of the personal computer as a tool for the democratization of information. In the process, however, it denuded that vision of its broader political critique, replacing a community-based ideal of shared information processing with an individualist fantasy of empowerment through consumption. This new ideological formulation paved the way for the libertarian techno-hype that dominated cybercultural discourse through the 1990s.

Chapter 6, "The Rise of Simulation Games," looks at computer programs themselves as texts. It concentrates on the "simulation" genre of computer games that emerged in the late 1980s, including *SimCity* and *Sid Meier's Civilization*. Drawing on film theory, reader-response theory, and the work of Donna Haraway and Fredric Jameson, it examines how computer games blur the boundary between reader and text. It argues that much of the pleasure of computer games comes from the feedback loop generated by the constant interaction between user and machine, which creates a distinct form of "cyborg consciousness." It concludes that computer games offer a distinct opportunity to develop new aesthetic practices that may be more capable than older cultural forms at representing the complexity of late capitalist society.

Finally, Part III, "The Interpersonal Computer," turns to the rise of the internet. Chapter 7, "Imagining Cyberspace," looks at the diffusion and changing meanings of "cyberspace," a term coined by science fiction writer William Gibson. In Gibson's 1984 novel *Neuromancer*, the term has dual, linked meanings, encompassing what we would now call "the internet" *and* "virtual reality." In the late 1980s, as "VR" became a hot fad, the term "cyberspace" became a useful term to describe the simulated environment produced through the combination of 3D goggles, motion-sensitive gloves, and other associated technologies. When the internet emerged as a mass medium in the mid-1990s, however, the use of the term shifted to this new, less tangible terrain. The chapter suggests that VR was perhaps a transitional point in the development of our notion of the internet, offering a more accessibly embodied model of an information landscape. It warns, however, that the transition from VR to the internet involves a possible loss: whereas VR at least acknowledged a link between mind and body, the internet offers the fantasy of completely disembodied knowledge—and in the process, often occludes the still very real bodies of programmers, communication workers, and users who make the internet possible.

Chapter 8, "Dot-com Politics," examines the ideology of the dot-com boom by looking at *Wired*, Silicon Valley's magazine of record in the 1990s. *Wired*, it argues, came to prominence by forging a common ground between "hackers" interested in exploring the democratic potential of new information technologies, and communication executives hoping to exploit these new media for maximum profit. That common ground was technolibertarian utopianism—a smug faith that unchecked laissez-faire capitalism could both maximize personal liberty and solve social ills through economic and technological development. (The irony of this rhetoric was particularly rich, given the enormous role of government funding in the rise of the computer industry and the internet.) Both groups got something out of this exchange: hackers won access to finance capital, while industrialists gained access to the subcultural capital that made cyberculture hip and marketable. The evasions of this ideological fantasy, however, eventually came home to roost, as the dot-com crash widely exposed its inadequacy and hypocrisy.

Chapter 9, "Napster and Beyond," turns from the computer industry to the music industry, to examine some of the broader consequences of the digitization of culture. It examines the rise and fall of the Napster on-line music service, which allowed millions of users to share digitally recorded songs over the internet. The crisis provoked by Napster, it argues, opened up the music industry as a utopian sphere, a space in which to experiment with new models of the relationship between culture and commerce. The chapter looks at four paradigms: first, the current, waning CD-oriented model, which conceives of music as tangible physical commodity; second, the pay-per-download model followed by online services such as iTunes and the new Napster, which conceives of music as an intangible bundle of rights; third, the subscription model of the competing online service Rhapsody, which conceives of music as a utility; and fourth, the file-sharing model of the original Napster and its descendants, which conceives of music as folk culture.

While the dot-com boom offered a technotopian vision based on a narrowly self-interested understanding of economic and technological development, Chapter 10, "Linux and Utopia," looks at the alternate cybertopian vision offered by proponents of "open source" software such as the Linux operating system. Such software, often called "freeware," is licensed in a way that allows any user to freely copy, distribute, and/or modify the software. Linux software is developed collaboratively, among a large group of volunteer programmers around the world, communicating via the internet. It has emerged as a viable alternative to Microsoft Windows and the Apple OS, particularly in developing countries. Linux takes the hacker ideal of the free flow of information and pushes it to its logical conclusion, offering a critique of the regime of copyright. The chapter looks at the debates within the Linux community between idealists who see Linux as a model for a new vision of intellectual property and economic relations, and accommodationists interested in incorporating Linux into the conventional framework of capitalism.

Finally, the conclusion, "Cybertopia Today," will look at several current cybertopian visions, including alternate fuel systems, blogging, and smart mobs.

PART I

Mainframe Culture

1

Charles Babbage and the Politics of Computer Memory

As we have seen, the dialectic of technological determination is both enabling and disempowering. It clears space to imagine wild visions of the future. But it closes off our ability to question our present options, since the future is presumed to be the inevitable result of inexorable technological progress. And it impoverishes our understanding of the past, robbing it of any sense of contingency. What happened had to happen, since it did happen.

This bargain has been good enough for technotopians from Edward Bellamy to Isaac Asimov (author of the *Foundation* series, which introduced the fictional predictive science of "psychohistory") to Gene Rodenberry (creator of *Star Trek*) to Louis Rosetto (founder of *Wired* magazine). But for some thinkers, the trade-off isn't worth it. Looking more closely at the history of computing, these skeptics notice the odd turns and dead ends that give the lie to the grand narrative of technological determinism.

This chapter will look at the struggle between the determinist mainstream and the critical margins to define the historical memory of computing. It will focus on the contested legacy of the so-called "father of computing," Charles Babbage. Before we get to Babbage, though, we'll need a little background. Let's start with a question: what is a "computer"?

The answer depends on how you define "computer." The term was originally used to label not machines, but people. For most of the past three centuries, a computer meant "one who computes," according to the *Oxford English Dictionary*, which traces this usage as far back at 1646.[1] Scientists engaged in large-scale projects involving many calculations, such as the computation of navigation tables, would hire rooms full of human "computers"—usually women—to crunch their numbers.[2] It was not until the 1940s, when new kinds of flexible calculating machines began to replace people for these large-scale projects, that the connotations of the word began to shift, as engineers labeled their new devices "computers." Even so, through the 1940s and 1950s, popular discourse more often referred to the machines as "giant brains," "electronic brains," or "mechanical brains." It wasn't until the 1960s that "computer" became standard usage. While a term such as "giant brains" may strike us today as a rather garish anthropomorphism, note that the seemingly more neutral term "computer" itself has its origins in anthropomorphism.

One version of the history of computing, then, is the story of computing as a process for the large-scale production and organization of information—a process performed sometimes by people, sometimes by machines. A second, more familiar version is the story of the computer as a mechanical calculating device. This chronology takes us from the abacus and other counting devices of the ancient world to the mechanical adding machines first developed in the seventeenth century, which used gears and levers to perform arithmetic. These two strands of computing history—computer as large-scale information processor, and computer as mechanical device—first came together in the work of a nineteenth-century British inventor named Charles Babbage.

Babbage's Engines

Babbage began his first project, the "difference engine," in the 1820s. A massive, steam-powered calculating machine and printer, it was designed to mechanize the process of computation and table-making, just as other inventions of the Industrial Revolution were mechanizing other labor processes. The British government invested a total of 17,000 pounds in his research; Babbage is estimated to have spent an equal amount of his own money. In 1833 Babbage produced a small-scale prototype that clearly demonstrated that the completed machine could work. But before Babbage could finish his machine, he was distracted by a new, more complex project. He never completed his difference engine.

Babbage's new idea was an "analytical engine." Rather than being hard wired to perform specific tasks, it was designed to be "a machine of the most general nature." Inspired by the Jacquard loom, Babbage came up with the idea of using a series of punched cards to input information into his machine. The cards would contain not only the raw numbers to be processed, but also logically coded instructions on how to process them. Input numbers could be held in the "store," a series of 1000 registers, each capable of storing one 50-digit number. Calculations of input numbers, or numbers taken from the store, would be performed by the "mill." The results would be displayed by the "output," an automated typesetter.

To contemporary computer users, Babbage's design sounds strikingly familiar. One can see in the punch-card "instructions" the equivalent of a contemporary computer program, in the "store" an analogue to computer memory, and in the "mill" a parallel to a central processing unit. It's worth being careful, however, in taking these parallels too far. As one historian of computing warns,

> at first sight Babbage's ideas are close to ours and one can almost imagine that he had invented the modern computer. However, it is too easy to read into his writings a modern interpretation. We assume that his thought ran along the same lines as ours would if we were faced with similar problems. In fact, it may have been running along quite different lines, lines that are hard for us to follow because we know the modern solutions.[3]

Similarly, R. Anthony Hyman explains,

> discussions of the Analytical Engines pose semantic problems because of the many features they have in common with modern computers. These abstract features of logical organization are almost impossible to discuss without using concepts which have been developed in modern computing. Such concepts as the stored program, programming, or array processing carry many implications to a modern computer person which may or may not in some measure have been clear to Babbage.[4]

Babbage worked on his Analytical Engine from 1834 to his death in 1871, but never completed the machine. He died a bitter, unappreciated man.

Babbage is a problematic figure in the historical memory of computing culture. He's been dubbed the "father of computing," or sometimes "the grandfather of computing." Today the largest computer museum in the United States is titled the Charles Babbage Institute, and a national software chain calls itself Babbage's. In England he's hailed as one of the country's great inventors. The bicentennial of his 1791 birth was celebrated with museum exhibitions, commemorative postage stamps, and, as we shall see, a successful attempt to build a working difference engine.[5] In a sense, Babbage invented the computer, since he developed a set of ideas that would ultimately see fruition in the twentieth century as what we now know as the computer.

But Babbage never successfully built his own machines, and no inventors followed in his footsteps. In fact, his work, now so widely hailed, was rediscovered too late to influence the development of the computer in the twentieth century. His writing was still obscure when the first digital computers were built in the 1940s. Most pioneers of the era, such as J. Presper Eckert and William Mauchly, have confirmed that they'd never heard of Babbage when they worked on ENIAC and UNIVAC, the machines widely considered to be the first true computers.[6]

Harvard's Howard Aiken, who developed another early computer, the Mach IV, was one of the few scientists of the time who did know something of Babbage's work. As a result, whiggish historians of technology have been quick to detect a direct lineage. The introduction to one collection on computing in 1953 claimed, "Babbage's ideas have only been properly appreciated in the last ten years, but we now realize that he understood clearly all the fundamental principles which are embodied in modern digital computers."[7] More recent scholarship, however, has complicated this story. I. Bernard Cohen's detailed study of the relationship between the work of Babbage and Aiken concludes that "Babbage did not play any seminal role in the development of Aiken's own ideas about machine architecture."[8] In fact, the Mark I "suffered a severe limitation which might have been avoided if Aiken had actually known Babbage's work more thoroughly."[9] As Stan Augarten concludes,

> Unlike most of the early computer pioneers, Aiken had heard of Babbage, and his proposal contained a brief, if rather inaccurate, summary of the Englishman's work. Aiken saw himself as Babbage's spiritual heir, yet his machines, the Automatic Sequence-Controlled Calculator (ASCC), or Harvard Mark I, had little in common with the Analytical Engine.[10]

So the figure of Babbage raises nagging questions for the technological determinism that operates as computer culture's common-sense theory of history. The logic of technological determinism presumes that if a technology can be developed, inevitably it will be—there's no sense in pausing to weigh a technology's promised benefits against its possible consequences, because technological momentum will keep pushing history forward, regardless. Raymond Williams identifies this perspective in *Television: Technology and Cultural Form:*

> [T]echnological determinism . . . is an immensely powerful and now largely orthodox view of the nature of social change. New technologies are discovered, by an essentially internal process of research and development, which "created the modern word." The effects of these technologies, whether direct or indirect, foreseen or unforeseen, are as it were the rest of history. The steam engine, the automobile, television, the atomic bomb, have *made* modern man and the modern condition.[11]

Technological determinism is a kind of essentialism, likening technological development to an unstoppable natural force. Cyber-pundit John Perry Barlow writes in his influential "Declaration of Independence for Cyberspace," "Cyberspace . . . is an act of nature and it grows itself through our collective actions."[12] Likewise, Nicholas Negroponte warns in *Being Digital,* "like a force of nature, the digital age cannot be denied or stopped."[13] But if technology is an unstoppable force, why didn't Babbage successfully build the first computer? Why did it take another century for Babbage's ideas to be realized? What happened to that force of nature for 100 years?

The technological determinist response is the converse of the assumption that "if it can be built, it will be built": "if it wasn't built, it must be because it couldn't have been built." For decades, writers looking back on Babbage's work concluded that while Babbage's engineering plans may have been sound, the Britain of his day just didn't have the technical capability to bring his design to fruition. In that era, the argument goes, rods, gears, and bearings couldn't be made to the precise specifications Babbage's design demanded. And so, Babbage's machines were doomed to failure: they simply couldn't be built with the existing technology.[14]

But more recent work has called this argument into question. In 1991 a team of historians succeeded in constructing a working difference engine from Babbage's designs, using parts no more precisely tooled than those available to Babbage.[15] As the project's leader, Doron Swade, puts it,

> In every history book which cites the reason Babbage failed, they say it was due to limitations in the technology of the time. . . . Our findings will oblige historians to look at more subtle reasons for the failure of the project, like the way governments are advised and the relationship between applied and pure science.[16]

Swade's *The Difference Engine* examines these subtle reasons, tracing Babbage's struggles with expensive machinists, skeptical government officials, and a conservative scientific establishment.

Charles Babbage, Icon of Contingency

Babbage's story, then, is a prime example of the contingency of history. Under slightly different circumstances, his invention could very well have been realized. As a result, for contemporary critics of the rhetoric of technological determinism, Babbage is a charged and compelling historical figure. When technological determinists point to examples such as the failures of Britain's Luddites to argue, "you can't stop history," critics of technological determinism can point to Babbage to demonstrate, "history doesn't always turn out the way you expected it to."

This critique is most fully elaborated in a science fiction genre known as "steampunk." A play on the label "cyberpunk," steampunk is a similarly revisionist science fiction genre. The difference is that is it set not in the future, but in the Steam Age. Steampunk imagines an alternate nineteenth century in which the Industrial Revolution and the Information Age happened simultaneously. The most influential steampunk novel is 1991's *The Difference Engine,* cowritten by William Gibson and Bruce Sterling, two of cyberpunk's most prominent novelists.

The Difference Engine proposes an alternate history in which Babbage succeeds in building both his difference engine and analytic engine. The result is a steam-powered Information Age, in which nineteenth-century "clackers" work on massive steam-driven computing machines. The effect of juxtaposing these two eras of technological change is to put each in relief, satirizing contemporary culture by garbing it in nineteenth century gear while forcing the reader to rethink clichés about the past by investing it with the urgency of the present. And by positing an alternative history in which Babbage did succeed, Gibson and Sterling force us to think of our own era as only one of many possible outcomes of history—and perhaps not the optimal one at that. As Gibson put it in one interview, "One of the things that *Difference Engine* does is to disagree rather violently with the Whig concept of history, which is that history is a process that leads to us, the crown of creation. . . . [I]t's about contingency leading to us."[17] Likewise, literary critic Herbert Sussman writes,

> The primary rhetorical effect of alternative history lies in the shock of defamiliarization. As much as contemporary theory has quite properly emphasized that we employ our own political agendas to organize the past, most readers . . . tend to naturalize past events, assuming that since events did happen they somehow had to happen, that social change and, given the emphasis of this novel, technological change are determined. One major effect of alternate history is to dramatize that what we accept as inevitable is only contingent, only one among an infinite number of possibilities, of forking paths.[18]

But if Gibson and Sterling successfully debunk technological determinism on one level, in another sense they nonetheless seem to succumb to it, demonstrating the tenacity of the logic of technological determinism. For, having granted Babbage the success of his difference engine, they proceed to extrapolate a nineteenth century vastly transformed by his invention in ways very comparable to the twentieth century's Information Age. In other words, while Gibson and Sterling critique the assumption that technological development follows only one invariable path, they nonetheless presume that once an invention is introduced, it will have inevitable social consequences—different in the nineteenth century because of the surrounding technological context (steam rather than silicon) but parallel and commensurate in effect.

As an alternative, imagine another scenario: Babbage builds his machines—but it doesn't matter much. Perhaps a few are reproduced, but they never catch on. And so Babbage dies, less broke and bitter, but just as obscure and unappreciated. Actually, this is pretty close to what did happen to the difference engine. Two Swedish inventors, the father and son team of Georg and Edvard Scheutz, managed to build a scaled-down version of a difference engine (with Babbage's encouragement) in 1854.

They sold it to an observatory in Albany, New York, where it was rarely used. A few other copies were made, including one for the British Register General, who used it to calculate actuarial tables for several years. In one of the earliest examples of "the productivity paradox" (discussed further in chapter 3), the investment in computer technology turned out to have a minimal payoff. The extra attention demanded by the delicate machine ate into the savings it offered over human "computers."[19] The Scheutzes failed to inspire a rash of orders, or imitators.

There just wasn't much of a market for the machine. Masses of human "computers" were already proving adequate to the production of tables. Other forms of organizational innovation seemed more pressing to businesses than the automation of information processing. As thrilling as the invention seemed to its inventors, the dream of a "mechanized brain" just didn't prove compelling to potential purchasers in the mid-1800s. As George Biddell Airy, the British Astronomer Royal, put it, "I believe the demand for such machines has arisen on the side, not of computers [meaning those who compute], but of mechanists."[20] In an 1857 report on the prospective usefulness of the Scheutzes' engines, Airy wrote, "In the Royal Observatory, the Machine would be entirely useless. . . . During the twenty-two years in which I have been connected with the Royal Observatory, not a single instance has occurred in which there was a need of such calculations."[21]

This perspective on Babbage's story—that Babbage produced a supply, but there was no reciprocating demand—suggests a theory of history even more at odds with technological determinism than steampunk's critique. Rather than granting technological momentum ultimate shaping power, it places technology in a broader social context, in which the diffusion (and ultimate social consequences) of a technology depends not merely on production, but also on consumption. Only when the development of a new technology is matched by consumer interest can the technology thrive; these two sides meet at what historian of technology Ruth Schwartz Cowan has called "the consumption junction, the place and the time at which the consumer makes choices between competing technologies."[22]

The history of technology is a story that must be told from both the top down (technological development) and the bottom up (consumer response), if we are to account for why some products prosper while others never catch on. The top-down historiography of technological determinism cannot explain Babbage's disappointments. And so the figure of

Charles Babbage continues to haunt computing culture, and to loom over the rhetoric of inevitability that comes so easily to today's cyber-pundits.

Ada Lovelace, "Enchantress of Numbers"

A parallel subject of historiographical struggle to Charles Babbage is Ada Lovelace, who collaborated with Babbage during the development of the analytic engine in the 1840s. Lovelace is sometimes described as the first computer programmer, although the degree of her input into Babbage's work is subject to debate among computer historians. In 1843 Lovelace published "Sketches of the Analytic Engine" in the British journal *Scientific Digests*. The work was a translation and expansion of an article written in French on the workings of Babbage's machine. Babbage biographer Dorian Swade describes the essay as "the most substantial account of the Analytic Engine published in English in Babbage's lifetime."[23]

Like Babbage's, Lovelace's story is one of thwarted hopes. "Sketches of the Analytic Engine" was her only scientific publication (although voluminous correspondence survives). Labeled a hysteric, she suffered a series of physical and mental ailments, leading to dependence on opium. Only in 1851 was the source of her pain, cervical cancer, diagnosed. She died a year later at age 36.

For many cyberfeminists, Lovelace is pioneering hero. As Sadie Plant, author of *Zeroes and Ones: Digital Women and the New Technoculture*, explains,

> Like everybody else, I had bought the story that computing had emerged from the worst, most obvious kinds of masculine desire and patriarchal organizations. When I found that a Victorian teenage girl (Ada Lovelace) had effectively invented the first computer, or certainly written the first computer software, it was obviously an amazing discovery. It immediately seemed to me that this fact in itself completely changed the whole picture.[24]

Plant's book places Lovelace at the center of what could be called a "herstory" of computing. Plant writes,

> [A]s it turns out, women have not merely had a minor part to play in the emergence of the digital machines. When computers were vast systems

of transistors and valves which needed to be coaxed into action, it was women who turned them on. They have not made some trifling contribution to an otherwise man-made tale: when computers became the miniaturized circuits of silicon chips, it was women who assembled them. Theirs is not a subsidiary role which needs to be rescued for posterity, a small supplement whose inclusion would set the existing records straight: when computers were virtually real machines, women wrote the software on which they ran. And when *computer* was a term applied to flesh and blood workers, the bodies which composed them were female. Hardware, software, wetware—before their beginnings and beyond their ends, women have been the simulators, assemblers, and programmers of the digital machines.[25]

For other computer historians, however, the Lovelace story is more myth than fact. Babbage biographer Bruce Collier writes,

> There is one subject ancillary to Babbage on which far too much has been written, and that is the contributions of Ada Lovelace. It would be only a slight exaggeration to say that Babbage wrote the "Notes" to Menabrea's paper, but for reasons of his own encouraged the illusion in the minds of Ada and the public that they were authored by her. It is no exaggeration to say that she was a manic depressive with the most amazing delusions about her own talents, and a rather shallow understanding of both Charles Babbage and the Analytical Engine. . . . I will retain an open mind on whether Ada was crazy because of her substance abuse . . . or despite it. I hope nobody feels compelled to write another book on the subject. But then, I guess someone has to be the most overrated figure in the history of the computer.[26]

Collier's venom is striking. What Collier so stridently ignores in dismissing Lovelace as the madwoman in the attic of computer history is that Lovelace holds significance to feminists not only for what she accomplished, but also for what she could not accomplish. Her life stands as a test case for the limits of women's opportunities to contribute to science in nineteenth-century England. Unable to pursue a traditional scientific education, Lovelace secured tutoring by Babbage and others in mathematics and engineering. (That she was able to carve out any scientific space for herself at all was undoubtedly due to the leverage afforded by her privileged class status—she was the daughter of Lord Byron.) Chafing against the limitations of Victorian society and suffering from a misdiagnosed "woman's ailment," she was labeled a hysteric. Her doctors pressured her to give up her scientific endeavors, blaming intellectual overexertion for her illness. Her one scientific publication was signed only in her initials, A. A. L., since it was considered inappropriate for a woman to be published in a scientific journal.

Whether or not Ada Lovelace was the first computer programmer, however we choose to define that term, she can certainly be seen as the "Shakespeare's Sister" of computing. Virginia Woolf in *A Room of One's Own* speculates on what would become of a female version of Shakespeare—equally talented, but struggling against the limitations of opportunity placed on women of her era, in which women were banned from higher education and the professional world.[27] Likewise, Ada Lovelace was a woman whose creative potential was squashed by patriarchal institutions.

This theme is explored in *The Difference Engine*, in which the success of Babbage's machine makes Lovelace a powerful woman. It's also the subject of the 1999 science fiction film *Conceiving Ada*, which contrasts the patriarchy of the nineteenth century with the more subtle forms of contemporary sexism. A female computer scientist discovers a way to "hack time," and is able to observe through her computer Lovelace's struggles with sexist scientific authority. Ultimately, she creates a "cyber-genetic clone" of Lovelace, finally bringing a woman who was ahead of her time into the computer age.

The Control Revolution

If Babbage the inventor was a failure, there is another sense in which Babbage the innovator was a raging success. In 1832 Babbage published *On the Economy of Machinery and Manufactures*, one of the most influential works of political economy of the nineteenth century.[28] In this study, Babbage laid out many of the concepts that would, 50 years later, become established as the principles of "scientific management" in the work of Frederick Taylor. Babbage was a pioneer in applying the principles of capitalist factory organization to knowledge work. In the chapter "On the Division of Mental Labor," Babbage writes, "We have already mentioned what may, perhaps, appear paradoxical to some of our readers—that the division of labor can be applied with equal success to mental as to mechanical operations, and that it ensures in both the same economy of time."[29] As communication theorist Nick Dyer-Witherford writes in *Cyber-Marx*, "Babbage's search for mechanical means to automate labor, both manual and mental, was the logical extension of the desire to reduce and eventually eliminate from production a human factor whose presence could appear to the new industrialists only as a source of constant indiscipline, error, and menace."[30]

While Babbage failed to produce a *mechanical system* to organize the production of knowledge, he helped lay the groundwork for the *bureaucratic* system that would organize *human* computers in response to the managerial challenges of the Industrial Revolution: the modern corporation. James Beniger in his masterful study of the historical roots of the information society, *The Control Revolution,* describes the creation of modern corporate bureaucratic structure as a kind of programming: the invention of structures and algorithms to process immense amounts of data. He writes of

> a crisis of control in office technology and bureaucracy in the 1880s, as the growing scope, complexity, and speed of information processing—including inventory, billing, and sales analysis—began to strain the manual handling systems of large business enterprises. This crisis had begun to ease by the 1890s, owing to innovations not only in the processor itself (formal bureaucratic structure) but also in its information creation or gathering (inputs), in its recording or storage (memory), in its formal rules and procedures (programming), and in its processing and communication (both internal and as outputs to its environment).[31]

Beniger describes the early-twentieth-century General Electric Company's "centralized, functionally departmentalized organizational structure" as a "new information processor, built of the collective cognitive power of hundreds of individual beings."[32]

In the beginning of this chapter, we looked at two versions of the history of the computer. One is the story of the computer as a mechanical calculating device. The other is the story of computing as a process for the large-scale production and organization of information. By the lights of the first version, Babbage was certainly a failure. In another sense, though, for better or worse, he was building computers all along.

2

Ideologies of
Information Processing
From Analog to Digital

So far, I haven't discussed how a computer processes information in much detail. In this chapter, I want to turn to this more technical subject, to look at the ideological conflicts underlying a critical transformation in information processing: the shift from analog to digital, which began in the 1940s and 1950s, and which continues to this day.

Instead of the proliferation of Babbage's digital computing devices, the nineteenth century saw the slow development of more limited calculating machines. The cash register was invented in 1879; by the turn of the century, it was used by most store owners in the United States.[1] In 1890 the U.S. Census Bureau hired Herman Hollerith to design a machine capable of collating demographic information about millions of people. Hollerith designed a system in which each person's demographic information was stored on an individual punch card. His successful company would ultimately change its name to International Business Machines, or IBM for short.

By the 1920s and 1930s, scientists were designing more sophisticated machines to handle more complex mathematical questions. The most famous of these was the differential analyzer, built by Vannevar Bush and his students at MIT in the 1930s. While many machines of this era were developed to calculate only specific equations, the differential analyzer was designed to be a more flexible machine. As Campbell-Kelly and Aspray write, it could address "not just a specific engineering problem but a whole class of engineering problems that could be specified in terms of ordinary differential equations."[2]

Machines such as the differential analyzer were in many ways what we would now call "computers." But most histories of computing pass quickly over these devices, treating them as a wrong turn in the development of computing technology.[3] That's because, unlike Babbage's devices, these were *analog* machines. Not until the era of World War II were the first *digital* computing devices successfully built. The transition from analog to digital after World War II (or, to put it another way, the return to Babbage's digital conception of computing) was a critical point in the history of computing, and the distinction between analog and digital continues to be a crucial—and ideologically loaded—concept in contemporary computing culture.

Analog and Digital

Let's start by clarifying the two terms. This useful distinction comes from Stan Augarten's *Bit by Bit:*

> [D]igital and analog . . . describe different methods of counting or measuring various phenomena, and the distinction between them is best illustrated by two gadgets that are found in almost every car: a speedometer and an odometer. As a recorder of miles traveled, an odometer is a digital device, which means that it counts discrete entities; as a measurer of miles per hour, a speedometer is an analog device, because it keeps track of velocity. When we count things, regardless of what those things may be, we are performing a digital operation—in other words, using numbers that bear a one-to-one correspondence to whatever it is we're enumerating. Any device that counts discrete items is a digital one. By contrast, when we measure things, whether to find their weight, speed, height, or temperature, we are making an analogy between two quantities. Any gadget that does this is an analog one. Scales, rules, speedometers, thermometers, slide rules, and conventional timepieces (the kind with hands) are all analog instruments, whereas odometers, . . . mechanical calculators, and the overwhelming majority of electronic computers are digital devices.[4]

Digital computers process information through mathematical calculations, following set, clearly defined rules (called "algorithms"), just as humans do when calculating with pencil and paper. The way in which analog computers process information is more difficult to explain. Here's Herman H. Goldstine's *The Computer from Pascal to von Neumann:*

[A]nalog machines depend upon the representation of numbers as physical quantities such as length of rods, direct current voltages, etc. . . . The designer of an analog device decides which operations he wishes to perform and then seeks a physical apparatus whose laws of operation are *analogous* to those he wishes to carry out. He next builds the apparatus and solves his problem by *measuring* the physical, and hence continuous, qualities involved in the apparatus. A good example of an analog device is the slide rule. As is well-known, the slide rule consists of two sticks graduated according to the logarithms of the numbers, and permitted to slide relative to each other. Numbers are represented as lengths of the sticks and the physical operation that can be performed is the addition of two lengths. But it is well-known that the logarithm of a product of two numbers is the sum of the logarithms of the numbers. Thus the slide rule by forming the sum of two lengths can be used to perform multiplications and certain related operations.[5]

Larry Owen explains how the differential analyzer operated:

The . . . machine consisted of a long table-like framework crisscrossed by interconnectible shafts. . . . Along one side were arrayed a series of drawing boards and along the other six disc integrators. Pens on some of the boards were driven by shafts so as to trace out curves on properly positioned graph paper. Other boards were designed to permit an operator, who could cause a pen to follow a curve positioned on a board, to give a particular shaft any desired rotation. In essence, the analyzer was a device cleverly contrived to convert the rotations of shafts one into another in a variety of ways. By associating the change of variables in an equation with a rotation of shafts, and by employing an assortment of gearings, the operator could cause the calculator to add, subtract, multiply, divide, and integrate.[6]

Like the slide rule, early analog computing machines could only process single types of equations; for each new problem, a new physical model had to be built. But more sophisticated models such as the differential analyzer could solve a wide range of problems that could be modeled in terms of differential equations.[7] As Alan Bromley writes,

In that the Differential Analyzer can be set up to solve any arbitrary differential equation and this is the basic means of describing dynamic behavior in all fields of engineering and the physical sciences, it is applicable to a vast range of problems. In the 1930s, problems as diverse as atomic structure, transients in electrical networks, timetables of railway trains, and the ballistics of shells, were successfully solved. The Differential Analyzer was, without a doubt, the first general-purpose computing machine for engineering and scientific use.[8]

Digital and Binary

Before going further, one other clarification is in order here: between *digital* and *binary*. Any discrete numerical system is digital. When I calculate a math problem on paper, I'm performing a digital operation in base ten, the "decimal" system. The "binary" system is another digital system: base two. It uses only two numerals, 0 and 1, rather than decimal's ten numerals. Just as base ten represents quantities by sequencing 0 through 9 in columns representing, from right to left, 10^0(ones), 10^1 (tens), 10^2 (hundreds), and so on, base two represents quantities by sequencing 0 and 1 in columns representing 2^0, 2^1, 2^2, and so on. Thus, the number *2* in base ten is written as *10* in base two; *5* in base ten is equivalent to *101* in base two; and so on. Base two can represent any quantity as a series of zeroes and ones.

Babbage's original design used base ten, as did some of the early digital computers of the 1940s. But soon computer engineers concluded that storing numbers in base two could be much more efficient—larger numbers can be stored using much less memory in base two. Today "digital technology" almost always means information translated into binary code and stored as a series of "on" and "off" charges, representing zeroes and ones, in electronic media such as magnetic disks and silicon chips. It's worth remembering, though, that *digital* does not inherently mean *binary*. There are possible digital systems with more than two stages, states between on and off. Morse code, for example, is a trinary system, made up of three states: no pulse, short pulse (dot), and long pulse (dash).[9] The binary system in a sense is the ultimate, Manichean extension of the logic of the digital. Just as digitization slices the holistic analog world into discrete, precise units, binarization represents those units through combinations of only two categories: 0 and 1.

From Analog to Digital

The demands of World War II inspired the development of new computing technologies. While most of this research took place in universities, it was bankrolled by the American and British militaries, motivated by the need for fast, accurate calculation of ballistics information for artillery and antiaircraft systems.[10] While Vannevar Bush perfected his analog differential analyzer at MIT, at the University of Pennsylvania's Moore School, J. Presper Eckert and William Mauchly developed the Electronic Numerical Integrator and Calculator, or ENIAC. By most historians' accounts, ENIAC is the first true digital computer.[11]

ENIAC was not completed in time to be used in the war. But the technical challenges of the conflict convinced the military to continue to pursue computing research. In fact, as Paul Edwards writes, "from the early 1940s until the early 1960s, the armed forces of the United States were the single most important driver of digital computer development."[12]

At the beginning of this period, however, it was by no means certain that this development would center on digital rather than analog computers. Analog computers seemed to have many advantages over the new digital computers.[13] The war had been fought with analog devices such as automatic pilots, remotely controlled cannon, and radar systems. As a result, many more engineers were versed in analog rather than digital techniques. And, as Edwards points out, "analog computers integrated very naturally with control functions because their inputs and outputs were often exactly the sort of signals needed to control other machines (e.g., electric voltages or the rotation of gears)."[14] Digital computers, on the other hand, required new digital-to-analog conversion techniques in order to control other machines. In addition, they were larger, more expensive, and unreliable compared to analog computers.

Digital computers, however, held the promise of greater precision, speed, and objectivity. Analog machines can be made to very precise levels of operation, but they are vulnerable to physical wear on their parts. And like any ruler, they offer only an approximation of measurement, based on the level of precision to which they are graded. A properly functioning digital machine, on the other hand, will always give the same answers with numerical exactitude. And while an analog machine is limited to processing equations for which a physical model can be built, a digital machine can process any algorithm. (Of course, as we'll discuss further, any algorithm is only as good as the information it's been fed.) By the end of the 1940s, digital computing research projects were winning funding, while analog systems were languishing.[15] In 1950 MIT shut down Bush's differential analyzer.

Most histories of computing treat the transition from analog to digital as the inevitable result of the superiority of digital technology. But Aristotle Tympas, in his study of the history of the electrical analyzer, argues that the transition from analog to digital was a matter of ideology, not necessity.[16] Tympas describes the battle between analog and digital laboratories to secure military funding as matter of bureaucratic infighting rather than technological merit. He quotes one of the digital researchers, George E. Valley, describing one critical confrontation:

> The director of the competing [analog] laboratory spoke first. . . . He had not learned, as I had learned . . . that in such situation[s] you stuck a cigar in your face, blew smoke at the intimidating crowd, and overawed the bastards. . . . From that time on the [digital] Lincoln system was truly accepted, but if anyone thinks that SAGE was accepted because of its excellence alone, that person is a potential customer of the Brooklyn Bridge. It was accepted because I shouted an impolite order at the leader of the competition, and he obeyed me. We were at the court of King Arthur, and I have prevailed.[17]

The transition from analog to digital computing had its trade-offs. Brute calculating force replaced hands-on experience. As one lifelong worker in electric power transmission put it:

> Digital computers and software development provide a tremendous increase in the calculating capability available to those performing network studies. In my opinion, however, this leap forward was not entirely beneficial. It resulted in the substitution of speed of calculation for the brains and analytical skill of the calculator; a decrease in the generation of innovative ideas and methods for the development of the network; and an emphasis on the process of the calculation rather than the functioning of the network. I believe that in some ways, digital computers have been harmful to the development of creative ideas for power system development.[18]

Likewise, Warren Weaver, director of the Natural Sciences Division of the Rockefeller Foundation, rued the passing of the differential analyzer:

[I]t seems rather a pity not to have around such a place as MIT a really impressive Analogue computer; for there is vividness and directness of meaning of the electrical and mechanical processes involved . . . which can hardly fail, I would think, to have a very considerable educational value. A Digital Electronic computer is bound to be a somewhat abstract affair, in which the actual computational processes are fairly deeply submerged.[19]

Historian of technology Larry Owens, in "Vannevar Bush and the Differential Analyzer: The Text and Context of an Early Computer," examines Bush's machine as a kind of text. He concludes that the differential analyzer reflects the values of early-twentieth-century engineering culture. Engineers' training of that era emphasized the crafts of machine-building and penmanship, and valued the tangible engagement with mathematical concepts offered through the drawing board and the slide rule. In that spirit, the differential analyzer drew out its solutions with pen on paper, in elegant curves. "Forged in the machine shop, the analyzers spoke the Graphic Language while they drew profiles through the landscape of mathematics."[20] The digital computer, by contrast, embodied an alternate set of values, reflecting the scientific and military culture of the post–World War II era: abstract rather than concrete, intangible rather than tactile.

Analog versus Digital Today

Fifty years after the transition from analog to digital computing, digital technologies continue to hold out the promise of perfection. What began in the 1940s with mainframe computers continues to this day, as music, books, and other media are relentlessly "digitized." Media recorded in digital format promise sharper clarity and less distortion (although this depends on the precision of the recording mechanism). And because digital files are stored as numerical quantities, they aren't subject to degradation in quality as copies are made. A fifth-generation digital sound file, properly copied and error-corrected, is identical to the first, while a fifth-generation cassette recording invariably will have more tape hiss than musical information. Digital data can also be easily transferred through a multitude of channels—telephone lines, fiber-optic cable, satellite transmissions—again without loss of quality. The result is an enormous economy of scale: almost all of the costs are in the general infrastructure, rather than in the individual product. All these advantages lead cyber-pundits such as Nicholas Negroponte to proclaim that an unstoppable, transforming era of digitization is upon us.

But against the digital bandwagon has emerged a backlash. Defenders of analog argue that digital's promise of precision is often just an illusion. A digital clock may be able to give you a readout to the tenth of a second, but that doesn't mean it's actually more accurate than an old-fashioned clock with hands. The ease with which digital information can be copied can lead to the illusion that the cost is "free," but to download a "free" MP3 audio file from the internet first requires quite a bit of infrastruc-ture—a computer, monitor, speakers, modem, network connection, inter-net account, and appropriate software. One thing digital delivery does to deliver its economy of scale is to transfer much of the infrastructure cost to the consumer—instead of just a CD player, you need all the above to enjoy the benefits of online audio.

The most vocal proponents of analog are music fans who trumpet the virtues of vinyl recordings over CDs and other digital formats.[21] CDs overturned vinyl as the record industry's best-selling medium in the 1980s, on a wave of publicity championing the superiority of digitally recorded music. (It didn't hurt that the major label distributors stopped allowing retailers to return unsold copies of vinyl records, making it im-possible for most stores to continue to stock vinyl versions of albums.)[22] CDs work by "sampling" a sound wave—taking a series of snapshots of sonic information, at a rate of 44,100 samples per second. When this choppy accumulation of sound snippets is played back, it appears con-tinuous, much in the way a film, composed of still frames, creates the il-lusion of fluid motion when projected at twenty-four frames per second. Vinyl, on the other hand, is an analog medium. It records sound waves continuously, replicating the waves themselves in the grooves of the disc. Vinyl enthusiasts argue that the piecework nature of digital recording cre-ates an arid, crisp sound, as the subtleties between samples drop out. Vinyl, by contrast, preserves a warmer, more whole sound. Even the im-perfections of vinyl—the hiss and pop of dust and scratches on the sur-face of the disc—can be seen as virtues, reminders of the materiality of the recording and playback process. Much contemporary dance music takes advantage of this evocation of materiality, sampling hiss-and-pop-filled vinyl drum loops to give beats a "dirtier" sound. (My all-digital synthesizer, the Roland MC-505 "Groovebox," even has a "vinylizer" feature, which adds simulated vinyl sounds to a track.)[23]

Eric Rothenbuhler and John Durham Peters make the provocative argument that analog recording is inherently more authentic than digital, because "the phonograph record and the analog magnetic tape do contain physical traces of the music. At a crude level this is visible with the naked eye in the grooves of the record. . . . The hills and valleys of those grooves are physical analogs of the vibrations of music."[24] By contrast, a CD contains only numbers. The CD player translates those numbers by following a decoding scheme established by the corporations that developed CD technology, Sony and Phillips. "These numbers are related to waveforms by a convention arrived at in intercorporate negotiations and established as an industry standard; but they could be anything."[25] Record albums, Rothenbuhler and Peters conclude, "bear the trace of a body and have an erotics impossible to CDs. . . . To favor phonography is to favor a particular kind of hermeneutic, one attentive to conditions of embodiment."[26]

The real world is analog, the vinyl enthusiasts insist. Digital, by offering the fantasy of precision, reifies the real world. This complaint can be extended to a more global critique of computer culture: the binary logic of computing attempts to fit everything into boxes of zeros and ones, true and false. Many ethnographers of computer programmers have remarked on how the binary mindset of computer programming seems to encourage a blinkered view of the world. As Tracy Kidder writes in *The Soul of a New Machine,* "Engineers have . . . a professional code. Among its tenets is the general idea that the engineer's right environment is a highly structured one, in which only right and wrong answers exist. It's a binary world; the computer might be its paradigm. And many engineers seem to aspire to be binary people within it."[27]

Computer usability expert Donald Norman argues that the root of users' frustrations with modern technology lies in the conflict between digital and analog modes of information processing. Computers are digital, but people are analog. In his rejoinder to Negroponte, "Being Analog," Norman writes,

> We are analog beings trapped in a digital world, and the worst part is, we did it to ourselves. . . . We are analog devices following biological modes of operation. We are compliant, flexible, tolerant. Yet we people

have constructed a world of machines that requires us to be rigid, fixed, intolerant. We have devised a technology that requires considerable care and attention, that demands it be treated on its own terms, not ours. We live in a technology-centered world where the technology is not appropriate for people. No wonder we have such difficulties.

From Bivalence to Multivalence

The rift between analog and digital, then, echoes a series of familiar oppositions:

analog	digital
slide rule	calculator
pencil	keyboard
paper	screen
material	ideal
modern	postmodern
natural	technological
real	virtual
index	symbol[28]
female	male
soft	hard
hot	cold
holistic	atomizing
nostalgic	futuristic
neo-Luddite	technotopian
body	mind
goddess	cyborg

But to neatly divide the world into categories of analog and digital is already to concede to digital's binary logic. And as with most binary oppositions, this one is susceptible to deconstruction. As Jonathan Sterne points out,

> today's sound media—whether analog or digital—embody and extend a panoply of social forms. It does not matter whether the machine is question uses magnetic particles, electromagnetic waves, or bits to move its information: sound technologies are social artifacts all the way down.[29]

Some of the most interesting recent developments in computer science suggest ways out of binary thinking. The field of "fuzzy logic" is one attempt to develop an alternative. Bart Kosko, author of *Fuzzy Thinking,* writes,

> in much of our science, math, logic and culture we have assumed a world of blacks and whites that does not change. Every statement is true or false. Every law, statute, and club rule applies to you or not. The digital computer, with its high-speed binary strings of 1s and 0s, stands as the emblem of the black and white and its triumph over the scientific mind. . . . This faith in black and the white, this *bivalence,* reaches back in the West to at least the ancient Greeks. . . . Aristotle's binary logic came down to one law: A OR not-A. Either this or not this. The sky is blue or not blue. It can't be both blue and not blue. It can't be A AND not-A.[30]

In contrast to bivalent Aristotelian logic, fuzzy logic is "multivalent." In fuzzy logic, an object may be both A AND not-A. The root of "fuzzy logic" is in the concept of "fuzzy sets," developed by Lotfi Zadeh.[31] Fuzzy sets are sets who elements belong to them to different degrees. An object may be partly A, and partly not-A. As Daniel McNeill and Paul Freiberger write, "Suppose two people in a living room are watching *Bonfire of the Vanities* on the VCR. The (fuzzy) set of annoyed people in the room is Sam/0.85 and Pam/0.80. Its complement, the set of not-annoyed people, is Sam/0.15 and Pam/0.20."[32]

Proponents of fuzzy logic compare its perspective to that of Eastern philosophies that reject binarism. Kosko suggests the yin-yang symbol, in which black and white are inextricably intertwined, as "the emblem of fuzziness."[33] Fuzzy logic also fits well with the challenges to traditional scientific positivism offered by such developments as Heisenberg's uncertainty principle and Gödel's incompleteness theorem, which demonstrate that not all scientific statements can be proven to be true or false.[34]

Beyond the philosophical challenges offered by fuzzy logic, the system has also turned out to be of great practical value. Ian Marshall and Danah Zohar write,

> Suppose engineers want to make an intelligent traffic light that can time itself to change from red to green at different intervals, depending on how light or heavy the traffic flow is. The binary switch of a digital computer is too crude to do this. Binary switches are either on or off. But

The yin-yang symbol. From Wikipedia, http://en.wikipedia.org/wiki/Image
:Yin_yang.png.

fuzzy chips that allow traffic lights to readjust constantly have now been invented. They also delicately adjust subway control systems, the loading sensors of washing machines, the contrast buttons of TV sets, and a whole host of other "smart" machines.[35]

Fuzzy logic does not abandon the world of the digital—fuzzy chips are digital devices, not analog ones. And in some ways, fuzzy logic may not be quite as fuzzy as proponents like Kosko claim. The mathematics of fuzzy sets allow for states between A and not-A. But they still presume the ability to know as an absolute truth where a value lies between A and not-A. In the VCR example, fuzzy logic allows for a state between annoyed and not-annoyed. But how can we know with mathematical certainty that Sam is precisely 85% annoyed, and Pam 80%? Perhaps we are only 90% certain that these numbers are accurate. But how certain can we be of that 90% figure? Pursuing this question further leads to an infinite regress of uncertainty—illustrating, to some of fuzzy logic's critics, the futility of attempting to deconstruct Aristotelian logic while retaining the fantasy of mathematical precision.[36]

But if fuzzy logic does not truly transcend the prison house of digital thinking, perhaps this is appropriate. Rather than a unilateral rejection of binarism, it may be best seen as an accommodation with it: a fuzzy bridge between the worlds of analog and digital.

3

Filming the "Electronic Brain"

In tracing the cultural history of computing, so far our focus has been on the discourses and legacies of technical elites: first the works of Charles Babbage and Ada Lovelace, then the debates of engineers over the relative merits of analog versus digital computing. This is because before the mid-1940s, computers were specialized technical objects unfamiliar to the general public. Computers weren't a part of popular culture.

With the emergence of mainframe digital computers in the years after World War II, computing machines entered public consciousness for the first time. Early digital computers such as ENIAC and UNIVAC were featured in *Life, Time,* and other newsmagazines. By the 1950s, the computerization of America had begun. Americans started to encounter the work of computers in their interactions with complex bureaucracies, including government agencies, banks, and other institutions. Representations of the huge, powerful, intimidating machines began appearing in science fiction and other forms of popular entertainment.

As computers moved out of the lab and into the workplace, they emerged in the American public sphere as figures of both hope and anxiety, offering the promise of technological salvation and the threat of mass unemployment. At first, even the name of the machines was up for grabs—up through the end of the 1950s, they were often called "electronic brains" or "giant brains." To understand popular ideas about computers in the mainframe era, this chapter will turn to turn an examination of representations of computers in popular film. We'll focus on two of the most commercially successful films of the 1950s and 1960s to feature computers: 1957's *Desk Set* and 1968's *2001: A Space Odyssey.*

Desk Set is a romantic comedy, the eighth of the nine films starring Katharine Hepburn and Spencer Tracy. Hepburn plays Bunny Watson, the head research librarian for a television network. Tracy is Richard Sumner, a consultant brought in to computerize the workplace. The comic tension in the film springs from Watson's fear that the new computer will replace her and her colleagues. Although her fears are revealed to be groundless in the film's conclusion, they resonate more deeply than does the movie's pat happy ending. The film is a fascinating snapshot of popular anxieties about computerization in the 1950s.

Desk Set is particularly interesting because it's one of the few movies about computers that isn't in any way part of the genre of science fiction. SF films typically address audiences' hopes and anxieties about technology through extrapolation, imagining the utopian and/or dystopian future consequences of new machines such as computers. (As we'll see in a moment, this is exactly the strategy of *2001*.) *Desk Set*, instead, is a romantic comedy set in the present. In the genre of romantic comedy, social conflicts are mapped onto the characters of a warring couple who alternately fight and love. This is the template for all of the Hepburn and Tracy comedies. In this case, *Desk Set* mines the audience's hopes and anxieties about computers as the source of comic (and romantic) tension and conflict between Hepburn and Tracy. As we shall see, this generic framework allows the film to directly address questions of gender and technology that almost always remain repressed in the science fiction genre.

2001 is Stanley Kubrick's filmed version of Arthur C. Clarke's science fiction novel, in which a group of astronauts travels to investigate a mysterious extraterrestrial object. Over the course of their journey, their artificially intelligent shipboard computer, HAL, begins to malfunction, murdering most of the crew before he can be deactivated. *2001* is a much darker story than *Desk Set*, with no happy ending for HAL (although the remaining astronaut goes on to his hallucinatory final journey in the film's famously psychedelic climax). But its legacy has been more complex than one might think. Despite HAL's villainy, he lives on as film's most fully realized artificially intelligent computer, and he remains an inspiration for generations of AI researchers who choose to focus on the inspiring technical accomplishment of HAL's creation, rather than his subsequent meltdown. The film, then, is another snapshot of the mixture of hope and anxiety in Americans' attitudes towards computers. Filmed in Kubrick's portentous style, it takes a very different approach from the frothy *Desk Set*. But still, in the differences between the two films, we can take some measure of Americans' deepening suspicions about computers in the years between 1957 and 1968.

These two films, of course, can't tell the whole story. But they're a good place to begin an effort to take stock of popular ideas about computers in this era, for several reasons. To begin with, films are more than isolated artifacts. They're rich, vibrant documents that contain traces of the concerns of multiple creators and multiple audiences. To use the language of Mikhael Bakhtin, we could say that popular film is inherently polyphonous[1]—it contains multiple, intersecting voices. Film is a richly collaborative medium. It is always more than individual expression. Examining a popular film can give us a sense not just of the ideas of one auteur, but of a community of creators—writers, actors, producers, and crew, as well as the director.

In addition, beyond the voices of its creators, film also must inherently echo the voices of its intended audiences. To appeal to a broad and heterogeneous viewership, popular texts must be able to encompass diverging perspectives, while speaking to deeply held hopes and fears. Films may not directly reflect audiences' ideas, but their underlying assumptions must share common values, hopes, and anxieties, if they are to resonate with audiences. The humor in *Desk Set* could only work because its audience shared its worries about technological unemployment. Without these worries, the jokes wouldn't be funny. Likewise, *2001* could only frighten an audience who shared a fear of and fascination with artificial intelligence. Otherwise, HAL wouldn't be a scary and compelling character. Looking more closely at these films, then, can help us understand popular feelings about computers in the eras they were made.

"Electronics for Plenty"?

The development of digital computers in the early and mid-1940s was financed almost exclusively by the American military. Most observers of the time saw little market for such powerful devices beyond the government and a few research universities. In the late 1940s, the developers of ENIAC, J. Presper Eckert and William Mauchly, made an attempt to build a commercial computer business, but despite the technological triumph of ENIAC's successor, UNIVAC, they had little commercial success. They were forced to sell out to a larger company, Remington Rand, in 1950.

By the early 1950s, however, IBM began to see a possible market in selling computers to businesses. IBM's skilled sales force and extensive technical support perfectly positioned the company to help corporations integrate computers into the workplace.[2] By the late 1950s, IBM was far and away the leader of the emerging computer industry, and its name was practically synonymous with computers.

Businesses of this era found computers useful not only for mechanizing routine office tasks, but also for automating factory work. The rapidly increasing processing power of the computer made it possible to mechanize the production line to an extent never before seen. The mainstream media celebrated this development as another step in the march of progress. A 1955 *Time* cover story on IBM, for example, proclaimed, "Automation: Electronics for Plenty," and promised, "automation of industry will mean new reaches of leisure, new wealth, new dignity for the laboring man."[3] But many critics vocally protested the possible consequences of automation for labor: lost jobs and the deskilling of those jobs remaining.

Among the critics of automation was one of the scientists who had made it possible: Norbert Wiener, the "father of cybernetics." In the years after World War II, Wiener grew increasingly concerned by the potential consequences to labor of large-scale automation, and refused to participate in corporate-backed automation research. In a 1949 letter to United Auto Workers president Walter Reuther, Wiener wrote,

> I do not wish to contribute in any way to selling labor down the river, and I am quite aware that any labor, which is in competition with slave labor, whether the slaves are human or mechanical, must accept the conditions of work of slave labor. For me to remain aloof is to make sure that the development of these ideas will go into other hands which will probably be much less friendly to organized labor.[4]

Desk Set is one of the few films of its era to take on these emerging labor conflicts. Even more unusually, it specifically addresses the consequences of automation for *women* in the workplace. Most of the discussion about technological unemployment and deskilling in the 1950s addressed its impact on blue-collar jobs, held almost exclusively by men. *Desk Set* is exceptional for its time (or any time, for that matter) for concentrating on the plight of "pink-collar" office workers—librarians in this case, though their situation clearly parallels that of the many secretaries, telephone operators, and even old-fashioned human "computers" whose livelihoods were threatened by new technologies in the years after World War II. This focus may help explain the dismissive response of the critics of the time. Bosley Crowther in the *New York Times* called the original play a "trifling charade";[5] *Time* magazine described the film as a "comedy about the milder terrors of technological unemployment."[6] It's hard not to ascribe these judgments to sexist condescension—presumably, the terrors were "milder" because the prospective victims were women.

Desk Set began in 1955 as a Broadway play by William Marchant. It attracted the attention of Hepburn and Tracy, who were looking for material for the next of their long-running series of romantic comedies. The duo had the property adapted by the screenwriting team of Henry and Phoebe Ephron (the parents of contemporary romantic comedy auteur Nora Ephron). Directed by Walter Lang, the film was a big-budget, high-visibility production. It was the first of their movies to be filmed in color, in glorious Cinemascope. As in all the Hepburn and Tracy films, comic tension and sexual chemistry spring from professional and ideological conflict. What makes *Desk Set* somewhat unusual in the Hepburn and Tracy canon, however, is that here the couple's primary conflict is as much about *class* as gender. In films such as *Adam's Rib* and *Woman of the Year,* Hepburn the feisty feminist butts heads with cuddly but chauvinistic Tracy. Here, on the other hand, Hepburn's independence is taken for granted. The drama is not over whether she'll lose her man, but whether she'll lose her job.

The action takes place in a glistening modernist skyscraper in New York City, home to a fictional television company, the Atlantic Network. Hepburn plays Bunny Watson,[7] head of the network's all-female research staff, who check facts, answer queries, and maintain an extensive in-house library. In a sparkling opening scene, Watson and her three colleagues prove their expertise by reciting, off the tops of their heads, answers to a range of questions phoned in by the writers of various network shows, from Ty Cobb's lifetime batting average to the text to Longfellow's "Song of Hiawatha."

Into this warm, intellectual, woman-centered workspace shambles Spencer Tracy as the genial but inscrutable Richard Sumner. Sumner is an efficiency expert, and it appears that he's come to install EMERAC, an "electronic brain" (the term "computer" is never used) in the library. His exact plans, however, are mysterious—Mr. Azae, president of the network, has made Tracy promise not to say anything about "this big thing that's coming up." As a result, Watson and her staff (along with the audience, which has been left equally in the dark) grow more and more anxious that the entire department will be replaced by the computer. Fellow

EMERAC disrupts the librarians' idyllic workspace. From *Desk Set* (Fox, 1957).

librarian Peg Costello (Joan Blondell) notes that after the payroll depart-ment's computer was installed, half of the staff was laid off. As Sumner mysteriously wanders the office measuring floor space and observing the librarians' work, he and Watson banter flirtatiously. Their growing at-traction, however, is threatened by Watson's fear that he's there to down-size her.

The mood in the office doesn't improve once the computer is installed. The staff now spend their time feeding the contents of their library into the machine, certain that once they're finished, they'll be fired. Finally, the day comes—pink slips arrive for everybody. Just then, more research re-quests come in; as Hepburn and her staff watch with bitter amusement, the computer proves overmatched without their expert guidance, spitting out page after page of irrelevant materials. Meanwhile, something seems odd about the pink slips—Sumner's received one too, and he's not even on the payroll. He calls up Azae, and learns that even the company president got a pink slip. The notices are the result of a mistake made by the computer in payroll. Nobody's going to be fired after all—the reason Sumner's been so coy isn't because of looming job cuts, but because the network is about to announce a merger, and Azae didn't want word of the acquisition of the new computer to leak out ahead of time. With the merger, there will be plenty of work for everybody, and they'll even be expanding the department. Her fears resolved, Bunny Watson can learn to love both EMERAC and Richard Sumner.

Technotopian Narrative, Technophobic Subtext

The surface moral of the film's narrative, then, is clear: computers make life better for everybody. This, presumably, is the message IBM found in the film when it agreed to act as a "consultant" for the movie. (The opening credits prominently thank IBM, and it appears that EMERAC is supposed to be an IBM product "invented" by Sumner.) But *Desk Set* puts up a mighty struggle on the way to narrative closure. Through most of the film, the librarians' fears seem perfectly justified. While Sumner and Azae know all along that nobody's job is in danger, the audience is never let in on their secret. Much of the film's humor is actually quite hard-hitting, puncturing corporate rhetoric of better living through computers. Lecturing a group of executives about the machine, Sumner expounds, "The purpose of this machine, of course, is to free the worker . . ." at which point Watson bitterly interjects, "You can say that again." Later, when asked by one executive her thoughts on the machine, Watson dryly replies, "I think you can safely say that it will provide more leisure for more people."

Note that both these jokes operate not through direct confrontation, but irony—Watson, and the audience, attribute a second, darker meaning to Sumner's sunny pronouncements. (Sumner, meanwhile, doesn't even notice Watson's jibes.) The conclusion of the film, then, seems to retroactively discredit Watson's sarcasm: it turns out that there never was a darker meaning to Sumner's comments, and Watson apologizes for misinterpreting his motives. On the other hand, her critique of the rhetoric of computerization was never groundless; after all, half the payroll department really was laid off.

From *Desk Set* (Fox, 1957).

Even though Watson's staff do retain their jobs, the film suggests that their idyllic workspace has been permanently disrupted by the giant machine. The scene introducing the computer begins with a series of forbidding signs being posted on the doors to the research department: "No Smoking," "Keep Door Closed," "Warning: Do Not Touch," all evoking that famously despised IBM phrase, "Do Not Fold, Spindle, or Mutilate." The machine itself, an intimidating vista of blinking lights and whirring tapes, is so huge it fills the Cinemascope screen, displacing desks and disrupting the familiar space of the research department. The machine is cared for by Sumner's assistant, Miss Warringer, a cold, uptight woman who reserves all her emotion for "Emmy," which she dotes over, petting it and calling it a "good girl." A nightmare (and sexist) vision of the dehumanizing effects of working with the machine, she is mockingly referred to by Watson's staff as "EMERAC's mother."

One aspect of *Desk Set*'s gender politics might seem surprising at first glance: structurally, its vision of a feminist workspace isn't *utopian,* but rather *conservative.* In *Desk Set,* it appears to be the status quo that's feminist, and "progress" in the form of computerization which threatens women. The film begins by demonstrating the autonomy and camaraderie Watson and her staff have already carved out for themselves within the patriarchal corporation. It's EMERAC, the wave of the future, that disrupts this feminist space. This seems a counterintuitive vision of women in the workplace, in an era when one might expect feminists to be fighting for a more equitable future rather than settling for the present.

But it reflects the threat of computerization at that time to pink-collar workspaces such as telephone operating centers and secretarial pools.

Nonetheless, if the film offers a critique of technological "progress," it does still associate its feminist workspace with the dream of a better future. From its very first shot of the shining tiles of a Mondrian-inspired office floor, followed by a cut to a gleaming New York skyscraper, the film announces its up-to-the-minute 1950s-style modernity. Likewise, the corporate setting, a television network, is in a fresh, new, glamorous industry. The women of *Desk Set* may be ambivalent about computers, but their lifestyles, even before the arrival of EMERAC, evoke the future more than the present or past.

The film's conclusion does attempt to reassure the audience that the computer will be a blessing rather than a curse for the librarians' work life. First, the computer fouls up without their help, demonstrating that it can't evaluate complex research requests without expert human guidance. Then, after the pink-slip confusion is resolved, the library receives a final query: "What is the weight of the earth?" Watson is dismayed—it's the kind of question that could take weeks of tedious data collection to answer. But not to fear, Sumner reassures her—this is exactly the kind of raw number crunching the computer can do in a flash! The computer's success demonstrates how it can help the librarians by taking over the most "mindless" kinds of labor, liberating them to concentrate on more intellectually challenging and fulfilling parts of their work. As Sumner explains, "EMERAC was never intended to replace you. It's here merely to free your time for research."

But even this happy ending contains a hint of dark humor. Before spitting out the weight of the world, EMERAC asks one question: "With or without people?" Watson is delighted—she sees the response as proof of the computer's sophistication. But it's hard for a contemporary viewer not to hear an echo of *2001*'s HAL in EMERAC's ominous query.

How do we reconcile the tensions and contradictions in *Desk Set?* One approach would be to follow the framework of Stuart Hall's classic cultural studies essay "Encoding, Decoding." Hall distinguishes among three possible readings of popular culture texts: hegemonic, negotiated, and oppositional. Under Hall's categories, we could label the conflicting pro-computer and anti-computer perspectives I've outlined here as hegemonic and oppositional readings of *Desk Set,* respectively. This framework suggests that while the majority of the film's viewers would likely come away reassured of computers' benevolence, a critical minority

Happily ever after? From *Desk Set* (Fox, 1957).

would embrace the alternate reading. Others might fall somewhere in the middle, settling for negotiated readings.

Evidence of audience reaction to the film confirms that the happy ending fails to close off all alternate interpretations. As one of the few librarian heroines in Hollywood history, Bunny Watson has developed something of a cult among contemporary information professionals, with several web sites devoted to her. The most interesting is titled "Top Ten Reasons Why 'Bunny Watson' Was Right about Computers in Libraries," by Craig A. Summerhill, a library systems coordinator. Adapted from a librarians' conference talk, the essay enumerates the technological problems facing librarians, embracing Bunny Watson as a model for "professionals who are at least partially skeptical about computer technology." What's particularly revealing is how Summerhill misremembers the plot of *Desk Set:*

> The film is a romantic comedy, and ultimately Hepburn and Tracy fall in love despite the fact that Tracy is sent into the company to optimize the library's performance and reduce the number of employees, including Hepburn's position as managing librarian. In the end, humanity also triumphs over the machine and Hepburn saves her job as well as the other library employees by outperforming the machine in a clutch situation.[8]

Actually, the conclusion of the film reassures us that the employees' jobs were never in jeopardy. But the author's selective memory demonstrates how much more compelling the film's depiction of job anxiety is, compared to the abrupt happy ending that tries to take it all back. Similarly, an article on "Classic Movies of the Workplace" from the feminist website electra.com noted, "It's a little surprising that IBM worked so closely with this film: not only do computers here (temporarily) fulfill everyone's fears of being replaced, but they screw up royally at their first chance out of the gate. Just like Windows 95!"[9]

But I think it's a mistake to follow a hermeneutic model which presumes that either the critic or the viewer can make a choice between rival interpretations. Rather, I think it's most accurate to see *Desk Set* as a cross section of simultaneously held hopes and fears about computers. The utopian and dystopian uneasily coexist in this film. It's the tension between these two visions that generates the film's humor and romance. Even Summerhill's essay reflects this conflict. While its title suggests a neo-Luddite attack on computerization, it's actually just a discussion of the challenges facing library technologists.

A chart mapping the hopes and fears underlying *Desk Set,* then, would look something like this:

Narrative: Technotopian hopes	*Subtext:* Technophobic fears
Computers generate new jobs, bringing prosperity to all.	Computers replace workers, producing widespread unemployment.
Computers free workers from "mindless" tasks, allowing for more fulfilling labor.	Computers regiment work, forcing workers to become more "machine-like."

Productivity Myths and Realities

In the utopian conclusion to *Desk Set,* all the film's dystopian fears are dismissed as having been baseless all along. The computer, it turns out, won't take jobs away, but will actually create new ones. This happy ending requires not only some suspension of disbelief, but also selective memory. After all, we've already been told that the computer in payroll *did* displace half the department's workers, so the endings don't turn out so happy all the time.

There is another possible reading of *Desk Set,* what one might call a more nuanced capitalist technotopian vision. One could see the film as allegorizing the economic argument for computerization: that while computers may cause some temporary anxiety and job displacement, in the long run they will actually create more jobs by boosting productivity, thereby expanding the economy. This is the argument that 1955 *Time* cover story makes: "In such progress, some workers may indeed be displaced by machines. But for every job lost, a dozen more interesting, better-paying jobs will open up in the making and servicing of machines."[10]

Under this reading of *Desk Set,* the merger that will bring more jobs to the research department represents, in deus ex machina form, the continued growth that computers and other forms of automation bring to the American economy. So, the argument would go, while in practice it may be a convenient fiction to imagine that nobody in Bunny Watson's department would be fired after the introduction of a computer (or, for that matter, downsized following the merger with another network, which presumably has its own, now redundant, research staff), in the long run, more jobs will be gained than lost by computerization, and so, in spirit, the film's utopian depiction of the consequences of computerization is on target.

Since the time of *Desk Set,* this vision of computerization has become economic doxa in the United States. In fact, the most surprising part of the film is that it presents any critique of automation at all. Today the rhetoric of growth and progress—and the silencing of the American labor movement—has drowned out just about any public discussion of technological unemployment and deskilling. And historical amnesia has made it very hard to recapture a sense of the debates of the past. In researching this discussion, I was surprised to discover just how widespread discussion of the consequences of automation was in the "placid" 1950s, when unions still had a sizeable voice in the American public sphere. One of the most jarring moments in *Desk Set* for a contemporary viewer is when librarian Peg Costello, outraged over learning of EMERAC, promises, "I'm going to go down to the union hall and see if there's a law against it!" The film doesn't take this promise very seriously; nowhere else does the film imply that the workers have any recourse to collective representation. Nonetheless, it's striking that the joke would be credible enough to be funny; a similar joke today would fall flat.

But if, outside these moments of tension, *Desk Set* presents a technotopian vision of computerization in which a rising tide of productivity lifts all boats, the reality for librarians in the years since the film's release has not been so kind. Stanley Aronowitz and William DiFazio write in *The Jobless Future,*

From the early days of office computers in the 1950s, there has been a sometimes acrimonious debate about their effects. Perhaps the Spencer Tracy-Katharine Hepburn comedy *Desk Set* best exemplifies the issues. . . . The film reiterates the prevailing view of the period (and ours?) that, far from posing a threat, computers promise to increase work by expanding needs. Significantly, the film asserts that the nearly inexhaustible desire for information inherent in human affairs will provide a fail-safe against professional and clerical redundancy. In contradistinction to these optimistic prognostications, new information technologies have enabled corporations, large law firms, and local governments to reduce the library labor force, including professional librarians. In turn, several library science schools have closed, including the prestigious library school at Columbia University.[11]

The numbers don't back up the technotopian economics of *Time* or *Desk Set*. From the 1950s through the mid-1990s, the computerization of the American economy did not lead to any marked increase in productivity. As economist Robert Solow famously observed in 1987, "You can see the computer age everywhere but in the productivity statistics."[12] Economists label this irony "the Solow productivity paradox." As Daniel E. Sichel writes in *The Computer Revolution: An Economic Perspective*,

> Since the late 1950s, . . . observers in the business press have often proclaimed optimistically that recent problems in getting full value from computers had largely been overcome and that a surge was just around the corner. Perhaps the optimists are right this time. But then again, perhaps this optimism should be discounted, since this genre of commentary on the computer revolution has been around for years.[13]

How could such powerful machines fail to boost productivity? Doug Henwood explains:

> On first, and even second, glance, it might seem that computers could contribute mightily to productivity, especially since the price of computing power has been dropping like a stone for decades. . . .
> But to focus on that price decline alone is to miss many significant points. . . . It says nothing about the costs of software, training, repairs, or support, which are declining much more slowly if at all. And their levels can be quite high; private consultants estimate, for example, that a

$2,500 PC costs a typical big business from $6,000 to $13,000 a year in such secondary expenditures. Miracles can easily disappear in overhead like that.

And the hardware price decline is itself a financial pitfall: it means that an investment made today depreciates very rapidly. . . . For an existing business, computers that come in the front door are often replacements for ones going out the back door. That pace of obsolescence can be very expensive, a fact that barely penetrates the cybertopians' prose.[14]

Much of information technology investment is a process of "running to stand still," as industry observer Gerry McGovern puts it.[15] Morgan Stanley economist Stephen Roach observed in a 1997 paper that "sixty percent of annual corporate IT budgets go toward replacement of outdated equipment and increasingly frequent product replacement."[16]

In the last decade, many economists have begun to argue that the productivity paradox has finally been resolved. Productivity rates started to rise significantly in the late 1990s. While productivity slackened during the 2001 recession, it rose markedly in the "jobless recovery" that followed. The significance of this recent productivity boom is still under debate. Some economists argue that only now that computers have thoroughly saturated the American economy can the full benefits of computerization be exploited. Paul David compares computerization to the electrification of the United States, which likewise took decades to make its full economic impact felt.[17] Other studies argue that the impact of computerization on the recent productivity boom has been overstated by cyberboosters. A detailed McKinsey Global Institute study of the factors behind U.S. productivity growth from 1995 to 2000 found the correlation between corporate IT spending and productivity performance to be "barely positive and statistically insignificant." It concluded that high-tech industries contributed just 27% of the total productivity acceleration.[18] As Doug Henwood writes in *After the New Economy*,

[Whether] the burst in reported productivity growth that started in the late 1990s . . . is a long-term thing or not isn't yet clear; it's going to take a few more years to tell whether the productivity slump of the 1970s and 1980s is over or not. But even enthusiasts rarely bother to delineate the mechanisms linking the net to the productivity burst. It may be that very unglamorous things—the cheapening of labor through outsourcing, the movement of much of production to low-wage countries, continued unwillingness of firms to share their good fortune with employees, and what the people at *Labor Notes* call "management by stress" (pushing human workers and work arrangements to their breaking point and maybe a little beyond)—are the real underlying mechanisms. It may also be that people are actually logging lots more hours on the job than get recorded in the official statistics. Or it may be that the productivity blip is a statistical illusion—a product of the way output is valued by statisticians.[19]

Much of the gains of productivity may be a reflection of how new technologies such as email, laptops, and cell phones put extra, uncompensated demands on workers, rather than making their lives easier. As Stephen Roach (hardly a radical critic) writes in the *New York Times,*

[P]roductivity measurement is more art than science—especially in America's vast services sector, which employs fully 80 percent of the nation's private work force. . . . Productivity is calculated as the ratio of output per unit of work time. How do we measure value added in the amorphous services sector?

Very poorly, is the answer. The numerator of the productivity equation, output, is hopelessly vague for services. For many years, government statisticians have used worker compensation to approximate output in many service industries, which makes little or no intuitive sense. Government data on work schedules are woefully out of touch with reality. . . . For example, in financial services, the Labor Department tells us that the average workweek has been unchanged, at 35.5 hours, since 1988. That's patently absurd. Courtesy of a profusion of portable information appliances . . . most information workers can toil around the clock. The official data don't come close to capturing this shift.

As a result, we are woefully underestimating the time actually spent on the job. It follows, therefore, that we are equally guilty of overestimating white-collar productivity. Productivity is not about working longer. It's about getting more value from each unit of work time. The official productivity numbers are, in effect, mistaking work time for leisure time.[20]

Even if we grant that computers have been a contributing factor to the productivity boom of the last few years, we're left with the question, productivity for what? Conventional economists assume that productivity growth is the key to a society's prosperity and happiness. Channeling that *Time* cover story of 1955, the *Economist* wrote in 2000, "Productivity growth is the single most important economic indicator. It determines how fast living standards can grow. The reason why the average American today is seven times better off than his counterpart at the turn of the century is that he is seven times as productive."[21] But it seems a stretch to so confidently equate a dollar figure with quality of life. As McGovern observes, "Back in the Fifties, we were promised a 3-day week. But the facts show that we are working longer hours than ever. We were promised the 'paperless office.' But we have never produced more paper and it's rising every year."[22] And as Henwood notes, "Even though at the dawn of 2003 the U.S. economy was four times larger than it was in 1980, and almost ten times larger than it was in 1970, in many ways we feel more strapped than we ever did in the past. We're constantly told we 'can't afford' universal health care or a civilized welfare state."[23]

Productivity growth is not a panacea. The question remains on whose backs that productivity is achieved, and how a society distributes the rewards of growth. As Henwood observes,

> During the 1960s, pay and productivity grew in tandem, but they separated in the 1970s. In the 1990s boom, pay growth lagged behind productivity by almost 30%. . . . With weak unions and strong bosses, productivity growth can just as easily show up in the pockets of creditors, stockholders, and CEOs as it can in fatter paychecks, as it clearly did. . . . Conceptually, productivity growth determines what an economy can produce over time, but how that growth is distributed depends on social institutions, and the institutions of American society tend to direct the booty upward.[24]

Computers and Power

So, if computerization failed to achieve major productivity gains for 40 years, and its impact remains debatable even today, why would corporations through this entire period continually push for greater and greater computerization? Sociologists of labor argue that the answer is *control*. Computerization is an extension of the process of deskilling—which, as we saw in chapter 1, Babbage himself pioneered in the nineteenth century.

Computers redistribute knowledge and skill from the shop floor to machines owned outright by management. As Aronowitz and DiFazio write,

> studies of the labor process reveal, time and again, the degree to which reducing the worker to an interchangeable part by means of "rational" organization and machine technology rationalization . . . is also paralleled and dominated by the struggle among the workers, management, and the owners for *power.* . . . As E. P. Thompson and Harry Braverman have suggested, the struggle of capital to dominate the labor process has for centuries been linked to breaking craft culture, not only by bitter tactics such as provoking strikes and lockouts to smash craft unions, but also by making mechanization and rationalization a "natural" process that is regarded as socially progressive. What could not be accomplished by Taylorism was finally achieved by computerization.[25]

Aronowitz and DeFazio come to precisely the opposite conclusion of *Time* and the *Economist:*

> For an ever smaller number of people in virtually all occupations, the qualifications required by computers have created new opportunities for satisfying and economically remunerative work. But for the immense majority, computerization of the workplace has resulted in further subordination, displacement, or irrelevance.[26]

Something of this critique surfaces in *Desk Set*'s satire of a computer-dominated workplace, where librarians must tiptoe around the demanding machine. But the film dulls its satire in its choice of target: the officious Miss Warringer, a scapegoat who diverts blame from both President Azae, who made the decision to bring the computer into the workplace (and who's presented as amiably ineffectual), and Sumner, who's in charge of the computer's installation. (The film suggests that all the rules and warning signs are the work of Miss Warringer. But as Sumner's subordinate, she's presumably acting under his instruction.)

Likewise, the film softens its critique of corporate power by fudging its representation of IBM in ways that humanize the giant corporation. Although the exact arrangement is never made completely clear, the film's several references to IBM imply that EMERAC is an IBM product, and Sumner an employee of IBM. But Sumner is also described as "the inventor and patent holder of EMERAC." Were EMERAC a real IBM product, the patent would almost certainly be held by the corporation, not an individual. And while Charles Babbage might fairly be said to have personally invented his difference engine, by the 1950s no corporate-built computer was the work of a single "inventor." As Kenneth Flamm explains in *Creating the Computer,*

> A complex computer system draws on many different technological elements, from many sources. The ownership rights to an advance produced by combining many disparate elements are often cloudy. Coupled with the marginal, incremental nature of many of the technical advances, which build on work done by others, determining which of many parallel and similar efforts was the "first" to generate a successful innovation is often rather arbitrary. Even defining the exact nature of a particular innovation, when similar and closely linked concepts are being explored in many different places, is difficult.[27]

The film further misrepresents IBM by naming its computer EMERAC—an obvious play on the real-life ENIAC machine. By implicitly giving IBM credit for ENIAC, the film appropriates the work of IBM's rivals, Eckert and Mauchly. At a time when IBM was consolidating its quasi-monopoly in the computer industry, *Desk Set* helped perpetuate the public impression that *all* computers are made by IBM, while at the same time portraying IBM as simply a home for independent inventors.

AI Anxiety as Allegory

Another way to divert blame from the people and institutions responsible for technological unemployment and deskilling is to blame the machines themselves. Characters in *Desk Set* sometimes treat EMERAC as if it were an autonomous entity functioning independently of the people who built and maintain it. At a sullen Christmas party right before the expected layoffs, Peg Costello wonders, "Do you think EMERAC will throw a party next year?" Granting EMERAC agency in some ways further obscures the roles of Sumner, Azae, and the other people responsible for building, buying, installing, and running the machine. Anthropomorphizing the computer also obscures the machine's origins in human labor. Thus, it is the ideological complement to the process of deskilling. First, workers' knowledge is appropriated into corporate-owned machines. Then, machines are fetishized as subjects independent of the labor that created them. Aristotle Tympas examines the historical consequences of this "ideology of intelligent machines":

> the ideology of intelligent machines aimed at presenting the computing machine as the source of value so as to relatively lower the part of the capital that went to computing wages, and, as a result, so as to allow for the extraction and accumulation of surplus computing value. The surplus computing value accumulated was transformed into new computing machines so that the capitalist mode of computing production could keep on expanding successfully—an expansion that was key for the expansion of the capitalist mode of production as a whole.[28]

But if treating the machine as a subject risks reifying relations of production, it has its critical uses, as well. Characters in *Desk Set* don't exactly anthropomorphize EMERAC; rather, they treat the computer as a potential *rival* to humanity. Bunny Watson worries not only about her job, but also about human beings' place in a universe of artificially intelligent machines. After viewing a demonstration of an IBM computer, she wonders whether "maybe, just maybe, people are becoming outmoded." Sumner jokingly answers, "Yeah, I wouldn't be surprised if they stopped making them altogether."

A brief history of the dream of artificial intelligence is worth recounting here. The fantasy of artificially replicating humanity has a lengthy history, from such folklore as the Jewish stories of the golem to nineteenth-century visions such as Mary Shelley's *Frankenstein* and Hoffman's tales. But while such an event has been predicted since the dawn of AI research, the more we learn about the complexity of human intelligence, the farther away the possibility of mechanically produced sentience appears.

The term "robot" dates from Karel Capek's 1921 play, *R.U.R.* In Czech it means "slave," but it quickly came to mean any artificial, mechanically constructed person. Early-twentieth-century science fiction such as Fritz Lang's film *Metropolis,* following in the tradition of *Frankenstein,* typically envisioned the robot as a nightmare doppelganger, a horrific warning against crossing the boundary between human and machine. In these stories, the threat of the robot is that it both looks like humans and thinks like humans, although its difference is usually highlighted by its metallic, machinelike exterior.

Isaac Asimov's "Three Laws of Robotics" broadened the possible uses of robots in fiction, not by blurring the boundary between human and machine, but by offering a more sophisticated policing mechanism. His stories, and the many others influenced by the laws he formulated, presume that all robots can be designed with built-in safeguards to ensure that they might never threaten human authority. However, Asimov continued the assumption that a being with artificial intelligence will look, for the most part, like a human; ENIAC hadn't even been built when he began writing his stories.[29]

The development of computers in the 1940s and 1950s broke the traditional imaginary link between artificial mind and artificial body. These new machines were clearly the most likely candidates to replicate human intelligence, and yet there was no reason for them to parrot human anatomy: they were simply huge boxes of processing power. They seemed not to be analogous to bodies, but rather to brains, and were often described as "big brains." By the 1960s, the malevolent computer (most famously Hal of *2001,* as we shall discuss below) had replaced the rebellious robot as the most threatening creation in science fiction.

AI research, growing out of the computing culture of the 1950s, took the notion of a computer as a "big brain" for granted, and, conversely, presumed that the human brain could be understood as a kind of very sophisticated computer.[30] By this logic, AI development would be a process of simply harnessing as much processing power as possible, until the computer could replicate the level of sophistication of the human brain.

This set of presumptions still guides much of AI research. But the empiricist optimism of early AI researchers was dashed by the difficulties discovered in replicating human intelligence. Consciousness, it started to seem, involves more than just processing information in the brain. Humans understand themselves not just through brain-based cognition, but through the experiences of the sensorium of the whole body. Our sense of ourselves can not be separated from our experience of living in our bodies. We make sense of the world, in large part, by physically relating to it, and this physical component cannot be abstracted from purely "mental" processes. More and more, contemporary AI researchers have come to conclude that in order to understand consciousness, and thus replicate it technologically, one must abandon the Cartesian separation of mind from body. And so the most recent AI research, while remaining within the empiricist constraints of scientific discourse, intriguingly echoes such poststructuralist ideas as Hélène Cixous's concept of "writing the body."[31] As

Vivasvan Soni writes in a compelling critique of the traditional assumptions of AI research, "Bodies . . . are not merely accidents that happen to befall abstract machines. More likely, it is intelligence that befalls bodies or arises from bodies which are trying to survive in the world. There is no such thing as an abstract and disembodied intelligence."[32]

So, if AI remains such a tough nut to crack, why do films from *Desk Set* to *2001* to *The Matrix* continue to take the bold predictions of the most arrogant AI pundits so seriously? Granted, the immediate content of these fears about computers can't be completely dismissed out of hand; it may be unlikely, but at least some credible researchers believe that artificially intelligent computers might some day develop self-awareness and independent thought.[33] But while such an event has been predicted since the dawn of AI research, the more we learn about the complexity of human intelligence, the farther away the possibility of mechanically produced sentience appears—despite the astonishing advances in computer processing power.

The roots of metaphysical anxiety over computer intelligence, I would argue, are less practical than allegorical. The AI allegory anthropomorphizes the machines that already seem so powerful in our lives. Depicting computerization as a struggle between humanity and anthropomorphized machines invests the contemporary consequences of computerization with an aura of urgency and moral weight. Allegorization draws a connection between the specific victims of computerization and the mass public: it suggests that computers threaten not merely some workers, but all humanity.

In exaggerating the powers of computers in order to reshape social struggle as a metaphysical battle, however, allegorization risks not only reifying relations of production, but also fostering a skewed understanding of computers' actual capabilities. In order to treat EMERAC as a kind of speaking subject, *Desk Set* fudges what a computer of the 1950s could actually do. At one point, to demonstrate the computer's skills, Sumner asks it several questions by typing in entire sentences—mirroring the way he would ask a member of the research staff a question. But as any contemporary computer user knows, even today's computers are very poor at responding to such "natural language" queries; Sumner would have had to do the intellectual work of formatting his query in the form of a Boolean search to get anywhere.

Of course, *Desk Set,* as a comedy set in its era's present, exaggerates computers' powers much less than a science fiction film would. The computer's power in *Desk Set* is only embellished, not extrapolated. EMERAC only provokes characters' AI anxieties; nobody actually considers the computer sentient. Allegories of AI anxiety become much more prominent in films that project computing power into the future, and imagine truly intelligent machines. It is to one of those films, *2001,* that we will now turn.

2001: Technophobic Narrative, Technotopian Subtext

First, a little background on the growth of computing in the intervening decade between the releases of *Desk Set* and *2001.* At the time of *Desk Set,* IBM was just emerging as the leader of this new field, and corporate America was beginning to purchase computers in large numbers. IBM cemented its dominance in 1964 with the introduction of System/360, a series of "third-generation" computers of different sizes designed to handle a broad range of computing needs. Costing IBM over $500 million in direct research, and over $5 billion in total costs to bring to market,[34] the effort was one of the largest civilian research projects ever undertaken.[35] Sales far exceeded IBM's expectations, and System/360 became the anchor of IBM's growth for the next 25 years. In 1951 there were 10 computers in the United States. By 1970 there were approximately 75,000.[36]

Protests over the Vietnam War had made Americans much more aware of computing's role in the military-industrial complex. In 1968 antiwar protesters marched on MIT's Tech Square, home of the university's famed Artificial Intelligence lab, one of many computer research institutions funded by the Defense Department's Advanced Research Projects Agency.[37] (ARPA was also the primary backer of ARPANET, the networking system that would become the internet.)

The most famous computer of the 1960s was undoubtedly HAL, the star of *2001.* Released in 1968, the film was immediately hailed by critics as visionary science fiction (although some complained about the plodding pace). It was a commercial success as well, becoming the second-highest-grossing film of the year.[38] Its reputation has only grown in the years since its release. In the American Film Institute's much-publicized 1998 poll of filmmakers and critics to determine "America's 100 Greatest Films," *2001* ranked at number 22.

Like *Desk Set, 2001* has an IBM connection: the company consulted on the likely design of computers in the future. According to some

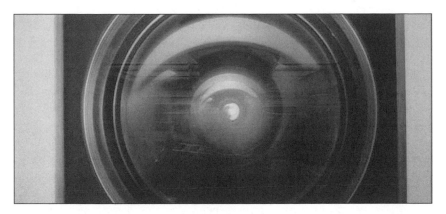

HAL. From *2001: A Space Odyssey* (MGM, 1968).

sources, in fact, IBM had planned on a product-placement deal in which the company's logo would be affixed to HAL, until they got wind of the machine's villainous role. IBM was further displeased after the film's release, when fans of the movie began to notice that "HAL" is "IBM" with the letters shifted down a character. Many commentators have taken this connection to be a subtle dig at the company, although director Stanley Kubrick and author Arthur C. Clarke insisted it's just coincidence. (Clarke has always maintained that HAL stands for "Holistic ALgorithm." Given Kubrick's notorious perfectionism, however, it's hard to believe the similarity of the initials to "IBM" went unnoticed during four years of screenplay revision and two years of production.)

Here's a brief review of the plot. In a prologue, a clan of prehuman primates discovers a mysterious monolith, which appears to somehow spur the development of tool building, war making, and, by implication, human evolution and civilization. Cut forward to the year 2001. A similar monolith has been discovered on the moon. Its only form of communication since its discovery has been to transmit a radio signal in the direction of Jupiter. The spaceship *Discovery* is sent to the planet to investigate. On board are two conscious crew members, three others in suspended animation, and the ship's artificially intelligent computer, HAL. During the mission, HAL begins to act strangely, ultimately killing four of the astronauts. The final survivor, commander Dave Bowman, only saves himself by disconnecting the rogue computer. He is subsequently picked up by the aliens who created the monoliths, and in the film's famously trippy climax, achieves some sort of transcendent post-human state.

In comparing *2001* and *Desk Set,* what's most striking is the inversion of narrative and subtext. In *Desk Set,* the authorized narrative endorses technological progress, while anti-computer anxiety bubbles beneath the surface. In *2001,* on the other hand, it is the surface narrative that appears anti-computer, while the subtext is technotopian.

HAL is the murderous villain of *2001.* As a machine gone bad, he seems a classic technophobic figure, a warning to those who would attempt to replicate human intelligence in silicon. With his unblinking lenses in every room, he is a nightmare vision of computer as Big Brother—a massive, omniscient presence, so pervasive that the crew must hide in a pod to get any privacy. Even then, there's no escape, as he reads their lips. HAL is also a vision of the dangers of human dependence on technology for survival. Floating in space, the crew is reliant on the systems HAL controls to provide air, food, water, and warmth. When HAL snaps, there's little they can do; three of the crewmen are killed without ever knowing what hit them, their life support cut off while they sleep in suspended animation. Only Dave survives, and just barely; it's not clear he would have had much hope if the aliens hadn't picked him up when he reached Jupiter.

But as many commentators have noticed, HAL is also the most sympathetic character in *2001.* The film's humans are famously dull. Even when his life's on the line, Dave can barely muster the emotion for a slight grimace. HAL, by contrast, continually shares his feelings with Dave, ultimately begging for his life and regressing to earliest memories as Dave methodically unplugs the memory banks that contain the computer's consciousness.

HAL's reception demonstrates the promise lurking beneath the film's pessimism. To artificial intelligence researchers, he has become the Holy Grail, the most inspiring example of what AI hopes to achieve. In 1997, the year of HAL's birth according to Clarke's novelization of the film,[39] a commemorative conference was held at HAL's birthplace, the University of Illinois at Urbana-Champaign, to, according to the organizers, "celebrate the roles of computers in people's lives."[40] That year also saw the release of a collection published by MIT, *HAL's Legacy: 2001's Computer in Dream and Reality.* Experts in different areas of AI address how close research in their subfield is to achieving what editor David G. Stork calls "the dream of making HAL."[41] Topics include HAL's apparent capacity

Dave disables HAL. From *2001: A Space Odyssey* (MGM, 1968).

to feel emotion, his ability to make plans, and his speech and voice recognition skills. In the collection's introduction, Stork describes how many of the contributors were in part inspired to become computer scientists by HAL:

> Implicit, and occasionally explicit, throughout this book is the fact that nearly all the contributors were deeply influenced by *2001* when it was released in 1968. I was myself introduced to the notion that a computer might someday be able to lipread by that famous scene in the pod, and I have spent years trying to devise computer lipreading systems. In that sense, many scientists are themselves a part of HAL's legacy.[42]

The upshot of HAL's lipreading is that he discovers the crew's plan to shut him down, spurring his own murderous actions. But the villainous context of HAL's skill was no barrier to Stork's inspiration. Nowhere in *HAL's Legacy* does anybody wonder whether making HAL would necessarily be a good thing, given what happened to the fictional version.

The divergent readings of HAL—HAL as villain versus HAL as prototype—demonstrate again, as we saw with *Desk Set*, how differently audiences may interpret a film. While viewers already suspicious of computers had their worst fears confirmed by HAL's treachery, the contributors to *HAL's Legacy,* budding scientists in 1968, easily discounted the narrative context, and saw only the promise of technological achievement. But, as with the reception to *Desk Set,* I want to guard against this easy division of interpretations, which I think misses the conflicts and contradictions within any one viewer's experience of the film. I think it is most useful to see *2001* as a cross section of often simultaneously held fears and hopes about computers. *2001* suggests that even in a climate of suspicion toward computers, an undercurrent of technotopianism ran beneath phobic narratives. It was this wellspring of hope that the personal computer would tap in the 1970s.

AI Anxiety Redux

2001 has been hailed by critics and scientists alike for its scientific verisimilitude. A pet peeve of many scientists about most SF movies, for example, is that their outer-space explosions produce thundering booms audible halfway across a solar system. There actually shouldn't be any noise at all—since space is a vacuum, the sound wouldn't carry. *2001* is one of the very few science fiction films to bother to get this kind of detail right. The outer-space sequences include no diagetic sound at all. As Stork writes,

> With most science fiction films, the more science you understand the *less* you admire the film or respect its makers. . . . But with other, less numerous films, the more science you know the more you appreciate a film and esteem its makers. *2001* is, of course, the premier example of this phenomenon. Director Stanley Kubrick and author Arthur C. Clarke consulted scientists in universities and industry and at NASA in their effort to portray correctly the technology of future space travel. They tried to be plausible as well as visionary. Every detail—from the design of the space ship, the timing of the mission, and the technical lingo to the typography on the computer screens and the space stewardesses' hats (bubble-shaped and padded to cushion bumps in the zero gravity of space travel)—was carefully considered in light of the then-current technology and informed predictions.[43]

But Clarke, Kubrick, and their many consultants got at least one scientific prediction wrong by a wide mark: we have now passed the supposed date of HAL's birth, but we are nowhere close to creating a self-aware artificially intelligent computer. Today, in an era of technological arrogance, we remain flummoxed by consciousness. Simson Garfinkel writes that the contemporary situation is

> a dramatic ideological reversal from the 1960s, when AI researchers were sure that solutions to the most vexing problems of the mind were just around the corner. Back then, researchers thought the only things they lacked were computers fast enough to run their algorithms and heuristics. Today, surrounded by much more powerful computers, we know that their approaches were fundamentally flawed.[44]

AI boosters, however, continue to see electronic sentience just around the corner. Influential AI researcher Ray Kurzweil sets the date at 2020 in *The Age of Spiritual Machines: When Computers Exceed Human Intelligence*. As I discussed above, this continued confidence may have less to do with a scientific judgment about the prospects of future research than with a desire in the present for a certain vision of the future. AI is so vivid a dream because it's so compelling as allegory. As a projection into the future, it helps us make sense of our present, objectifying and personifying technology that so often seems invisible and nameless. HAL is an embodiment of anxieties and hopes about computers in the 1960s.

But who is to blame for HAL's murders? Do HAL's actions overshadow any understanding of the men and women behind the machine? To put it in the terms I used earlier, does the allegorical resonance of anthropomorphism outweigh the danger of reifying relations of production—of blaming machines and letting people off the hook?

Michael Bérubé, addressing this question in his essay "Paranoia in a Vacuum: *2001* and the National Security State," argues no:

> HAL has been programmed to conceal the purpose of the mission *even from the astronauts on board*. At the same time, he has been programmed to perform flawlessly; as he puts it to a BBC interviewer, "no 9000 computer has ever made a mistake or distorted information." Lurking beneath the human/machine binary, in other words, is a specific set of instructions in HAL's software, all written by very human members of the US national security apparatus. HAL does not rebel against his mission. . . . He simply seeks to reconcile contradictory mission imperatives, and he does so with nothing more emotional than the microchips in his logic centers; behind the "conflict" between men and machines in *2001* are still more men.[45]

Those men include not only the computer scientists directly responsible for HAL's programming, but all the functionaries of the "national security state":

> the decision to withhold mission information from the *Discovery* crew has the highest security clearance. It is not the work of a Strangelove in Mission Control, but of the entire institutional apparatus of national security, including the president, NASA (the NCA) and the National Security Council (with the possible exception of the vice-president, who no doubt will claim to have been out of the loop).[46]

The murders, then, are an expression of the national security state's pathological logic of secrecy and paranoia, what another critic calls "the bureaucratization of evil in the form of the whole computer system."[47]

But as Bérubé admits, he's in the minority in his argument. Most critics describe the film (often admiringly) as depoliticized compared to Kubrick's earlier *Dr. Strangelove*. As Bérubé puts it,

> critics' readings of HAL . . . tend to underread the sources (and the effect) of his programming, while ascribing too much "ineffably human" pluck and initiative to Bowman's eventual victory over HAL.
>
> Kubrick's explicators are almost uniformly silent on what we might call the "social context" of the Jupiter mission. Norman Kagan writes that "when he begins to acquire emotions, an ego, and the beginnings of a personality, when he starts to be a man, HAL begins to misbehave because of the precariousness of his self-worth, his own emptiness"; Thomas Allen Nelson claims that "once programmed to be human," HAL "becomes imbued with a consciousness of his own fallibility"; Daniel De Vries says, "he is proud and willful, and when his pride is hurt and his life threatened, he does what any other human being would do: he becomes murderous"; and Michel Ciment concludes that HAL is a creature "which, rebelling against its mission, falling prey to anxiety and the fear of death, wreaks vengeance on those who no longer have confidence in it by finally sinking into criminal madness."[48]

My own conclusion is that while Bérubé is correct to say that Kubrick leaves *2001* open enough for viewers to connect the dots leading HAL's behavior back to the choices of his makers, the affective experience of the film discourages this reading, as Bérubé's own research demonstrates.

HAL, as I've pointed out, is in many ways the most human character in *2001*. If any character in *2001* appears to have autonomous agency, it's HAL.

Philosopher Daniel Dennett, in an essay in *HAL's Legacy* titled "When HAL Kills, Who's to Blame?" argues that HAL must bear the ethical responsibility for the murders, because he exhibits independent intentionality. In framing the question as to whether HAL is responsible for his own actions, Dennett (despite his essay's title) hardly even bothers to wonder what culpability HAL's makers might share. The essay perfectly demonstrates how easily the allegory of AI, to the extent that it grants the computer agency, lets the computer's makers off the hook.

Gendering the Mainframe

In a charming scene in *Desk Set,* Richard Sumner administers a psychological test to Bunny Watson as part of his evaluation of her department. The first question he asks is "What is the first thing you notice in a person?" Watson quickly answers, "Whether the person is male or female." Sumner seems tickled by the answer, as if he thinks of gender as so transparent a category, he hadn't even thought it counted as something to notice. Like Poe's purloined letter, gender seems too obvious to notice—or rather, to notice that you've noticed, particularly if you're a successful man comfortable with the invisible privileges of patriarchy. For Watson, though, as a woman working in a company run by men, gender is always visible—it's the only explanation, after all, for why she reports to a thick headed male boss (who doubles as her uninspiring boyfriend before Sumner's arrival), when as President Azae himself admits, she's really the one who runs her department.

But if gender is the first thing we notice about a person, what do we notice when the "person" is a computer? As disembodied boxes of circuits, computers have no physical marks of gender. In fact, it doesn't make much sense to talk about computers, however artificially intelligent, as having gender at all. As Tyler Stevens puts it, "*Whatever their subjectivities, present or future, computers have no gender. That's not a fact we live with easily.*"[49]

Sumner's question intriguingly echoes the famous Turing Test, designed by computer scientist Alan Turing in 1950 as a way to determine researchers' success in replicating "human" intelligence.[50] AI theorists had been bogged down on the tricky, perhaps unanswerable question of sentience—how to tell if a computer actually knows it thinks. Turing suggested that rather than try to answer the question by looking at the mechanics of the computer's computational process, one could best answer the question experimentally, by seeing if the computer could be programmed to respond just as a human would to a series of questions. Thus, Turing turned the question of identity away from a model of interiorized subjectivity, instead defining identity as performative.

The test itself is explicitly a form of *passing*. A questioner is connected, via a monitor, to two hidden parties: a computer and a human. The challenge for the computer is to fool the questioner into thinking it's human. If it consistently can, then, in a performative sense, it has achieved human intelligence.

At least, that's how the Turing Test is carried out today. But the original version, as Turing formulated it, is even more intriguing in what it suggests about the centrality of identity transgression to the formative fantasies of AI research. It involves two stages. First, the questioner addresses the computer and a woman; then, a man and the same woman. Turing argued that if the computer could fool the questioner into thinking *it* was the woman as often as the man could fool the questioner into thinking *he* was the woman, then it had demonstrated a kind of human intelligence. Identity here is defined not just as performance, but specifically as the performance of *gender,* abstracted from biology.[51]

For a computer, gender is always a copy for which there is no original.[52] This aspect of AI subjectivity can be an unsettling reminder of gender's instability. As Stevens writes, "Disarmingly, this reflects back to us, to our re-negotiation of our own subjectivities, our own pleasures within and across our subjectivities, in the realization that every conversation is an imitation game, every form of representation is a Turing technology."[53] Allegories of artificial intelligence, then, can offer another cybertopian hope: a queertopian vision of a world of fluid gender roles.

The instability of gender in cyberspace has been a source of inspiration for a generation of queer theorists. Today, it's easy to be a straight woman in one online chat room, a gay man in another, a transsexual in a third. Users tied to the specificity of their bodies in the "real world" find the space to blur their gender identities. The computer has become an icon of gender fluidity.

This fluidity, however, is also threatening to many who cling to traditional gender roles. The genderlessness of the computer can be perceived not as an open space for play and experimentation, but an ominous void. Coming from this angle, allegories of artificial intelligence can spin into homophobic panic.

Desk Set doesn't precisely take either of these routes. Rather, in a movie in which gender conflict often parallels class conflict, EMERAC is cast not only as a rival for Watson's job, but also as a rival for Sumner's affections. (In England, the film was released under the alternate title, *His Other Woman.*) Watson complains, "Emily EMERAC. She's all you ever think about." Later, when Sumner finally proposes, Watson wavers, complaining, "You're not in love with me, you're in love with her." To prove his love, Sumner ends the movie by throwing the switch that blows Emmy's circuits as he and Watson kiss. (Keep in mind that all this talk of EMERAC as a romantic rival is thoroughly metaphoric and tongue-in-cheek. Unlike HAL, EMERAC isn't actually sentient, and doesn't even talk; if the characters didn't tell us it was "female," there'd be no other way to know.)

Gender anxiety in *Desk Set* is embodied not by EMERAC itself, but by Miss Warringer, EMERAC's officious keeper. To mark off the homosocial space of the librarians' all-female office, the film goes to some lengths to assert the heterosexuality of each of the librarians. All four flirt with, dance with, and talk about men. Miss Warringer's coldhearted, lesbian-coded androgyny further accentuates the librarians' straightness, while providing a homophobic warning of what might happen if they failed to retain an interest in men.

In *2001,* the homophobia is much closer to the surface. As a few critics have noted, HAL, with his softy menacing tone (voiced by actor Douglas Rain), evokes the devious, gay-coded characters once played by actors such as George Sanders and Peter Lorre, with perhaps a hint of Anthony Perkins in *Psycho.*[54] As Wayne Gale puts it in an essay for the online magazine *Suck,* "Balanced on the knife edge between snide and anodyne, the computer's sibilant tone and use of feline phrases like 'quite honestly, I wouldn't worry myself about that' contain more than a hint of the stereotypically bitchy homosexual."[55] Frank tells Dave in the conversation HAL lipreads, "I can't put my finger on it, but I sense something strange about him." As HAL grows upset, he takes on the tones of a jilted lover. When Dave asks him, "What's the problem?" he petulantly responds, "I think you know what the problem is just as well as I do." Fitting into the long tradition of Hollywood films featuring gay-coded killers from *Dracula's Daughter* to *Silence of the*

Lambs,[56] the movie veers from moments of pathos to climactic scenes of revulsion and revenge. Kubrick at least leaves room for some sympathy for HAL at the climax. As he loses his mind, HAL famously sings "Bicycle Built for Two," his once-crisp voice slowing and slurring: "Daisy, Daisy, give me your answer do. I'm half crazy, all for the love of you. . . ."

PART II

The Personal Computer

4

The Many Creators
of the Personal Computer

The 1970s saw the emergence of a radically different kind of machine from the mainframes depicted in *Desk Set* and *2001*. The "personal computer" was small, self-contained, designed for individual use, and priced for consumer purchase. It broadly expanded the public availability of computing power, and transformed American notions about computing.

So how did we get from the mainframe to the PC? Rather than a smooth, linear development, the history of the PC is marked by false starts, dead ends, and unpredicted moments of convergence. Sociologists of technology have developed a helpful model for understanding the emergence of new technologies, labeled Social Construction of Technological Systems ("SCOT"). Trevor Pinch and Wiebe Bijker write,

> In SCOT the developmental process of a technological artifact is described as an alternation of variation and selection. This results in a "multidirectional" model, in contrast with the linear models used explicitly in many innovation studies and implicitly in much history of technology. Such a multidirectional view is essential to any social constructivist account of technology. Of course, with historical hindsight, it is possible to collapse the multidirectional model on to a simpler linear model; but this misses the thrust of our argument that the "successful" stages in the development are not the only possible ones.[1]

In tracing the multidirectional path of PC development in the 1970s, this chapter will examine a series of technological projects, including the development of the ECHO home computer system, the emergence of minicomputers and time-sharing, the formulation of Moore's Law, the marketing of the microprocessor, and finally, the invention of the Altair, hailed by most observers as the "first personal computer." As we shall see, each project reflected an intersection of multiple, often conflicting visions of computing. What we think of today as the PC is not the result of any single dominating vision. Rather, we live in the legacy of numerous struggles, alliances, and negotiations, out of which emerged contemporary notions of the personal computer.

ECHO: Making Room for a "Home Computer"

The first computer designed specifically for home use was the ECHO IV, the project of a Westinghouse engineer named Jim Sutherland.[2] Borrowing surplus controller hardware and memory from his job, Sutherland pieced together a complete computer system in his house in 1965. The guts of the computer resided in his basement, in four large wooden cabinets weighing a total of 800 pounds. Wires connecting input stations and output terminals ran throughout the house—there was a keyboard in the living room, a teletype in the kitchen, and several binary displays that hung over doorways and on ceilings.

In 1966 Westinghouse began publicizing its employee's futuristic project, and the Sutherland family appeared in a series of newspaper and magazine articles. As a story in the *IEEE Annals of the History of Computing* recounts,

> The accompanying photo from an early article on the machine shows Jim Sutherland at the console with his wife [Ruth] putting a raincoat on daughter Sally while [son] Jay and daughter Ann look on. The food [on the table in front of them] is supposed to symbolize how ECHO had the potential to track the groceries, and the raincoat was in case ECHO learned to predict changes in the weather, which it never did.[3]

Jim and Ruth Sutherland also made a series of presentations to meetings of home economists, discussing the computer's impact on their family's lives.

The ECHO raised for the first time the question of what it might mean to computerize a home. Where would you put a computer? What would it do?[4] We can see in the uses to which ECHO was put some early attempts to answer the question.

One answer was the kitchen. While installing 800 pounds of computing equipment in the basement and running wires up to a terminal in the kitchen just to make out shopping lists and file recipes in binary form may seem like comical overkill, ECHO wasn't the only kitchen computerization project of 1966. That year also saw the introduction (and quick failure) of the Honeywell Kitchen Computer, a powerful 16-bit machine that came with a built-in cutting board.[5] The cumbersome attempts to computerize the kitchen of the 1960s may seem silly in retrospect; after all, the kitchen of today remains largely PC-free (though, as I'll discuss below, today's microwave ovens, stoves, and even toasters often include microprocessors vastly more powerful than ENIAC). But they were a logical attempt to model the home computer along the lines of most of the new machines successfully marketed to American families in the twentieth century: "labor-saving" household appliances such as washing machines, dishwashers, and refrigerators.[6]

Despite the failure of the kitchen computer to catch on with the public, the idea of computerizing the kitchen has refused to die. Programs to organize recipes were among the first applications proposed for the Altair. (The January 1976 issue of *Byte,* for example, featured a complex flow chart diagramming a "Total Kitchen Information System."[7]) Likewise, early articles in general-interest magazines on why you'd want to buy a PC invariably included the supposed benefits of storing recipes on disk. During the dot-com boom of the late 1990s, multiple start-up companies attempted to sell "information appliances" that promised to connect the kitchen to the internet.[8]

A second space for ECHO was in the living room: one terminal was hooked up to work as a remote control for the TV, and the computer was programmed to control the family's TV antenna, making automatic adjustments to provide optimum reception for each channel. The computer could also automatically switch channels at scheduled times, the way a VCR does today. This second vision for the home computer—as part of a living room entertainment center—would become another model for PC marketing, along the lines of the selling of the television itself in the 1940s and 1950s. But while TV marketers successfully convinced Americans to remodel their living rooms around the television, establishing the TV as a kind of "electronic hearth,"[9] the PC has remained peripheral in the home, shunted off to a side desk in a corner of a living room, kitchen, or bedroom. Only recently, with the advent of the "home office" as a distinct room category (a reflection, like the PC itself, of blurring boundaries between work and leisure), has the PC begun to establish a room of its own in model American homes.[10]

What seems perhaps most quaint to contemporary eyes about the ECHO is its ubiquity. Not only were there terminals in the kitchen and living room, but three binary displays were posted over doorways, while a fourth, in a scenario that sounds like a technophile's version of a Las Vegas honeymoon suite, hung from the ceiling of the master bedroom, so that Jim Sutherland could check on the status of ECHO during the night. The PC, as it would emerge in the 1970s, was a much more self-contained product. What happened instead to computerize the home was the proliferation of microprocessors within products: tiny individual chips in clocks, TVs, and kitchen appliances would accomplish more than the ECHO's mainframe ever could. But the fantasy of a completely networked, centrally controlled "smart house" has never disappeared from computer magazines, despite repeated failures to take the consumer market by storm. Using your PC to control your appliances, like recipe organizing, was another ubiquitous recommendation in early articles about the uses of PCs. And "smart houses" in which PCs control lighting, audio/video systems, and security cameras continue to be popular subjects of photo layouts in computer magazines, as well as in more specialized publications such as *Audio/Video Interiors* and *Electronic Home*.[11] The archetype for these domestic fantasies is the home of Bill Gates, in which computers monitor the movements of guests, adjusting lighting, music, and digitally displayed artwork to match each guest's preference.[12]

The smart house ideal is a vision of domestic space as panopticon, and home surveillance technology as a cure for domestic troubles. The idea of a smart house often appeals to parents anxious to monitor their children's movements, for example. But the smart house has yet to really catch on as more than a technophile's daydream. More compelling to most than the fantasy of technology-enhanced domestic authority is its flip side, the fear of the hyper-technologized home as a high-tech gothic nightmare. Indeed, the computer that takes over the house has been a staple of recent SF. *2001* itself is a kind of Orwellian gothic nightmare, in which HAL haunts and controls the claustrophobic domestic space of the *Discovery*.[13] One can also include in this subgenre the film from which the title of this book is borrowed, *Electric Dreams,* in which a lovesick artificially intelligent PC battles its owner for the affection of a comely upstairs neighbor. It ultimately snaps, HAL-like, threatening the entire apartment building before it is unplugged.

Minicomputers and Time-Sharing: "Mental Models" of Personal Computing

While Jim Sutherland, and perhaps a few other kindred spirits who never made it into the papers, were playing with the idea of putting a computer in the house, a more widespread development in the 1960s was the emergence in university computing centers of a different kind of "personal" computing: time-sharing. As first designed, a mainframe computer could only be operated by one user at a time. As demand for computing increased in the 1950s, a system called "batch processing" was established: if you wanted a moment of the computer's processing power, you would have to program instructions on punch cards and hand them over to the technicians who controlled access to the computer. After the batch was processed, you could pick up the results of the operation. As John Kemeny, author of the BASIC programming language, complained,

> Machines were so scarce and so expensive that man approached the computer the way an ancient Greek approached an oracle. . . . A man submitted his request . . . and then waited patiently until it was convenient for the machine to work out the problem. Only specially selected acolytes were allowed to have direct communications with the computer.[14]

In this setup, there was little opportunity to interact with and learn from the computer. If you'd made a mistake in your program, or if the results had inspired a new question, you'd have to make a new batch of punch cards and start all over again.

In the 1960s access to computers became somewhat less constricted as smaller, relatively less-expensive "minicomputers" were developed by IBM rivals such as Digital Equipment Corporation. Steven Levy writes of the reaction of MIT's "hackers" to the introduction of DEC's first machine in 1961:

> The PDP-1 (the initials were short for Programmed Data Processor, a term considered less threatening than "computer," which had all kinds of hulking-giant connotations) would become known as the first minicomputer, designed not for huge number-crunching tasks but for scientific inquiry, mathematical formulation . . . and hacking. It would be so compact that the whole setup was no larger than three refrigerators—it

wouldn't require as much air-conditioning, and you could even turn it on without a whole crew of sub-priests being needed to sequence several power supplies in the right order or start the time-base generator, among other exacting tasks. The retail price of the computer was an astoundingly low $120,000—cheap enough so people might stop complaining about how precious every second of computer time was.[15]

Levy writes of how MIT's hackers grew to love the power of being able to directly interact with the computer. Inspired by this power, and anxious to increase opportunities for access, programmers at MIT and other institutions began developing "time-sharing" systems that would allow multiple users at multiple locations to simultaneously use a single computer. The computer would divide its resources, apportioning a portion of its processing power to each user. As Paul Ceruzzi writes of DEC's PDP-10, one of the first computers specifically designed for time-sharing, it "succeeded in creating the illusion that each user was in fact being given the full attention and resources of the computer. That illusion created a mental model of what computering could be—to those fortunate enough to have access to one."[16]

This illusion inspired many users to begin to imagine how computers might become tools used by large numbers of people. In California, an organization called the People's Computer Company brought time-sharing to local communities, pioneering the provision of low-priced computing access to nonprofit organizations and curious individuals.[17] Few involved in the development of time-sharing, though, would have imagined that this model would come to be popularized through the sale of discrete "personal" devices, rather than the establishment of a network of terminals and mainframes.[18]

Moore's Law: The Rush to Miniaturize

What would make the concept of an individually owned "personal" computer possible was the miniaturization of the circuitry that once took up whole rooms onto a mass-produced set of silicon chips. This section will look at the ideological assumptions and cultural consequences of the rush to miniaturization. First, though, we'll need some technical background.

It's important to remember that, at heart, a computer is simply a series of on/off switches, strung together in sequence to represent logical operations and numerical values. Given a set number of switches, the size of the computer depends on how large the switches are; the processing power depends on how quickly they can switch from one state to another (representing the binary values 0 and 1); and the price depends on how cheaply the switches can be manufactured and combined.

Charles Babbage's difference engine used electromechanical switches. ENIAC used vacuum tubes, which could operate much more quickly, but required large amounts of space, and were subject to frequent blowouts. The miniaturization of electronic devices that characterized the second half of the twentieth century began in 1947 with the invention of the transistor, which exploited the properties of certain materials called semiconductors. Transistors are much smaller, faster, more durable, and more energy efficient than vacuum tubes.

Over the subsequent decade, engineers investigated ways to streamline electronics design even further by putting multiple transistors on a single piece of semiconductor materials. The result of this research was the integrated circuit: a single "chip" upon which could be installed all the components to create a complete electronic circuit designed for a specific task. The IC was invented by Jack Kilby of Texas Instruments in 1958. The manufacturing process was subsequently refined by Robert Noyce of Fairchild Semiconductor, who figured out how to print all the connections on the chip in a single step through a photolithographic process, allowing the complex circuits to be mass-produced, rather than etched by hand.[19]

Through the 1960s semiconductor companies consistently found ways to imprint finer and finer circuitry into wafers of silicon. In 1965, looking back on the pace of miniaturization since the invention of the integrated circuit, semiconductor engineer Gordon Moore noticed a pattern: the number of transistors that could be built on a piece of silicon of a given size had consistently doubled every year.[20] That shrinking in the size of transistors translates pretty directly into a doubling of speed. Studying what his organization had in its pipeline, Moore saw that the pattern would apparently hold for the foreseeable future. Extrapolating further, Moore predicted that the pattern would hold indefinitely, with computer processing power continually increasing at an exponential rate. This prediction has become known as "Moore's Law," and it has held up astonishingly well in the decades since its formulation.

The exact pace of Moore's Law is subject to some dispute. Moore himself later revised his figure to two years, then settled on eighteen months.[21]

Since many different kinds of chips are always in production simultaneously, and benchmark tests to measure processing speed can vary, the measurement of the rate of Moore's Law depends on what points of reference are chosen. And microprocessor speed is only one aspect of computer performance. Hard-drive storage capacity has actually been growing at an even greater rate than microprocessor speed, doubling every year since 1997.[22] These advances have made the digital storage of massive multimedia files practical much sooner than once expected. On the other hand, laptop battery life has hardly budged in two decades. Nonetheless, it is the inexorable logic of Moore's Law that has come to define the pace—and worldview—of the computer industry.

Moore's Law is the centerpiece of the technological determinism that is computer culture's common-sense theory of history. Its unbroken period of predictive success seems to prove that the pace of technological change is not a socially determined phenomenon, but the function of the intrinsic properties of semiconductors. The invocation of Moore's Law serves to make continued technological change appear natural and inevitable, outside of the realm of human intervention. A typical offhand passage in the *New York Times* gives an example of how Moore's Law serves to divorce technology from history: "Moore's Law . . . has been the basic force underlying the computer revolution and the rise of the Internet."[23]

But of course, Moore's Law is not a "force" or a "law" in the same sense as, say, the Second Law of Thermodynamics. The rate of miniaturization of integrated circuits is a function of the labor and capital invested in researching methods of shrinking circuits and building new plants to manufacture those circuits. If research priorities and economic incentives shifted, integrated circuits would not go on shrinking on their own. By now, Moore's Law has become a kind of self-fulfilling prophesy. As *Slate* magazine reports, "Chipmakers and industry analysts now set their goals and forecasts based on Moore's Law."[24]

The logic of Moore's Law reveals much about the dynamics of postmodern culture. First, note that Moore's Law reflects not simply an increasing *rate of change,* but an increasing *rate of acceleration.* Electronic devices are not only speeding up, but the rate at which they are speeding up is continually increasing. This helps explain why it is that, despite the fact that technological change has been a constant aspect of modernity, writers on the Information Age from Marshall McLuhan in the 1960s to Nicholas Negroponte today have consistently perceived themselves to be at the center of a moment of *unprecedented* change. They're always right, in the sense that the rate of technological development they see is always moving more quickly than it has in the past.

At the same time, though, Moore's Law promises a level of predictability to technological change. Employing Moore's Law, executives, engineers, and futurists can with some certainty—or at least the illusion of certainty—extrapolate the processing power of computers five, ten, or even twenty years into the future. A knowledge of Moore's Law, in fact, may be one of the foundations of technological literacy separating those who operate within the computer industry from the majority who observe, with trepidation, from outside. While the rate of technological change may seem a mystifying, unpredictable phenomenon to outside observers, those working within the industry retain a mental schedule of where computers are going, and at what speed.

There's no reason why increased processing power should in itself necessarily imply greater creativity, efficiency, or ease of use, to say nothing of social utility. In fact, many computer users complain that increased processing power in the absence of compelling innovations making use of that power leads only to "bloatware"—overstuffed, sluggish software that expands to fill available space, but offers only superficial improvement over previous versions. Owners of older computers often notice that their PCs run some simple programs, such as word-processing software, faster than more recent PCs run their "updated" versions, even though the older computer's microprocessor speeds may be dozens of times slower. Meanwhile, the emphasis on speed above all else helps nurture a cutthroat, hypercompetitive corporate culture always afraid of falling behind. Tellingly, Intel CEO Andy Grove titled his autobiography *Only the Paranoid Survive*.

Nonetheless, the computer industry has consistently proved able to sell consumers faster and faster models, even if the practical uses of that speed aren't immediately apparent. Moore's Law is a great deal for the computer industry; it's postmodern culture's paradigm for planned obsolescence, a technological, quantifiable, "objective" justification for computer buyers to purchase new versions of the same machines every few years. (The software industry does its part to keep this process going, periodically "upgrading" software so that it will no longer run on older computers, thereby forcing purchasers of new software to buy new computers as well.)

The research and investment decisions reflected in Moore's Law mean that semiconductor companies such as Intel have been willing to continually build faster and more powerful chips with faith that a market for those chips will follow. As industry journalist Michael S. Malone wrote in 1995, "One of the great truths of the electronics revolution is that the great breakthroughs almost always precede the need."[25] (Although "need" is perhaps putting it a bit strongly.) In the wake of the dot-com crash, however, observers such as Malone have begun to question whether the computer industry's obsession with keeping up with Moore's Law has blinded it to other priorities. Writing in the final issue of the now-defunct tech industry magazine *Red Herring* in 2003, Malone concluded, "Forget Moore's law because it has become dangerous. It is a runaway train, roaring down a path to disaster, picking up speed at every turn, and we are now going faster than human beings can endure. If we don't figure out how to get off this train soon, we may destroy an industry."[26] Industry leader Intel has begun de-emphasizing "clock speed" in its promotion of some chips, highlighting other improvements such as lower power requirements for longer laptop battery life.[27] Nonetheless, as Intel faces increased competition from upstart chip manufacturers such as Advanced Micro Devices, it seems unlikely any chip company will be willing to halt the processor-speed race unless or until forced to by insolvency.

If Moore's Law celebrates a particularly blinkered vision of "progress" as pure speed, its blithe confidence that if you build it, they will come, has opened up the opportunities for other manufacturers and users to develop unanticipated uses. This example of the dialectic of technological determinism helps explain the development of the instrument that would, unintentionally, make the personal computer technically possible: the microprocessor.

The Microprocessor

Through the 1960s semiconductor companies had been manufacturing a wide array of chips of ever-increasing power for manufacturers of calculators, clocks, and other new electronic devices. Traditionally, the chip for each product had to be custom-designed. But as miniaturization reached the point where manufacturers could include thousands of transistors on a single chip, engineers at Intel, a new company started by Robert Noyce, Gordon Moore, and other refugees from Fairchild, came up with a more efficient design approach. They proposed developing one powerful, flexible chip that could be programmed to perform a range of tasks, depending upon the product in which it was embedded. The result, in 1971, was the introduction of the first microprocessor, the Intel 4004.

With hindsight, historians of computing have recognized the introduction of the microprocessor as the critical technological development that made the personal computer possible. But the microprocessor was introduced in 1971; the Altair, the first device to look like what we might now call a personal computer, would not appear until 1975. And when it did appear, it was the product of a small company that designed kits for electronics hobbyists. The technological development of the microprocessor was not, in itself, enough to usher in the age of the personal computer.

The designers of the microprocessor themselves did recognize that the chip, as a programmable device capable of carrying out complex subroutines, contained the core capabilities of an actual computer. Early on, in fact, some engineers described the 4004 as a "microprogrammable computer on a chip."[28] To Intel management, however, the part was simply a more flexible version of the chips it already sold. As Leslie Haddon writes,

> Fundamentally their vision was not of a future with products promoted as "microcomputers"; rather it was a future of microchips as embedded parts of other products. They . . . saw the microchip as general component, not the core of an actual computer. The overall role of these companies as component suppliers led them to locate the microprocessor in such terms; indeed, the device had been designed partly to overcome a component supply problem.[29]

Likewise, the established computer companies could have taken advantage of Intel's new chips and brought out personal computers themselves in the early 1970s. In fact, a few engineers at Hewlett-Packard and Digital lobbied their companies to build low-cost microcomputers.[30] Digital's experimentation went the furthest. David Ahl, the company's manager of education sales, organized a pilot program and produced two prototypes. Each was about the size of a television; one had a handle and was designed to be portable. He planned to sell the devices to both schools and individual consumers, at $5000 each. He even made initial contacts with specialty retailers Hammacher Schlemmer and Abercrombie & Fitch, who were both intrigued with the idea of selling a home computer.[31] In May 1974 Ahl appeared before Digital's operations committee to make the case for what would have been the first computer marketed directly to home users. Stan Augarten writes,

> The committee was split. About half of the members came from the engineering side of the firm; dedicated tinkerers themselves, they had a weakness for interesting new gadgets and were gung ho about Ahl's proposal. But the other half of the committee came from the sales department, and they were much more hard-nosed. Why would a school buy such a limited machine when a time-sharing minicomputer was much more cost effective? . . . Likewise, the salesmen didn't see a market for the gadget in the home; again, what would you do with it? . . . [Digital CEO Ken] Olsen—a fallible human being, just like the rest of us—ended the debate by coming down on the side of the salesmen, and Ahl's project was scuttled.[32]

The mainframe model of computing made it practically impossible for computer executives to imagine that a tiny chip could truly be the core of a computer. Ted Hoff, the developer of the microprocessor, recalls to Michael S. Malone,

> People were used to thinking of computers as these big expensive pieces of equipment that had to be protected and guarded and babied and used efficiently to be worthwhile and cost-effective. So there was this built-in bias in people that any computer had to be treated that way. I remember one meeting in which there was all this concern about repairing microprocessors and I remember saying, "A light bulb burns out, you unscrew it and throw it away and you put another one in—and that's what you'll do with microprocessors." But they just couldn't accept doing that with a computer.[33]

As Malone concludes, "Design engineers looked at the sliver of silicon and couldn't make the cognitive leap from the room-sized computer down the hall."[34]

The Altair: Playing with the Future

By most popular accounts, the dawn of the age of the personal computer can be dated to the January 1975 issue of *Popular Electronics*.[35] The

The introduction of the Altair. Cover of *Popular Electronics*, January 1975. Courtesy of the Computer History Museum.

cover of the hobbyist magazine announced, "Project Breakthrough! World's First Minicomputer Kit to Rival Commercial Models. . . ." The image on the cover was of a rectangular metal box. On its front was a series of switches and lights. On the upper left hand corner was the product's name, the "ALTAIR 8800." Inside, the magazine explained how to put together a kit available via mail order from a small Albuquerque, New Mexico, company called Micro Instrumentation Telemetry Systems, or MITS, to create a computer of one's own for only $397.

The Altair was the brainchild of Ed Roberts, president of MITS. Roberts had founded the company in the late 1960s to build electronic instruments for model rocketry hobbyists. By the early 1970s the company had moved into the booming hobbyist field of personal calculator kits; a series of their projects ran in *Popular Electronics*. In 1974, however, large companies such as Texas Instruments started coming out with low-cost calculators, and suddenly fully made devices were available for less than MITS's kits. In need of a new product, Roberts came up with the idea of a low-cost digital computer kit. At the same time, *Popular Electronics* was looking for a minicomputer kit project. It was a perfect fit.

The Altair was not the first hobbyist project to build upon the Intel 8008 microprocessor, the successor to the 4004. The Scelbi 8-H was advertised in the March 1974 issue of *QST*. The ad promises, "Kit prices for the new Scelbi-8H mini-computer start as low as $440!"[36] In July 1974 Jonathan Titus published a piece in *Radio-Electronics* on how to build what he called the Mark-8.[37] The cover announced, "Build the Mark-8, Your Personal Minicomputer."[38] About 10,000 readers sent in $5.50 to Titus for a 48-page booklet with more detailed instructions on how to build the machine. About a quarter of those also paid $47.50 for circuit boards designed by Titus; the other components, including Intel's 8008, had to be purchased directly from the companies. Stan Augarten estimates that between one and two thousand Mark-8's were successfully built.[39]

Titus actually contacted *Popular Electronics* about his project as well, but they turned him down, considering his device to be more of an educational project than a useful machine. The Scelbi 8-H and Mark-8 had less memory and less flexibility than the Altair, and were much more difficult to build. Nonetheless, in many ways they could be described as the first "personal computers." The Altair, however, was the first machine to develop a strong user base to support further development of software and peripherals, initiating the personal computer industry.

The Altair was a success beyond the wildest dreams of MITS. Ed Roberts had hoped to sell 400 machines; he sold that many in a single afternoon. Although statistics vary from source to source, it appears that in all, 2,000 Altairs were shipped in 1975, and over 10,000 were sold in the following two years. Newsletters and magazines for Altair users began to be published. Companies popped up to write software for the Altair, including the fledgling Microsoft, which translated a version of the BASIC programming language for the machine. And the success of the Altair was enough to inspire the development of competitors, such as the IMSAI 8080 and Processor Technology's SOL, culminating in the release in 1977 of the first computer to gain truly wide distribution, the Apple II.

The bare-bones Altair did not contain all the components of what we would now think of as a complete personal computer. It had no keyboard: the only way for the user to input data into the machine was to flick a series of switches, corresponding to instructions in binary code. In order to input a simple program, the user had to flick the switches thousands of times; a single mistake would make the entire program meaningless. It had no system for long-term memory storage: every time the power was turned off, all the information entered into the computer was erased, meaning all those switches would have to be flicked all over again the next time the computer was used. And it had no monitor: the output of the program was represented by the lights on the front of the machine, which had to be translated back from binary code. It did, however, have an "open bus" architecture. This meant that plug-in expansion cards could easily be produced (by MITS and any competitors) to attach a keyboard, monitor, and other peripherals. This easy expandability and compatibility would be a crucial influence on the development of the PC industry, opening up room for a range of small companies to sell a variety of peripherals.

But when the Altair first hit the market, no expansion cards were yet available. So why would the readers of *Popular Electronics* be interested in buying this awkward device? The issue's opening editorial answered this question in terms of utility. Editorial director Art Salsberg explained,

We were determined *not* to present a digital computer demonstrator with blinking LED's that would simply be fun to build and watch, but suffer from limited usefulness. . . . What we wanted for our readers was a state-of-the-art minicomputer whose capabilities would match those of currently available units at a mere fraction of the cost.[40]

Salsberg listed several possible applications for the computer, including "an accounting system, navigation computer, time-shared computer, sophisticated intrusion system."

There's an awkwardness to this list, however, suggesting an air of defensiveness. A "sophisticated intrusion system" is just a roundabout way of saying "burglar alarm." A "time-shared computer" is just a computer with multiple simultaneous users—you're still left with the question of what each individual user would want to do with the computer. The repetition of the words "system" and "computer" demonstrate the degree to which a language had not yet even emerged in which to talk about the uses of a home computer. The terms are jargon, evoking the power and importance associated with computers, without pointing to any specific uses. While Salsberg promised "a minicomputer that will grow with your needs," it wasn't really clear that anybody had much "need" for a personal computer. What's most interesting from a contemporary perspective is what isn't on the list: no word processor, no spreadsheet. These applications simply hadn't been invented yet.

From its inception, then, we see a tension in the appeal of the personal computer: between the practical, immediate uses to which it can be put, and the long-range hopes and fantasies it embodies and inspires. As Leslie Haddon and David Skinner write of early British computer hobbyists, "The language of utility . . . hides and, to some extent, justifies the pleasure of exploring the machine."[41]

So, what did this pleasure entail? What other motivations may have lurked beneath the surface rhetoric of immediate utility for the builders of Altairs? On the most practical level, building the Altair was an opportunity to develop technical skills. The readers of *Popular Electronics* were self-identified "hobbyists." A hobby exists on the boundaries of work and leisure; it's a way to experiment with a task, to learn through play. It doesn't promise immediate practical reward, but it does offer the long-range opportunity for "self-improvement." Indeed, issues of *Popular Electronics* in the mid-1970s were filled with advertisements for technical education courses, including many designed to teach computer skills to those without access to actual computers. One ad in the Altair issue, for "NRI's Complete Computer Electronics Course," promised, "NRI is the only school to train you at home on a real digital computer."[42] (The "computer" in question was actually a "digital multimeter"—the kind of learning tool the Altair article dismissed as a "souped-up calculator.") Other ads in the same issue ran for International Correspondence Schools[43] and Bell and Howell Schools.[44] For readers with interest in computers but without the credentials and status to gain direct access, building a computer was a way to join an elite fraction of the professional-managerial class—either directly, by developing the skills needed to get computer jobs, or in spirit, by gaining access to the cultural capital that set that elite apart.

For those hobbyists not specifically interested in the computing profession, building a computer provided a more general opportunity to explore and understand a powerful technology. In a direct, tactile way, it allowed them an opportunity to transcend their sense of alienation from this powerful technology, and to gain a sense of control and mastery.

Many of these hobbyists saw their own new access to computing as part of a larger movement with political consequences: the democratization of technology. As an editorial in the Altair users' newsletter, *Computer Notes,* put it, "You may have noticed some strange things happening in technology lately. Ordinary people have been gaining the use of technology that was previously limited entirely to the use of experts."[45] Advocates of "computer liberation" began to emerge, especially among bohemian technophiles in California's Bay Area, home to both the counterculture and research institutions such as Stanford University.[46] An organization dubbed the Homebrew Computer Club became the meeting place for idealistic Altair enthusiasts in the Bay Area. Many of the pioneers of Silicon Valley, including Apple's Steve Wozniak, developed their ideas about computing at the group's biweekly meetings.[47]

Technophilia and radical politics met in the pages of publications such as *The Whole Earth Catalog* and *Co-Evolution Quarterly.* These magazines promoted the "appropriate technology" movement, which advocated the use and development of new, democratizing, environmentally friendly tools such as solar power and Buckminster Fuller's geodesic domes. (As we shall see in chapter 8, the publishers of *The Whole Earth Catalog* would go on to found *Wired* magazine in the dot-com 1990s.)[48] The personal computer was a logical extension of this left-wing technotopianism. A writer named Ted Nelson explored this vision in his 1974 self-published manifesto, *Computer Lib/Dream Machines.* As *Whole Earth Catalog* originator and *Wired* founding editor Stuart Brand writes, with typical hyperbole, in the introduction to a 1987 edition of the book (reissued by Microsoft Press),

From Ted Nelson, *Computer Lib/Dream Machines* (Microsoft Press, 1987).

It was all quite ironic. At the very time in the late '60s through the mid-'70s that the New Left was noisily advocating populist political revolution and conspicuously failing, a tiny sub-subculture of the Counter-Culture was quietly, invisibly fomenting a populist computer revolution, and the shock of *their* success was heard 'round the world.

The one fomenter who was not quiet was Ted Nelson, accurately depicted as the Tom Paine of the personal-computer revolution. His 1974 tract, *Computer Lib/Dream Machines,* had the same effect as Paine's *Common Sense*—it captivated readers, informed them, and set them debating and eventually marching, rallying around a common cause many of them hadn't realized was so worth or even a cause before. . . .

The enemy was Central Processing, in all its commercial, philosophical, political, and socio-economic manifestations. Big Nurse.[49]

What's important to note is the difference between this libertarian vision of democratized technology and the earlier mainframe time-sharing model. The time-sharing model was based on a *communitarian* vision of computing: the computer as a shared public resource, bringing users together. The hobbyists, however, embraced an *individualist* democratic vision, in which each user had his (or, more rarely, her) own, *personal* computer, and used it in isolation.[50]

It was this new privatized concept of computing that made it possible to imagine the computer as a commodity (like, say, a car), rather than as a utility (like a transit system). This shift, culminating in the rise of the personal computer industry, fostered the decentralization of computing, making computer power accessible to many more people than ever before. But by establishing an understanding of the computer as an expensive private investment rather than as a shared public resource, the commodification of computing guaranteed that access to computing would be stratified by income level. This development was quintessentially American in its individualism and consumerism. Compare, by contrast, the French Minitel system, which treated the computer as an extension of the government-backed phone system, and which as a result reached a much larger percentage of the French population in the 1980s. Only recently, as prices for computers have fallen below $1,000, have computers penetrated the majority of American households.

The commodification of computing established a vision of computing as an atomized, "personal" task—much different from the time-sharing model, in which the computer is a medium of communication among many users. Despite the availability of modems from very early on, "connectivity" was widely seen as only a peripheral role for computers. Only with the rise of the internet in the mid-1990s did this model start to shift, as personal computing finally began to develop into something like "interpersonal" computing. Even today, the American interpersonal model remains rooted in the assumption that each individual user is anchored to a personal computer. While in many parts of the world, the majority of users log on to the internet through publicly available computers at cybercafes, in the United States cybercafes in locations such as Starbucks and Borders instead offer WiFi access—the user is expected to bring her own laptop.

Finally, I want to point to one other, less definable aspect to the hobbyists' vision of computing: the promise that building an Altair would be a way to participate in the making of the future. The text of the *Popular Electronics* article began, "The era of the computer in every home—a favorite topic among science-fiction writers—has arrived!"[51] This language cast the builders of the first Altairs as the stars of their own SF epics, pioneers launching a new age of technology.

Les Solomon, an editor at *Popular Electronics* in 1975, tells the story of how the Altair was named:

> After dinner one night I asked my twelve-year-old daughter, who was watching *Star Trek*, what the computer on the Enterprise was called.
> "Computer," she answered.
> That's a nice name, I thought, but not sexy. Then she said:
> "Why don't you call it Altair? That's where the Enterprise is going in this episode."[52]

This is a nifty little creation story that combines intergalactic SF utopianism with the figure of the child as harbinger of the future. A competing version of the story keeps the theme of intergalactic exploration, while toning down the utopianism. According to computer historian Stan Veit, "Forest Mims said the name came from two editors of *Popular Electronics* in New York. One of them, Alex Burawa, who was an astronomy fan, said, 'It's a stellar event, so give it a star name—Altair.'"[53] The latter story is confirmed by other participants, some of whom resent Solomon's perceived embellishments. Arthur Salsberg writes in a feature titled "Jaded Memory," "Solomon weaves a nice story about his daughter's naming the machine while watching *Star Trek*, but it seems that this is just a story."[54] Nonetheless, Solomon's version makes a more mythically resonant story, and it's stuck. Most computer histories print the legend.[55]

What marvels would this future of computers in every home hold? How would the world be changed? Here, *Popular Electronics* fell silent, as did most of the hobbyist community. In fact, reading through years of *Popular Electronics, Byte,* and *Computer Notes,* what's striking is the juxtaposition of vivid enthusiasm for the technologies of the future with very little examination of the possible consequences of those technologies. The fascination in these hobbyist texts is clearly for the technology in itself, rather than for what it might bring. Their mute awe at the promise of the future is in some ways equivalent to the "sense of wonder" described by science fiction critics,[56] or what David E. Nye calls the "American technological sublime."[57] It is the utopian impulse at its most basic and unfocused: a vague sense that the world is not all that it can be, and a deep hope for fundamental change. Out of this vague yearning, other groups would attempt to craft more fully articulated visions of the future.

5

Apple's *1984*

From an emphasis on technology in the previous chapter, this chapter turns to the initial marketing of this new product, the personal computer. How did fledgling PC companies attempt to define a product that had never before existed? How did marketers engage and redirect the available visions of computing? Why would anybody buy one of these bizarre new devices? We will trace the changing promotional strategies of personal-computer manufacturers from the "invention" of the PC in the mid-1970s to its firm establishment as a mass-produced consumer item in the mid-1980s. We'll zoom in on what was undoubtedly the single most influential personal computer advertisement: the award-winning "1984" ad, which introduced the Apple Macintosh computer to an audience of 96 million viewers[1] during the 1984 Super Bowl.

Apple II and VisiCalc

Before we get to 1984, let's look at the years between the Altair and the Mac. The commodification of computing in the form of the PC made information processing available for the first time to millions of potential consumers. Following the success of the Altair, a number of other small computer manufacturers started up, selling to the growing hobbyist market. Not until the Apple II, however, did a computer emerge that reached a broader consumer base.

Apple Computer was founded in 1976 by Steve Jobs and Steve Wozniak. Jobs was a brilliant salesmen, Wozniak a talented engineer interested in designing PCs for users without the technical skills of the hobbyists. Their first product, the Apple I, was released later that year. A custom-built product in a wooden case, it sold only a few copies.

The Apple II was a much slicker package. In one molded-plastic box, it gave a beginner everything needed to begin computing. The Apple II was released in 1977. The following chart shows its subsequent diffusion:[2]

Year	Total Users
1977	570
1978	8,170
1979	43,270
1980	121,370
1981	301,370
1982	580,370
1983	1,000,000
1984	2,000,000

Stan Veit, the founder of one of the first stores for personal computers in the wake of the Altair's success, recalls,

The Apple II changed the entire business. No longer did solder iron wielding techies hang out at our store—the Apples came completely built and ready to run. . . . The Apple users were much more oriented toward software and graphic applications. They were more interested in what a computer did than how it did it.[3]

What users were interested in doing, more than anything else, was to use a new kind of computer program: *VisiCalc,* the first spreadsheet. Written by Dan Bricklin and Robert Frankston, *VisiCalc* was a combination of calculator and ledger sheet, allowing financial planners to create complex documents composed of interlocking mathematical relationships. *VisiCalc* exploited the interactive properties of computing, allowing users to explore a range of financial scenarios by just changing just one or two variables.

In the language of the computer industry, *VisiCalc* was the first "killer application," a software program so compelling it inspired consumers to buy computers just to run it. (Subsequent killer apps include word processing, desktop publishing, and, more recently, email and web browsing.) Released in October 1979, *VisiCalc* sold 200,000 copies in two years.[4] Only available for the Apple II, it caused an explosion in Apple II sales. As Veit recalls, "The Apple disk system was priced within everyone's price range, and soon there was a lot of very useful software for it, led by *VisiCalc,* the most important program. Businessmen would come into the store to buy 'A *VisiCalc* Machine' and that's all they used it for."[5]

VisiCalc exploited the unique interactive qualities of computer software much as computer games do. Bricklin's original model for the program, in fact, was a computer game. Computer industry journalist Robert X. Cringely writes,

> What Bricklin really wanted was . . . a kind of very advanced calculator with a heads-up display similar to the weapons system controls on an F-14 fighter. Like Luke Skywalker jumping into the turret of the Millennium Falcon, Bricklin saw himself blasting out financials, locking onto profit and loss numbers that would appear suspended in space before him. It was to be a business tool cum video game, a Saturday Night Special for M.B.A.s, only the hardware technology didn't exist in those days to make it happen.[6]

So Bricklin settled for the metaphor of a sheet of rows and columns instead of a fighter cockpit.

The IBM PC and the Rise of Microsoft

In August 1981 the world's largest computer company finally responded to the personal computer boom when IBM introduced its own personal computer. The IBM PC was an immediate success, selling out distributors and pushing the company to ramp up production far beyond initial plans. In 1981 IBM sold 35,000 PCs. In 1983 they sold 800,000, making the IBM PC the most popular computer in the world.[7]

IBM's entry into the PC market legitimized the machine for many conservative corporate purchasers skeptical about personal computers and wary of smaller, less established suppliers. As industry wags put it, "Nobody ever got fired for buying IBM." IBM's entry also helped establish technical standards for an industry still very much in flux. Instead of making competing, incompatible devices, many manufacturers began producing IBM-compatible peripherals and software.[8] More problematically for IBM, companies also began developing IBM-compatible "clones," lower-priced PCs reverse-engineered for complete compatibility with all IBM PC hardware and software.[9]

In order to catch up with the rapid pace of the PC industry, IBM ditched its traditional product development strategy in designing their personal computer. Normally, developing a new product at IBM took three years. One reason for the slow pace was that IBM preferred to man-ufacture all parts in-house, to capture as much of the profits as possible. The IBM PC, by contrast, went from conception to store shelves in only one year.[10] IBM managed this feat by outsourcing much of the development, bringing in parts and software from outside vendors.

One component IBM outsourced, to its everlasting chagrin, was the underlying software that allowed programs to function: the operating system. At the time, this didn't seem distinctly important—no more, say, than the Intel microprocessor or the Zenith power supply. And so, IBM ended up licensing its Disc Operating System from a small software company named Microsoft. Microsoft actually didn't have the resources to develop the software itself, either—instead, it bought the rights to MS-DOS from a local software company, Seattle Computer Products, for $30,000.[11]

Microsoft received a royalty of between $10 and $50 for every computer sold with its software installed.[12] It was the revenue and leverage provided by this arrangement that allowed Microsoft to become the dominant company in the computer industry within a decade. IBM's market share and profit margins were quickly squeezed by low-cost clone makers such as Compaq and Dell.[13] MS-DOS, on the other hand, was needed not just to run an IBM PC, but any "IBM-compatible" PC. PC hardware turned out to be a commodity business, in which competition among multiple producers of interchangeable, easily-copied products drives prices into the ground.[14] Software was where the real profit margins lay. The only computer company to successfully buck this development was Apple, which in 1984 introduced a new piece of hardware that contained proprietary software—the Macintosh Operating System—miles beyond anything available for the IBM-compatible PC.

Early PC Ads

VisiCalc and the Apple II launched the personal-computer industry as a multibillion dollar segment of the American economy. With this economic clout came access, through advertising and public relations, to the American public sphere. PC companies hoped to reshape public perceptions about computing. Marketers had the chance to counter the suspicions evident in *Desk Set* and *2001* by popularizing the technotopian vision of the Homebrew Computer Club and Ted Nelson—a new vision of computing as decentralized, democratic, and empowering. This transformation, in turn, might expand the PC market beyond spreadsheet users, inspire the development of new killer apps,[15] and make the PC as ubiquitous in American households as the television.

But the shadow of HAL hovered over early PC advertising. Marketers shied away from any SF-style bold promises of the future, fearing that when Americans thought of computers and science fiction, they would think of *2001*. Instead, companies bent over backwards to reassure consumers that computers were simple, unthreatening devices. This was why IBM's advertising agency, Chiat/Day, ran as far in the other direction as they could, associating the IBM PC with the quaint struggles of Charlie Chaplin. Campbell-Kelly and Aspray write,

> [IBM's] market research revealed that although the personal computer was perceived as a good thing, it was also seen as intimidating—and IBM itself was seen as "cold and aloof." The Chiat Day campaign attempted to allay these fears by featuring in its advertisements a Charlie Chaplin lookalike and alluding to Chaplin's famous movie *Modern Times*. Set in a futuristic automated factory, *Modern Times* showed the "little man" caught up in a world of hostile technology, confronting it, and eventually overcoming it. The Charlie Chaplin figure reduced the intimidation factor and gave IBM "a human face."[16]

Rewriting the story of the dystopian *Modern Times* to give it a *Desk Set*–style happy ending was an act of astounding gall, but judging from the IBM PC sales, it was quite successful.

Apple's early print campaigns for the Apple II looked back even further: one ad starred Thomas Jefferson, another Benjamin Franklin. The ads that first introduced Apple to most consumers were self-consciously nonthreatening: they starred Dick Cavett giving self-deprecating testimonials to the power of the Apple II. Later campaigns centered around what were called "lifestyle" ads, in which attractive yuppies—including a young Kevin Costner—make their lives easier and more productive with Apple computers. None of these innocuous early spots attempted to communicate the broader California vision of the liberating possibility of personal computing.

Charlie Chaplin shills for IBM. IBM ad from *Byte*, October 1984.

Introducing the Macintosh

By 1983 Apple had reached annual sales of over $1 billion.[17] But its spot as the PC market leader was in jeopardy, thanks to the brisk sales of the IBM PC. Apple's first attempt at a next-generation product that could reestablish the company's preeminence was the Lisa. A $10,000 computer designed for the business market, it was a flop. The Macintosh was a streamlined version of the Lisa, rushed out by Jobs's development team in the wake of the Lisa debacle. It was built to be compact, relatively affordable, and easy to use. Jobs hyped it as "the people's computer." It was designed to look not like an imposing piece of machinery, but an "information appliance." In its sleek, inviting shape, it bore the influence of another high-tech product of the early 1980s: the Cuisinart food processor.

What made the Macintosh and Lisa different from previous commercially available personal computers was a new technological feature: the mouse. The point-and-click interface replaced the cumbersome command-line text interface with an intuitive, elegant means of interaction.[18] The mouse was first developed by Douglas Engelbart of the Stanford Research Institute in the 1960s,[19] and perfected by researchers at the Xerox Palo Alto Research Center in the 1970s.[20] Steve Jobs toured Xerox PARC in the late 1970s and was amazed by the Alto, its prototype mouse-based computer. But Xerox never committed to developing a commercial version of the Alto, and so it was left to Apple to introduce the world to the mouse.

One might presume that the mouse was such a brilliant idea that it was inevitable the Mac would succeed. But keep in mind that the Lisa, the first PC with a mouse, failed. Many computer industry insiders dismissed the mouse as a toy, a gimmick nobody could ever take seriously. This attitude persisted even after the initial success of the Mac. As software usability expert Jacob Neilsen writes,

> In 1986, I asked a group of 57 computer professionals to predict the biggest change in user interfaces by the year 2000. The top answer was speech I/O, which got twice as many votes as graphical user interfaces. It may be hard to remember, but in 1986, there was no guarantee that the graphical user interface would win the day. It was mainly used by the "toy-like" Macintosh machines—not by the "serious" systems used by IT professionals.[21]

The Macintosh. Macintosh marketing brochure.

After a frenetic design period, the Mac was ready to be introduced in January 1984. Apple wanted a marketing campaign that would make the product stand out while communicating the broader vision of the California technotopians. The Chiat/Day advertising agency, known for its edgy work, scripted the ad. Film director Ridley Scott was hired to direct, fresh off *Blade Runner,* and given an unheard-of production budget of $900,000.[22]

The ad opens on a gray network of futuristic tubes connecting blank, ominous buildings. Inside the tubes, we see cowed subjects marching towards a cavernous auditorium, where they bow before a Big Brother figure pontificating from a giant TV screen. But one lone woman remains unbroken. Chased by storm troopers, she runs up to the screen, hurls a hammer with a heroic roar, and shatters the TV image. As the screen explodes, bathing the stunned audience in the light of freedom, a voice-over announces, "On January 24th, Apple Computer will introduce the Macintosh. And you'll see why 1984 won't be like *1984.*"

After seeing Scott's work, Jobs and his new handpicked president of Apple, John Sculley, were sure they had a hit. They purchased one and a half minutes of ad time for the Super Bowl, annually the most-watched television program in America. In December 1983 they screened the com-

From "1984" (Chiat/Day, 1984).

mercial for the Apple board of directors. To Jobs's and Sculley's surprise, the entire board hated the commercial. Panicked, Sculley ran back to Chiat/Day to try to get them to sell back the ad time. Chiat/Day, still enthusiastic about their ad, dragged their feet, and only managed to sell off 30 seconds. Rather than take a loss on the 60-second ad, Apple decided to go ahead and run "1984."[23]

Despite the board's fears, Super Bowl viewers were overwhelmed by the startling ad. The ad garnered millions of dollars worth of free publicity, as news programs rebroadcast it that night. It was quickly hailed by many in the advertising industry as a masterwork.[24] *Advertising Age* named it the 1980s' Commercial of the Decade,[25] and it continues to rank high on lists of the most influential commercials of all time.[26] As we'll see further in chapter 8, the ad—and the fantasy behind it—became a touchstone for the dot-com hype of the 1990s, anchoring the images of technology corporations ranging from "spunky" start-up companies like Monster and eBay to multinational telecommunications empires such as AT&T, WorldCom, and Intel.

"1984" was never broadcast again after the Super Bowl, adding to its mystique. Unintentionally, Chiat/Day had invented the phenomenon known as "event marketing," in which a high-visibility commercial garners mountains of extra free publicity. "1984" also inaugurated the phenomenon of showcasing commercials on the Super Bowl. And, most importantly for Apple, the ad brought consumers into the stores. It kicked off a successful $15 million, 100-day marketing blitz for the Mac.[27] Apple's sales in the first 100 days of the Macintosh's release exceeded their already high expectations,[28] and launched the Mac as a product and icon.

What "1984" accomplished was to tackle the specter of HAL head-on. It turned the confusing complexity of the Information Age—the ambivalence of *Desk Set* and *2001*—into a Manichean battle of good versus evil. There's the bad technology—centralized, authoritarian—which crushes the human spirit and controls people's minds. Read, IBM. But we can be liberated from that bad technology by the good technology—independent, individualized—of the Mac.

One irony of the commercial, though, is that what seemed to really impress TV viewers—what cost so much money to put on the screen—was

IBM as Big Brother. From "1984" (Chiat/Day, 1984).

the vision of the bad technology. It's the futuristic gloss of that technology that is so compelling; all we get of the good technology is a hammer and the Mac logo on the athlete's tank top. The schema of the "1984" ad allowed Apple to harness the visual fascination of a high-tech future, while dissociating itself from its dystopic underside.

The ad "1984" also worked by re-gendering computing in important ways. The lone runner is female. As far as we can see, every single one of the drones, as well as Big Brother himself, is male. In the Manichean framework of the ad, women are on the side of the angels. This setup helps identify the Mac user as the underdog, the member of an oppressed group. It also distinguishes the Mac from all those other, male-identified computers. Despite the fact that the person described by some as the very first computer programmer, Ada Lovelace, was a woman, modern computing has been culturally gendered as a male activity. Women remain a minority of all computer programmers, and young girls continue to receive less encouragement to use computers. The Mac signaled from the beginning that it stood for something different, affiliating Apple with the goal of equal access to computing for women.

But this isn't all the ad did. In the allegorical framework of the ad, two levels of representation are at work. In one sense, the running woman stands for Mac users; in this interpretation, the Mac is the equivalent to the hammer, the tool she uses to destroy Big Brother. In another sense, though, the woman can be considered the personification of the Mac itself. The tank top she wears, which displays the Mac logo, suggests this correspondence. The ad does two things, then. It genders the archetypal Mac *user* as female. And it genders the Mac *itself* as female.

Gendering the Mac user as female implied that Apple stood for equal access to all for computing. It also helped open up an untapped market of potential women consumers. But just as importantly, gendering the Mac itself as female associated the Mac with a host of feminine-identified qualities that helped make the Mac seem more user-friendly for all users. Other computers were associated with the traditionally male-gendered sphere of the workplace; the Mac was the home computer. Other computers were rigid, imposing; the Mac was soft, curvaceous, easy to use. Other computers were emotionless; the Mac was the personal computer. If gendering the Mac user as female implicitly presumed women had equal interest in using computers, gendering the Mac itself as female bucked computer conventions while still evoking a traditional gender

Apple as feminist, feminine freedom fighter. From "1984" (Chiat/Day, 1984).

model: the image of the computer as the friendly secretary, the able assistant with a smile on her face.

The star of the "1984" commercial isn't just a woman; she's an athlete, in clear control of her own body. The "1984" star is an early example of a media image now ubiquitous after a generation of Title IX: the woman empowering herself through achievement in sport, what we might call the "Reebok feminist." In contrast to the body of the athletic hero of "1984," the bodies of the oppressors have been colonized by technology. The Big Brother figure, his face hidden by reflected glasses and framed by blinking letters and numbers, seems almost to be a creature of the TV screen itself, rather than a flesh-and-blood person. The storm troopers' entire faces are covered by masks the shade of an unplugged TV screen. And the drones' bodies are covered in drab gray garments. Some drones even wear what appear to be gas masks. The drones' masks, in fact, evoke the breathing apparatus of that quintessential cyborg nightmare of the era, Darth Vader. And their resemblance is even more striking to a subse-

Star Trek's Borg: A nightmare vision of the hyper-technologized body. From "The Best of Both Worlds, Part I," *Star Trek: The Next Generation* (Paramount, 1990).

quent popular vision of the horrors of the hyper-technologized body, the Borg of *Star Trek*.

Compared to these figures, the running woman, unencumbered in shorts, sneakers, and tank top, might seem to represent the body freed from technology. But that's not completely right. Rather, she's an example of the new kind of athletic ideal that emerged in the 1980s: the athlete who employs Nautilus, Stairmaster, and the other technologies of exercise to hone the body to perfection. This "robo-cized" athlete is the flip side of the cyborg nightmare. Rather than the technology wearing her, she wears the technology.

This vision of technology serving the body was most fully expressed in another 1980s phenomenon: the Walkman. The Walkman wasn't just portable technology—it was wearable technology. The rise of the Walkman in the 1980s was a quintessential example of the phenomenon Raymond Williams describes as "mobile privatization": the use of technologies to insulate the individual from larger social groups, turning even public spaces into private experiences.[29] With your Walkman on, you can imagine yourself as alone and self-sufficient, even in the middle of a bustling city.

As we have seen, the rise of the personal computer was a quintessential example of privatization, turning a public resource into a personal commodity. Granted, the personal computer in 1984 was not exactly mobile; it still tied the user to a desk. But the promise of cyberspace offered a new kind of fantasy of mobile privatization: that you could sit at the computer, in the comfort of your own home, and fly through data from around the world as swiftly and self-sufficiently as the running woman, making physical movement and interpersonal interaction unnecessary.

Alongside this fantasy of mobility through cyberspace, in the years since 1984, the development of laptops, PDAs, and wireless internet connections has made computing truly mobile in the same physical-world sense as the Walkman. Reflecting these developments, for the twentieth anniversary of the Mac, Apple rereleased the "1984" ad on its website with one new digital addition: an iPod swinging from the running woman's waist.[30]

A final irony of "1984" is the fact that the villain of the commercial is a television image. In the framework of the ad, TVs are bad, PCs are good. This would become a perennial theme of computer commercials—buy a PC so your kids will do something more constructive than watching TV commercials. (Of course, in the 1990s, once large numbers of

The 2004 version, with iPod. From "20 Years of Macintosh: 1984-2004," http://web.archive.org/web/20040109083640/www.apple.com/hardware/ads/1984/.

American children gained access to computers, parents began to worry that it was the internet that would rot their children's brains.) Allegorizing the TV-viewing experience was a clever way to engage the Super Bowl audience—especially since, by the third quarter of the typically one-sided game, most viewers were likely to feel something like zombies themselves. The commercial really did accomplish in real life what it dramatized on-screen, blowing the dazed viewers out of their chairs.

The odd part is that more viewers didn't resent the implication that they were nothing but drones in need of deliverance. Presumably, this didn't rub viewers the wrong way because it left open the possibility for everyone to identify with the hammer-thrower. Even if you didn't rush out the next day to buy a Mac, you could imagine yourself as the kind of person who would, eventually. But the arrogance implicit in "1984" would come back to haunt Apple the following year. Apple and Chiat/Day's much-anticipated follow-up for the 1985 Super Bowl, a spot called "Lemmings,"[31] was a flop. In that ad, a stream of blindfolded businessmen is seen walking, one after another, off a cliff, to the tune of a dirgelike rendition of "Heigh-ho, Heigh-ho" from *Snow White and the Seven Dwarfs*. Finally, one person steps out of the line, lifts his blindfold, and asks, "Why am I doing this?" The implication was that IBM PC users were the lemmings, Mac users the rebel. But many IBM users resented the attack, which seemed blunt and personal compared to the "1984" allegory. John Sculley writes,

> The day after the Super Bowl, our telephone lines were overloaded with calls from irate people claiming they would never buy an Apple product again. They believed the commercial insulted the very people we were trying to court as customers in corporate America. Dealers flooded us with calls saying they were getting complaints from prospective customers.[32]

Mac sales, which had begun to slow down at the end of 1984, continued to stagnate, and soon Apple fired Chiat/Day and moved its account to BBD&O. There was no blockbuster Mac commercial during the 1986 Super Bowl.

The audience as drones. From "1984" (Chiat/Day, 1984).

Flash Forward

Cut to August 1997. In a hotel ballroom in Boston, the assembled Apple faithful, convened for the annual MacWorld Expo convention, received a jarring dose of déjà vu. Onstage was Steve Jobs. Jobs had been forced out of Apple shortly after the introduction of his pet project, the Mac. But as Apple struggled to survive following the introduction of Microsoft's hugely successful, Mac-like Windows 95 operating system, Jobs emerged once again as the company's designated savior.

Jobs took the podium to announce a deal he promised would turn Apple around. He turned to the enormous video screen behind him, and up popped a giant image none other than Bill Gates, CEO of the hated Microsoft, IBM's successor as Apple's archrival.

Gates had agreed to invest $150 million in Apple, in return for Apple's endorsement of Microsoft's Internet Explorer web browser. That ominous image of Gates on the giant screen recalled another image from Apple's history: the Orwellian despot of "1984." The crowd, getting the

MacWorld Expo, 1997. From *Newsweek*, August 18, 1997.

Fan-created image of Bill Gates blended with Locutus of Borg. From Witzige Bilder, http://joergnaedele.bei.t-online.de/witzpics/micro/borg.jpg.

irony right away, was stunned. Many booed. Jobs, it seems, had made a deal with the devil.

So, had Apple betrayed what it promised in "1984"? Yes, but only in the sense that by 1997, some of the contradictions implicit in the original ad had begun to come home to roost. For many other technology companies, the reckoning came a few years later, after the NASDAQ crash of 2000.

As we've seen, the ideology of "1984" was built on a series of Manichean dichotomies. The heroic individual versus the despotic institution. The spunky start-up versus the smothering monopoly. Casting IBM as a monolithic threat to freedom allowed Apple, already a $500 million company at the time, to present itself as a lone underdog by comparison. (I'm sure that smaller computer manufacturers, such as Commodore, saw the picture somewhat differently.) Apple may present itself as a smaller, kinder, gentler corporation, but it operates by the same rules of the marketplace as everybody else. In comparison to a smothering monopoly, entrepreneurialism can look pretty exciting. But that doesn't much affect the underlying inequities of capitalism. While Apple celebrated its computers' ability to empower knowledge workers, the manual laborers who built the Mac's chips, assembled its hardware, and swept up after its programmers were not so liberated by the promise of individual computation. For those workers, the difference between the era of IBM hegemony and the hypercompetition of today's marketplace is that the pace of the "New Economy" increases job instability, which in turn makes unionization incredibly difficult. Unions don't fit in well with the libertarian fantasy of the "1984" ad—workers are somehow supposed to empower themselves individually. High technology, in fact, is the least unionized industry in the United States.[33]

The framing of the battle of monopoly versus competition, then, elides another conflict—that between labor and management. It also avoids another alternative to competition: state regulation. In Orwell's original scenario, the *state* is Big Brother, the source of oppression. In Apple's version of 1984, the target is not so clear—Big Brother is most obviously IBM, but more generally seems to represent any conglomeration of centralized power. This recognition that multinational corporations may be more powerful and dangerous than nation-states is a theme the ad shares with its literary contemporary, cyberpunk fiction, and is part of what makes the ad feel so compelling and relevant, even two decades after its release. But by lumping in the state with the megacorporation as just another monopoly of power, the ad presumes that the only route to liberation is unregulated competition—the free market. In the guise of countercultural idealism, the ideology of "1984" has come to mean endorsing the most unrestricted, brutal forms of capitalist competition.

So perhaps it's not worth crying for Apple's loss of innocence in the 1990s and beyond. Steve Jobs promised to change the world, but for all his supposed idealism, Apple never questioned the rules of competition. This is no surprise; Jobs was a businessman with a company to run. If he were any more of an idealist, he would have been out of a job even quicker than he was. But the collapse of Jobs's utopian rhetoric suggests the limitations of dreams dictated by the marketplace.

6

The Rise of the Simulation Game

Following the success of the Apple Macintosh, the IBM PC, and their many imitators, the personal computer in the 1980s emerged as a full-fledged mass-consumer product, purchased for American homes in the millions.[1]

But once they brought these objects home, what could users do with these strange new machines? In the wake of *VisiCalc,* financial management was one obvious application, although few home users had much need for the powerful data crunching made possible by spreadsheets. Word processing was another popular choice. The opportunity to instantly alter an already-typed document through cutting and pasting was a profound change in the dynamics of writing. The famously prolific science fiction writer Isaac Asimov moaned that if he'd had his Radio Shack TRS-80 for his entire career, he could have published three times as much.[2] Other commentators worried about trading the permanence of handwriting and typing for the eternal fluidity of computer text, with its endless temptation to tweak and tinker.[3]

But these applications, as new and influential as they were, only scratched the surface of the PC's ever-expanding graphics and processing power. For the many users who sought not just utility, but the opportunity to test the possibilities of these new machines, it was a less immediately practical genre of software which offered the greatest opportunity for exploration: the computer game.

The computer game is a paradigmatic example of a cybertopian space. Computer games allow players to lose themselves in imaginary worlds, with incredible flexibility to mold characters and environment. And because the computer game is such a new medium, these worlds are in continual flux, as new game designs imagine new ways to shape a world.

In the late 1980s a fresh genre of computer game emerged that took this always-implicit "world-building" aspect of gaming to a whole new level: the simulation game. *SimCity,* first released in 1987, placed the player in the role of "mayor" of an imaginary town, responsible for developing and managing all aspects of the city as it grows. *Sid Meier's Civilization,* released in 1991, expanded this model even further, putting the player in the role of leader of an epoch-spanning empire. This chapter will look at these two pioneering simulation games, to understand how the computer made it possible to build new kinds of worlds. We'll then turn to more recent games to examine the legacy of these two innovators.

Before going further, a historiographical note. Since their original release, these two games have become popular franchises. *SimCity* has spawned the direct sequels *SimCity 2, SimCity 3000,* and *SimCity 4,* along with spin-offs *SimEarth, SimAnt, SimLife, SimFarm, SimHealth, SimGolf, SimTown, SimTune, SimIsle, SimCopter, SimThemePark,* and *Streets of SimCity.* The most successful spin-off, *The Sims,* has become a franchise in its own right, generating numerous add-on packages, the sequel *The Sims 2,* and *The Sims Online. Civilization* has spawned *Civilization II, Civilization III,* and many add-ons and imitators. Each new version of these games has added more user options, more sophisticated artificial intelligence, and more sparkling graphics. As each new generation is released, the previous generation is sent to the bargain bins, and earlier generations disappear altogether. Eventually, old software becomes unplayable. Games programmed for Windows 3.1 crash on new Windows XP systems. Games stored on 5 1/4 inch floppy drives are uninstallable on contemporary 3 1/2 inch drive systems, to say nothing of computers with only CD-ROM drives.

This situation is much different from that of other media such as film and television. In this postmodern age, the history of Hollywood lives on as a palimpsest in video stores and cable channels, as contemporary movies play on next to 1970s disaster flicks, 1950s comedies, and even silent films. Computer game culture, on the other hand, embraces the cult of the new, as each new release is hyped for pushing the boundaries of graphic technology.

This situation is beginning to change a little at the margins, as computer game culture grows old enough to develop historical memory and nostalgia. Fans of "retrogames" argue that more recent games have lost the elegance and simplicity of earlier games, becoming more examples of "bloatware." Recently, companies have begun marketing recreations of beloved games from the 1970s and 1980s. Thanks to Moore's Law, an entire library of original Atari games can now fit inside a single joystick, which plugs directly into your TV to provide a complete stand-alone retrogaming system. Meanwhile, die-hard retrogamers circulate bootlegged ROM files containing the digital code originally stored on old game machines' chips. To play a game stored on a ROM file, the file is fed into a software emulator such as MAME (Multiple Arcade Machine Emulator), running on a modern computer.[4] The result is not just a recreation of the original game, but a resurrection, allowing the old software to live again.

Some earlier generations of games remain commercially viable in new technological contexts. The original *SimCity* would be considered horribly primitive by contemporary computer game standards. But it's now available on the PalmPilot PDA, whose memory, microprocessor, and graphics can't handle the more complex software of recent games. It's also available for free online as a Java program, playable online without a permanent download.

This chapter will try to avoid the twin temptations of whiggism and nostalgia—the conviction that everything's getting better, or that everything's getting worse. Instead, I'll try to understand the original *SimCity* and *Civilization*—ancient by contemporary standards—in the context of their own times. At the same time, I'll attempt to assess their legacy for today's games.

In addition to these historical challenges, writing about computer games also brings up methodological questions. What, exactly, is the "text," when every game may come out differently? How much can we generalize from one game player's experience? My own solution is to attempt a mix of phenomenology, reader-response criticism, and textual analysis. I have chosen to write much of this chapter in the second person, to try to capture the experience of playing the game. Not every player, of course, will experience a game in the same way—that's part of the magic of interactive art. But games depend on rules, structures that control every player's field of choices. This analysis will attempt to understand how these games structure players' range of possible experiences, and to what effect.

The Power of Interactivity

First, though, let's talk briefly in more general terms about the medium of the computer game, and how it may differ from other mediums.

There was a great Nintendo commercial in the 1990s in which a kid on vacation with his Game Boy started seeing everything as *Tetris* blocks. Mount Rushmore, the Rockies, the Grand Canyon—they all morphed into rows of squares, just waiting to drop, rotate, and slide into place. The effect was eerie, but familiar to anyone who's ever played the game. The commercial captured the most remarkable quality of interactive software: the way it seems to restructure perception, so that even after you've stopped playing, you continue to look at the world a little differently.

This phenomenon can be dangerous—as when I once finished up a roll of quarters on the arcade racing game *Pole Position*, walked out to my car, and didn't realize for a half mile or so that I was still driving as if I were in a video game, darting past cars and hewing to the inside lane on curves. Likewise, when the whole world looks like one big video game, it may become easier to lose track of the human consequences of real-life violence and war. One powerful exploration of this theme is Orson Scott Card's classic science fiction novel *Ender's Game*, in which videogaming children are recruited to fight a remote-control war. In a perverse case of life imitating art, the U.S. military has now begun sponsoring the development of computer games as both training systems and recruitment tools. *America's Army*, the "Official U. S. Army game," is available as a free download from the Army's website, and is also handed out by local Army recruiters. *Full Spectrum Warrior* was first developed in-house by the Army, then outsourced to a computer game designer.[5] And commercials for Microsoft's X-Box Live, a networking add-on to the game system, portray teenage gamers unwittingly losing to American soldiers stationed halfway around the world.

But if computer games can be exploited to glamorize violence while evading its consequences, the distinct power of software to reorganize perception also has great potential. Computers can be powerful tools for communicating not just specific ideas, but structures of thought—whole ways of making sense of the world. Just as *Tetris*, on the simple level of spatial geometry, encourages you to discover previously unnoticed patterns in the natural landscape, more sophisticated programs can teach you how to recognize more complex interrelationships.

Any medium, of course, can teach you how to see life in new ways. When you read a book, in a sense you're learning how to think like the author. And as film theorists have long noted, classical Hollywood narrative teaches viewers not just how to look at a screen, but how to gaze at the world. But for the most part, the opportunities for these media to

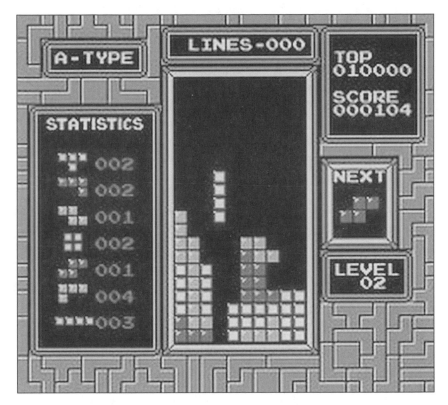

From *Tetris* (Spectrum Holobyte, 1987). Image from http://www.allgame.com/
cg/agg.dll?p=agg&SQL=GIH|||||1331.

reorient our perceptions today are limited by their stylistic familiarity. A particularly visionary author or director may occasionally confound our expectations and show us new ways to read or watch. But in general, the codes of literary and film narrative are set. We may learn new things in a great book or movie, but we almost always encounter them in familiar ways.

Software, by contrast, is a relatively new medium. And because the computer industry keeps following Moore's Law, doubling processor power every 18 months, the ground keeps shifting under the medium's accepted norms and structures.[6] At the time *SimCity* and *Civilization* were released, genres had begun to form (adventure, sports, arcade, etc.), but they remained fluid, open-ended. Even today, when the industry appears much more "mature," there's still plenty of room to invent entire new game forms, as Will Wright did with *The Sims* in 2000. The rules and expectations for computer applications are still not set in stone. Each new program must rethink how it should engage the user, and the best software succeeds by discovering new structures of interaction, inventing new genres. What would be avant-garde in film or literature—breaking with familiar forms of representation, developing new modes of address—is standard operating procedure in the world of software. Every software developer is always looking for the next killer application—the newest paradigm-buster.

What makes interaction with computers so distinctively powerful is the way computers can transform the exchange between "reader" and "text" into a feedback loop. Every response you make provokes a reaction from the computer, which leads to a new response, and so on, as the loop from the screen to your eyes to your fingers on the keyboard to the computer to the screen becomes a single cybernetic circuit.

Granted, there are many different kinds of software, and different levels of engagement with computers. Using a word processor is a fairly disengaged activity. You see the words appear on the screen as you type, but the rest is up to you. Surfing the internet offers a moderate degree of engagement, as the term "browsing" implies. The feedback is incremental rather than fluid—each new page offers a series of discrete options, each surfing choice brings up a new page of hyperlinks. And then there are computer games, where the computer responds almost instantaneously to every action of the player, which in turn provokes a new reaction from the player, and so on.

If the feedback loop between user and computer is what is most distinctive about human-computer interaction, then computer games are in many ways the quintessential software products. Looking more closely at the dynamics of computer games, then, can help us understand the new interactive possibilities opened up by computer software.

The Early History of Video Games and Computer Games

Playing games on computers was first made possible by the introduction of minicomputers in the late 1950s. Freed from the IBM punch card bureaucracy, programmers for the first time were able to explore the possibilities opened up by hands-on interaction with computers. Games were among the first programs attempted by the original "hackers," under-graduate members of MIT's Tech Model Railroad Club. The result, in 1962, was the collaborative development of the first computer game: *Spacewar,* a basic version of what would become the *Asteroids* arcade game, played on a $120,000 DEC PDP1.[7] Computer designer Brenda Laurel points out this early recognition of the centrality of computer games as models of human-computer interaction:

> Why was *Spacewar* the "natural" thing to build with this new technol-ogy? Why not a pie chart or an automated kaleidoscope or a desktop? Its designers identified action as the key ingredient and conceived *Space-war* as a game that could provide a good balance between thinking and doing for its players. They regarded the computer as a machine naturally suited for representing things that you could see, control, and play with. Its interesting potential lay not in its ability to perform calculations but in its capacity to represent action in which humans could participate.[8]

As computers became more accessible to university researchers through the 1960s, several genres of computer games emerged. Program-mers developed chess programs sophisticated enough to defeat humans. The first computer role-playing game, *Adventure,* was written at Stanford in the 1960s: by typing short phrases, you could control the adventures of a character trekking through a magical landscape while solving puz-zles. And in 1970 *Scientific American* columnist Martin Gardner intro-duced Americans to *LIFE,* a simulation of cellular growth patterns writ-ten by British mathematician John Conway. *LIFE* was the first "software toy," an open-ended model of systemic development designed to be end-lessly tinkered with and enjoyed.[9]

In 1972 *Pong,* a tennis game designed by Nolan Bushnell, became the first hit arcade videogame. By the mid-1970s, the videogame arcade had emerged as a new kind of public space. The first home videogame system, the Magnavox Odyssey, was also released in 1972, but home videogames didn't really take off until the release of a home version of *Pong* in 1975. Atari followed this up with a cartridge-based system that allowed one unit to play a range of individually purchased games. At the same time, the rise of the personal computer created another market for game software. By the 1980s, computer game software production had become an industry.

How to make sense of these new kinds of texts? As designers, fans and critics began to think about the computer game medium in the 1980s and

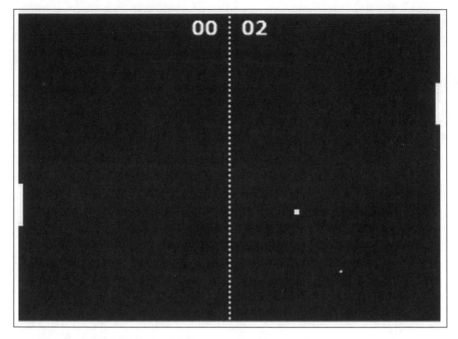

From *Pong* (Atari, 1972). Image from http://www.pong-story.com/pcpong.htm.

1990s, one popular perspective was to describe computer games as being like movies, only more so. Computer game development companies, the argument went, were the "New Hollywood."[10]

The New Hollywood analogy helped conceptualize the process of computer game design. Although in the industry's infancy it was possible for one programmer to write and market a game single-handedly, by the mid-1980s computer game production had become a complex collaborative process among many specialists. The introduction screens for modern games read like movie credits, listing producers, programmers, artists, musicians, and actors. At the top of the credits are the designers, the equivalent to movie directors. In the computer gaming world, designers like *Ultima*'s Lord British and *SimCity*'s Will Wright are respected as auteurs with unique personal visions.

The difference between the New Hollywood and the Old, according to the analogy, is that computer games are "interactive cinema," in which the game player takes on the role of the protagonist. But how to define interactive? How can the designer give the player a sense of control over the game, while still propelling the player through a compelling narrative? The solution, dating back to *Adventure* and *Zork*, has been to set up the game as a series of challenges, tasks, and puzzles. You muddle through the universe of the game—exploring settings, acquiring objects, talking to characters, battling enemies—until you've accomplished everything necessary to trigger the next stage of the plot. In the process, you're expected to regularly make mistakes, die, and restart the game in a previously saved position.[11] Out of the flaws in this system, a whole cottage industry of hint books and websites has developed, to help players stuck halfway through their adventures.

While the phrase "interactive cinema" has lost favor today, the related concept of "role playing" continues to be an influential framework for thinking about the player's relationship with the characters onscreen. This model presumes that identification in computer gaming works like identification in movie watching, only more intensely. When you watch a movie, you can only fantasize about being the hero. But when you play a computer game, you can actually "be" the hero, at least in the sense of controlling all the hero's onscreen actions yourself.

But this common-sense assumption of how identification in computer games works distorts critical differences between the way we experience the two mediums of games and films. Classic Hollywood cinema is structured in every way to facilitate losing yourself in the fantasy onscreen. The stop-and-go nature of the puzzle-solving paradigm, on the other hand, discourages this level of identification. Contemporary role-playing games such as the *Final Fantasy* series develop complex narratives that alternate interactive gameplay with "cut scenes"—computer-animated episodes that advance the game's storyline. But while these games can be compelling, rarely are the characters memorable in the way that a favorite film character is memorable. The marriage of interactive gameplay and static, scripted scenes remains an awkward match. Often, players will skip past the cut scenes after they've played them through once, anxious to get back to the gameplay. Revealingly, the most successful current mix of gameplay and cut scenes, the *Grand Theft Auto* series, resolves this dilemma with camp. The game's lighthearted, self-mocking tone makes it easy to laugh off the stagey dialogue and hackneyed characters. What's not clear yet is whether adventure game designers can create characters players can actually care about within the constraints of the gameplay/cut-scene format.[12]

From *Grand Theft Auto: Vice City* (Rockstar Games, 2002). Image from
http://www.rockstargames.com/vicecity/main.html#.

If the role-playing model is of limited use for explaining how identification works in adventure games from *Zork* to *Grand Theft Auto*, it falls
apart completely when we turn to games that are even less movie-like.
Simulation games could never be mistaken for interactive cinema. There
are no characters and story, in the conventional sense. Instead, as we shall
see, there is only process and space.

Simulation and Subjectivity

SimCity actually had its start as a wargame. As the game's creator, Will
Wright, explains,

> *SimCity* evolved from *Raid on Bungling Bay,* where the basic premise
> was that you flew around and bombed islands. The game included an is-
> land generator, and I noticed after a while that I was having more fun
> building islands than blowing them up. About the same time, I also

came across the work of Jay Forrester, one of the first people to ever model a city on a computer for social-sciences purposes. Using his theories, I adapted and expanded the *Bungling Bay* island generator, and *SimCity* evolved from there.[13]

Nervous that the product Wright came up with would appear too educational, distributors Broderbund took extra steps on *SimCity*'s initial release to make sure it would be perceived as a game, adding "disaster" options and prepackaged scenarios—earthquakes, nuclear meltdowns, even an attack from Godzilla. But as a 1989 *Newsweek* article on the game points out, "these are excess baggage."[14] What turned *SimCity* into a giant software hit, spawning numerous bootlegs, imitations, and spin-offs, was the pleasure Wright discovered in the simulation process itself.

Here's a description of the original game from a Maxis catalog:

> *SimCity* makes you Mayor and City Planner, and dares you to design and build the city of your dreams. . . . Depending on your choices and design skills, Simulated Citizens (Sims) will move in and build homes, hospitals, churches, stores and factories, or move out in search of a better life elsewhere.[15]

Beginning with an undeveloped patch of land and an initial development fund, you create a city by choosing where and what kind of power plants to build; zoning industrial, commercial, and residential areas; laying down roads, mass transit, and power lines; and building police stations, fire departments, airports, seaports, stadiums, and so on. While playing the game eventually comes to feel entirely intuitive, the system is quite complex. Every action is assigned a price, and you can only spend as much money as you have in the city treasury. The treasury begins at a base amount, then can be replenished yearly by taxes, the rate of which you can adjust. As you become more familiar with the system, you gradually develop strategies to encourage economic growth, build up the population of the city, and score a higher "approval rating" from the Sims. Which of these or other goals you choose to pursue, however, is up to you; Maxis likes to refer to its products as "software toys" rather than games, and insists,

> when you play with our toys, you set your own goals and decide for yourself when you've reached them. The fun and challenge of playing

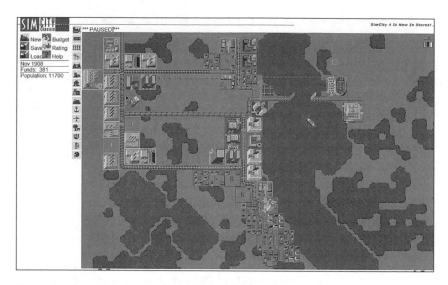

From *SimCity Classic Live*, http://simcity.ea.com/play/simcity_classic.php.

with our toys lies in exploring the worlds you create out of your own imagination. You're rewarded for creativity, experimentation, and understanding, with a healthy, thriving universe to call your own.[16]

Expanding upon the "software toy" ideal, science fiction writer and computer game critic Orson Scott Card argues that the best computer games are those that provide the most open-ended frameworks to allow players the opportunity to create their own worlds:

Someone at every game design company should have a full-time job of saying, "Why aren't we letting the player decide that?" . . . When [designers] let . . . unnecessary limitations creep into a game, gamewrights reveal that they don't yet understand their own art. They've chosen to work with the most liberating of media—and yet they snatch back with their left hand the freedom they offered us with their right. Remember, gamewrights, the power and beauty of the art of gamemaking is that you and the player collaborate to create the final story. Every freedom that you can give to the player is an artistic victory. And every needless boundary in your game should feel to you like failure.[17]

Playing *SimCity* is a very different experience from playing an adventure game. The interaction between player and computer is constant and intense. Gameplay is a continuous flow. It can be very hard to stop, because you're always in the middle of dozens of different projects: nurturing a new residential zone in one corner of the map, building an airport in another, saving up money to buy a new power plant, monitoring the crime rate in a particularly troubled neighborhood, and so on. Meanwhile, the city is continually changing, as the simulation inexorably chugs forward from one month to the next (unless you put the game on pause to handle a crisis). By the time you've made a complete pass through the city, a whole new batch of problems and opportunities has developed. If the pace of the city's development is moving too fast to keep up with, the simulation can be slowed down (i.e., it'll wait longer in real time to move from one month to the next). If you're waiting around for things to happen, the simulation can be speeded up.

As a result, it's easy to slide into a routine with absolutely no down time, no interruptions from complete communion with the computer. The game can grow so absorbing, in fact, that your subjective sense of time is distorted.[18] David Myers writes, "From personal experience and interviews with other players, I can say it is very common to play these games for eight or more hours without pause, usually through the entire first night of purchase."[19] You look up, and all of a sudden it's morning.

It's very hard to describe what it feels like when you're lost inside a computer game, precisely because at that moment your sense of self has been transformed. Flowing through a continuous series of decisions made almost automatically, hardly aware of the passage of time, you form a symbiotic circuit with the computer, a version of the cyborgian consciousness described by Donna Haraway in "Manifesto for Cyborgs." The computer comes to feel like an organic extension of your consciousness, and you may feel like an extension of the computer itself.

This isn't exactly the way the *SimCity* user's manual puts it. The manual describes your role as a "combination Mayor and City Planner." But while that title suggests that you imagine yourself playing a specific role along the lines of the interactive cinema model, the structures of identification in simulation games are much more complex. Closer to the truth is the setup in the simulation game *Black & White,* where you're simply a god—omnipotent (within the rules of the game), omniscient, and omnipresent. While in some explicitly political simulations, like *Hidden Agenda* and *Crisis in the Kremlin,* your power and perspective is limited to that of a chief of state, in games like *SimCity* you're personally responsible for far more than any one leader—or even an entire government—could ever manage. You directly control the city's budget, economic and residential growth, transportation, police and fire services, zoning, and even entertainment (the Sims eventually get mad if you don't build them a stadium, along with other amenities). While each function is putatively within the province of government control, the game structure makes you identify as much with the roles of industrialist, merchant, real estate agent, and citizen, as with those of mayor or city planner.

For example, in *SimCity*, the way a new area of town is developed is to "zone" it. You decide whether each parcel of land should be marked for residential, industrial, or commercial use. You can't make the zones develop into thriving homes or businesses; that's determined by the simulation, on the basis of a range of interconnected factors including crime rate, pollution, economic conditions, power supply, and access to other zones. If you've set up conditions right, an empty residential zone will quickly blossom into a high-rise apartment complex, raising land values, adding tax money to the city's coffers, and increasing the population of the city. If the zone isn't well-integrated into the city, it may stay undeveloped, or degenerate into a crime-ridden slum. But while you can't control the behavior putatively assigned to the resident Sims, the identification process at the moment of zoning goes beyond simply seeing yourself as the Mayor, or even as the collective zoning commission. The cost of zoning eats up a substantial portion of a city's budget—much more than it would cost a real city. This is structurally necessary to limit your ability to develop the city, so that building the city is a gradual, challenging process (something close to a narrative, in fact). The effect on gameplay is to see the process less as zoning than as buying the land. Not to say that you think of every *SimCity* building as being owned by the government. But at the moment of zoning, you're not playing the role of mayor, but of someone else—homeowner, landlord, or real estate developer, perhaps.

We could see playing *SimCity*, then, as a constant shifting of identifications, depending on whether you're buying land, organizing the police force, paving the roads, or whatever. This is part of what's going on. But this model suggests a level of disjunction—jumping back and forth from one role to the next—belied by the smooth, almost trancelike state of gameplay. Overarching these functional shifts is a more general state of identification: with the city as a whole, as a single system.

What does it mean to identify with an entire city? Perhaps attempting to map roles onto the player's on-screen identification misses the point. When a player zones a land area, she or he is identifying less with a *role* than with a *process*. And the reason that the decision, and the continuous series of decisions the gamer makes, can be made so quickly and intuitively, is that you have internalized the logic of the program, so that you're always able to anticipate the results of your actions. Losing yourself in a computer game means, in a sense, identifying with the simulation itself.

Cyborg Consciousness

To get a better sense of what it might mean to identify with a process, let's turn to *Sid Meier's Civilization*. Meier is the game's inventor and original designer, and is known in the computer gaming world for his skill in designing absorbing, detailed simulations. His early games *Pirates* and *Railroad Tycoon* each helped shape the emerging genre in the 1980s. *Civilization* was hailed on its release as one of the greatest computer games ever. The sequels have been similarly honored.

The manual for the original *Civilization* introduces the game this way:

> *Civilization* casts you in the role of the ruler of an entire civilization through many generations, from the founding of the world's first cities 6,000 years in the past to the imminent colonization of space. It combines the forces that shaped history and the evolution of technology in a competitive environment. . . . If you prove an able ruler, your civilization grows larger and even more interesting to manage. Inevitable contact with neighbors opens new doors of opportunity: treaties, embassies, sabotage, trade and war.[20]

What does it feel like to be cast "in the role of ruler of an entire civilization through many generations"? The game follows the conceit that you play the part of a single historical figure. At the beginning of the game, you're given a choice of nation and name. From then on, from the wanderings of your first settlers to your final colonization of outer space, the computer will always call you, for example, "Emperor Abraham Lincoln of the United States." Of course, nobody lives for 6,000 years, and even the most powerful real-life despots—to say nothing of democratically elected leaders—could never wield the kind of absolute power that *Civilization* gives even titular presidents and prime ministers, just as the "mayor" in *SimCity* is so much more than a mayor. In *Civilization,* you're responsible for directing the military, managing the economy, controlling development in every city of your domain, building Wonders of the World, and orchestrating scientific research (with the prescience to know the strategic benefits of each possible discovery, and to schedule accordingly). You make not just the big decisions, but the small ones, too, from deciding where each military unit should move on every turn to choosing which squares of the map grid to develop for resources. In *Civilization,* you hold many jobs simultaneously: king, general, mayor, city planner, settler, warrior, and priest, to name a few.

How does this tangle of roles become the smooth flow of gameplay? The answer, I think, is that you do not identify with any of these subject positions so much as with *the computer itself.* When you play a simulation game like *Civilization,* your perspective—the eyes through which you learn to see the game—is not that of any character or set of characters, be they kings, presidents, or even God. The style in which you learn to think doesn't correspond to the way any person usually makes sense of the world. Rather, the pleasures of a simulation game come from inhabiting an unfamiliar, alien mental state: from learning to think like a computer.

Let me clarify that in talking about "thinking like a computer," I don't mean to anthropomorphize, or to suggest that machines can "think" the way humans do. As discussed in chapter 3, artificial-intelligence researchers have learned, often to their chagrin, the limitations of computer cognition. Contemporary computers can only systematically, methodically crunch numbers and follow algorithms. They can't replicate the less linear, more fluid ways the human mind works. My point is that using simulation games can help us intuitively grasp the very alien way in which computers process information, and so can help us recognize how our relationships with computers affect our own thoughts and feelings.

In describing computers as, in a sense, nonhuman actors with associated states of consciousness, I'm borrowing a technique of Bruno Latour's, who in his novelistic history *Aramis, or the Love of Technology,* tells the story of a failed French experimental mass transit program from several perspectives—including that of the train itself. Latour writes,

> I have sought to show researchers in the social sciences that sociology is
> not the science of human beings alone—that it can welcome crowds of

nonhumans with open arms, just as it welcomed the working masses in the nineteenth century. Our collective is woven together out of speaking subjects, perhaps, but subjects to which poor objects, our inferior brothers, are attached at all points. By opening up to include objects, the social bond would become less mysterious.[21]

Latour's conceit is one way to attempt to account for the interpenetration of our lives with technology, to make visible the often unnoticed role of technology in our daily experience and sense of selves.

The way computer games teach structures of thought—the way they reorganize perception—is by getting you to internalize the logic of the program. To win, you can't just do whatever you want. You have to figure out what will work within the rules of the game. You must learn to predict the consequences of each move, and anticipate the computer's response. Eventually, your decisions become intuitive, as smooth and rapid-fire as the computer's own machinations.

In one sense, the computer is your opponent. You have to know how to think like the computer because the computer provides the artificial intelligence that determines the moves of your rival civilizations. Like Kasparov playing Deep Blue, IBM's championship-winning chess computer, you have to figure out how the computer makes decisions in order to beat it.

But in this role of opponent, the computer is only a stand-in for a human player. When multiple players compete, the AI isn't even needed. And in terms of strategy, the computer opponents in *Civilization* are no Deep Blue. Their moves are fairly predictable. The confrontation between player and AI masks a deeper level of collaboration. The computer in *Civilization* is not only your adversary, but also your ally. In addition to controlling your rivals, it processes the rules of the game. It tells you when to move, who wins each battle, and how quickly your cities can grow. It responds instantly to your every touch of the mouse, so that when you move your hand along the mousepad, it seems as if you're actually physically moving the pointer on the screen, rather than simply sending digital information to the computer. It runs the universe that you inhabit when you play the game. "Thinking like the computer" means thinking along with the computer, becoming an extension of the computer's processes.[22]

This helps explain the strange sense of self-dissolution created by computer games, the way in which games suck you in. The pleasure of computer games is in entering into a computerlike mental state: in responding as automatically as the computer, processing information as effort-lessly, replacing sentient cognition with the blank hum of computation. When a game of *Civilization* really gets rolling, the decisions are effort-less, instantaneous, chosen without self-conscious thought. The result is an almost-meditative state, in which you aren't just interacting with the computer, but melding with it.

The connection between player and computer in a simulation game is a kind of *cybernetic circuit,* a continual feedback loop. Today, the prefix "cyber" has become so ubiquitous that its use has diffused to mean little more than "computer related." But the word "cybernetics," from which the prefix was first taken, has a more distinct meaning. Norbert Weiner coined the term to describe a new general science of information pro-cessing and control.[23] (He took it from the Greek word *kybernan,* mean-ing to steer or govern.) In particular, he was interested in *feedback*: the ways in which systems—be they bodies, machines, or combinations of both—control and regulate themselves through circuits of information. As Steve J. Heims writes in his history, *The Cybernetics Group,*

> [The cybernetic] model replaced the traditional cause-and-effect relation of a stimulus leading to a response by a "circular causality" requiring negative feedback: A person reaches for a glass of water to pick it up, and as she extends her arm and hand is continuously informed (negative feedback)—by visual or proprioceptive sensations—how close the hand is to the glass and then guides the action accordingly, so as to achieve the goal of smoothly grabbing the glass. The process is circular because the position of the arm and hand achieved at one moment is part of the input information for the action at the next moment. If the circuit is in-tact, it regulates the process. To give another stock example, when a man is steering a ship, the person, the compass, the ship's engine, and the rudder are all part of the goal-directed system with feedback. The machine is part of the circuit.[24]

The constant interactivity in a simulation game—the perpetual feedback between a player's choice, the computer's almost-instantaneous response, the player's response to that response, and so on—is a cybernetic loop, in which the line demarcating the end of the player's consciousness and the beginning of the computer's world blurs.

There are drawbacks to this merging of consciousness. Connected to the computer, it's easy to imagine you've transcended your physical body, to dismiss your flesh and blood as simply the "meat" your mind must inhabit, as the protagonist of *Neuromancer* puts it.[25] This denial is a form of alienation, a refusal to recognize the material basis for your experience. The return of the repressed comes in the form of carpal tunnel syndrome, eyestrain, and other reminders that cyberspace remains rooted in physical existence.

But the connection between player and computer does enable access to an otherwise unavailable perspective. In the collaboration between you and the computer, self and Other give way, forming what might be called a single *cyborg consciousness*. In "Manifesto for Cyborgs," Donna Haraway proposed the figure of the cyborg—"a hybrid of machine and organism"—as an image that might help us make sense of the increasing interpenetration of technology and humanity under late capitalism. Haraway's point was that in this hyper-mechanized world, we are all cyborgs. When you drive a car, the unit of driver-and-car becomes a kind of cyborg. When you turn on the TV, the connection of TV-to-viewer is a kind of cybernetic link. The man steering the ship in Heims's example is a cyborg. And most basically, since we all depend on technology to survive this postmodern world—to feed us, to shelter us, to comfort us—in a way, we are all as much cyborgs as the Six Million Dollar Man.

Simulation games offer a singular opportunity to think through what it means to be a cyborg. Most of our engagements with technology are distracted, functional affairs. We drive a car to get somewhere. We watch TV to see what's on. We use the office computer to get work done.[26] Simulation games, on the other hand, aestheticize our cybernetic connection to technology. They turn it into a source of enjoyment and an object for contemplation. They give us a chance to luxuriate in the unfamiliar pleasures of rote computation and depersonalized perspective, and grasp the emotional contours of this worldview. To use the language of Clifford Geertz, simulation games are a "sentimental education" in what it means to live among computers.

Geertz's famous essay "Deep Play: Notes on the Balinese Cockfight" discusses how a game can encapsulate and objectify a society's sense of lived social relations:

Like any art form—for that, finally, is what we are dealing with—the cockfight renders ordinary, everyday experience comprehensible by presenting it in terms of acts and objects which have had their practical consequences removed and been reduced (or, if you prefer, raised) to the level of sheer appearances, where their meaning can be more powerfully articulated and more exactly perceived.[27]

This dynamic is particularly powerful because it is not just an intellectual exercise, but a visceral experience:

> What the cockfight says it says in a vocabulary of sentiment—the thrill of risk, the despair of loss, the pleasure of triumph. . . . Attending cockfights and participating in them is, for the Balinese, a kind of sentimental education. What he learns there is what his culture's ethos and his private sensibility (or, anyway, certain aspects of them) look like when spelled out externally in a collective text.[28]

Through the language of play, computer games teach you what it feels like to be a cyborg.

Cognitive Mapping

In *The Condition of Postmodernity*, geographer David Harvey argues for the primacy of spatialization in constructing cognitive frameworks: we learn our ways of thinking and conceptualizing from active grappling with the spatializations of the written word, the study and production of maps, graphs, diagrams, photographs, models, paintings, mathematical symbols, and the like.[29] Harvey then points out the dilemma of making sense of space under late capitalism: "How adequate are such modes of thought and such conceptions in the face of the flow of human experience and strong processes of social change? On the other side of the coin, how can spatializations in general . . . represent flux and change?"[30]

Representing flux and change is exactly what a simulation can do, by replacing the stasis of two- or three-dimensional spatial models with a map that shifts over time to reflect change. And this change is not simply the one-way communication of a series of still images, but a continually interactive process. Computer simulations bring the tools of narrative to mapmaking, allowing the individual not only to observe structures, but to become experientially immersed in their logic.

Simulations may be the best opportunity to create what Fredric Jameson calls "an aesthetic of cognitive mapping: a pedagogical political culture which seeks to endow the individual subject with some new heightened sense of its place in the global system."[31] Playing a simulation means becoming engrossed in a systemic logic that connects a wide array of causes and effects. The simulation acts as a kind of map-in-time, visually and viscerally (as the player internalizes the game's logic) demonstrating the repercussions and interrelatedness of many different social decisions. Offering an escape from the prison house of language, which seems so inadequate for holding together the disparate strands that construct postmodern subjectivity, computer simulations point to a radically new quasi-narrative form through which to communicate structures of interconnection.

Sergei Eisenstein hoped that the technology of montage could make it possible to film Marx's *Capital*. But the narrative techniques of Hollywood cinema developed in a way that directs the viewer to respond to individuals rather than abstract concepts. A computer game based on *Capital*, on the other hand, is possible to imagine. As Chris Crawford notes (paraphrased by David Myers), "Game personalities are not as important as game processes—'You can interact with a process. . . . Ultimately, you can learn about it.'"[32]

A simulation doesn't have characters or a plot in the conventional sense. Instead, its primary narrative agent is geography. Simulation games tell a story few other media can: the drama of a map changing over time. You begin *Civilization* with a single band of prehistoric settlers, represented as a small figure with a shovel at the center of the main map which takes up most of the computer screen. Terrain is delineated on this map by icons representing woods, rivers, plains, oceans, mountains, and so on. At the beginning of the game, however, almost all of the map is black; you don't get to learn what's out there until one of your units has explored the area. Gradually, as you expand your empire and send out scouting parties, the landscape is revealed. This process of exploration and discovery is one of the fundamental pleasures of *Civilization*. It's what gives the game a sense of narrative momentum.

In "Nintendo and New World Travel Writing," Henry Jenkins and Mary Fuller, scholars of American popular culture and the English Renaissance, respectively, compare two seemingly disparate genres which share a strikingly similar narrative structure.[33] Nintendo games and New World travel narratives, like simulation games, are structured not by plot or character, but by the process of encountering, transforming, and mastering geography. Fuller writes, "Both terms of our title evoke explorations and colonizations of space: the physical space navigated, mapped and mastered by European voyagers and travelers in the sixteenth and seventeenth centuries and the fictional, digitally projected space traversed, mapped, and mastered by players of Nintendo video games."[34] Borrowing from the work of Michel de Certeau,[35] Jenkins labels these geographical narratives "spatial stories." He describes the process of geographic transformation as a transition from abstract "place" into concrete "space":

> For de Certeau, narrative involves the transformation of place into space.[36] Places exist only the abstract, as potential sites for narrative action, as locations that have not yet been colonized. Places constitute a "stability" which must be disrupted in order for stories to unfold. . . . Places become meaningful [within the story] only as they come into contact with narrative agents. . . . Spaces, on the other hand, are places that have been acted upon, explored, colonized. Spaces become the locations of narrative events.[37]

Likewise, gameplay in *Civilization* revolves around the continual transformation of place into space, as the blackness of the unknown gives way to specific terrain icons. As in New World narratives, the process of "colonization" is not simply a metaphor for cultural influence, but involves the literal establishment of new colonies by settlers (occasionally with the assistance of military force). Once cities are established, the surrounding land can be developed. By moving your settlers to the appropriate spot and choosing from the menu of "orders," you can build roads, irrigate farmland, drill mines, chop down trees, and eventually, as your civilization gains technology, build bridges and railroads. These transformations are graphically represented right on the map itself by progressively more elaborate icons. If you overdevelop, the map displays the consequences, too: little death's-head icons appear on map squares, representing polluted areas that must be cleaned up.

In its focus on the transformation of place into space, *Civilization* seems like an archetypal spatial story. However, *Civilization* differs from the geographic narratives Jenkins and Fuller describe in an important way, one which demonstrates the distinctive qualities of simulation games. In addition to the categories of space and place, Jenkins borrows two other terms from de Certeau, maps and tours:

> Maps are abstracted accounts of spatial relations ("the girl's room is next to the kitchen"), whereas tours are told from the point of view of

the traveler/narrator ("You turn right and come into the living room").[38]
Maps document places; tours describe movements through spaces.[39]

Tours, in other words, are the subjective, personalized experiences of the spaces described abstractly in maps. You start your journey with a map. Then, as you navigate the geography, that abstract knowledge becomes the embodied firsthand experience of a tour. The maze of the Nintendo screen gives way to a familiar, continually retraced path that leads from the entrance to safety. The daunting expanse of the New World is structured by the personal account of one traveler's journey.

In the spatial stories Jenkins and Fuller discuss, then, the pleasure comes from two transitions, one involving geographic transformation, the other individual subjectivity. *Place* becomes *space* as unfamiliar geography is conquered through exploration and development. And *maps* become *tours* as abstract geography is subjectively situated in personal experience. As we have seen, *Civilization* is certainly engaged in the trans-

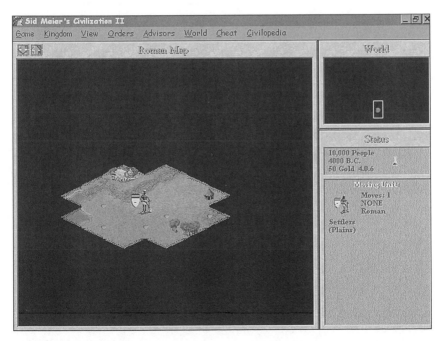

You begin *Civilization* with a single band of settlers, the unexplored terrain a black void. From *Sid Meier's Civilization II* (Microprose Software, 1996).

formation of place into space. But in simulation games, the map never becomes a tour. The game screen documents how the player has changed the landscape, but these transformations are always represented in the abstract terms of the map. The point of view always remains an overhead, god's-eye perspective.

What's the import of this distinction? We might assume that the continued abstraction of the map would indicate a measure of detachment, compared to the ground-level engagement of a tour. But as we have seen, simulation games seem singularly skilled at "sucking you in" to their peculiar kind of narrative. The difference is that the pleasure in simulation games comes from experiencing space as a map: of at once claiming a place, and retaining an abstracted sense of it. The spatial stories Fuller and Jenkins discuss respond to the challenge of narrating geography by getting inside the map—they zoom in from forest level so we can get to know the trees. Character may not be a primary criterion for these stories, but the stories still depend on individual subjective experience as the engine for their geographic narrative. Geography itself is not the protagonist; rather, the protagonist's experience of geography structures the narrative.

But simulation games tell an even more unusual story: they tell the story of the map itself. Drawing a steady bead on the forest, they teach us how to follow, and enjoy, its transformations over time. We need never get distracted by the trees. Because simulation games fix the player in a depersonalized frame of mind, they can tell their story in the abstract, without ever bringing it to the level of individual experience. The map is not merely the environment for the story; it's the hero of the story.

The closest analogue I can think of to the distinct kind of spatial story that simulation games tell are works of "environmental history" such as William Cronon's *Changes in the Land*.[40] Cronon attempts to tell a version of American history from the perspective of the land, turning the earth itself into his protagonist. The limitations of the written word, however, make it difficult to fully treat an abstract entity as a character. You can't easily employ the devices normally used to engage the reader with a human protagonist. As a result, the book is still a rather dry read. It may offer a new perspective, but it can't engage the reader enough to give an emotional sense of what this perspective *feels like*.[41]

The clearest way to conceptualize space is not with words, but with images. A map captures the abstract contours of space; any verbal description begins the process of turning that map into a tour. This is why

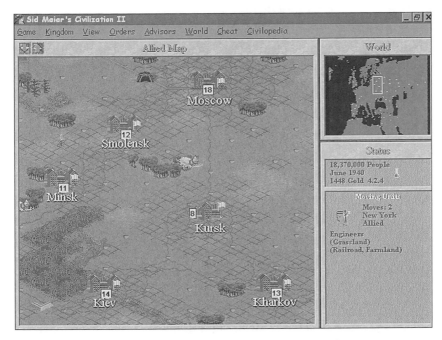

As your civilization grows, you can transform the lands with roads, bridges, mines, irrigation, and other "improvements." From *Sid Meier's Civilization II* (Microprose Software, 1996).

any good work of geography is full of maps; the reader is expected to continually check the words against the images, translating language back into visual understanding. Simulation games are a way to make the maps tell the whole story. As a still frame is to a movie, as a paragraph is to a novel, so is a map to a simulation game. Simulation games are maps-in-time, dramas that teach us how to think about structures of spatial relationships.[42]

Ideology

In one sense, every map is always already a tour. As geographer Denis Wood points out in *The Power of Maps*,[43] a map is the cumulative result of many subjective judgments. Maps always have a point of view. The ideological work of the "scientific," god's-eye view map is to make the traces of those subjective decisions disappear. Critics of computer games worry that the technological aura of computers further heightens this reification, leaving game players with the impression that they have encountered not just one version of the way the world works, but the one and only objective version.[44]

This perspective would leave little room to imagine resistance. But the structure of the computer gaming experience does allow for variant interpretations. You can win *Civilization* in one of two ways. You can win by making war, wiping the other civilizations off the map, and taking over the world. Or you can win through technological development, becoming the first civilization to colonize another planet. I haven't emphasized the military aspect of *Civilization* because I don't enjoy wargames all that much myself. My strategy for winning *Civilization* is to pour all my efforts into scientific research, so that my nation is the most technologically advanced. This allows me to be the first to build Wonders of the World that, under the game's rules, force opponents to stay at peace with me. In the ancient world, the Great Wall of China does the trick. By modern times, I have to upgrade to the United Nations.

That's just one strategy for winning. I think it's probably the most effective—I get really high scores—but, judging from online discussions, it doesn't appear to be the most popular. Most *Civilization* players seem to prefer a bloodier approach, sacrificing maximum economic and scientific development to focus on crushing their enemies.

The fact that more than one strategy will work—that there's no one right way to win the game—demonstrates the impressive flexibility of *Civilization*. But there still remain baseline ideological assumptions that determine which strategies will win and which will lose. And underlying the entire structure of the game, of course, is the notion that global coexistence is a matter of winning or losing.

There are disadvantages to never seeing the trees for the forest. *Civilization*'s dynamic of depersonalization elides the violence of exploration, colonization, and development even more completely than do the stories of individual conquest described by Fuller and Jenkins. Military units who fight and die in *Civilization* disappear in a simple blip; native peoples who defend their homelands are inconveniences, "barbarian hordes" to be quickly disposed of.

What makes this palatable, at least for those of us who would get squeamish in a more explicit wargame, is the abstractness of *Civilization*. Any nation can be the colonizer, depending on who you pick to play. Barbarian hordes are never specific ethnicities; they're just generic natives. It's interesting to note that Sid Meier's least successful game was a first attempt at a follow-up to the original *Civilization,* the 1994 release *Sid Meier's Colonization.* A more historically detailed game, *Colonization* allows you to play a European nation colonizing the New World. In addressing a more concrete and controversial historical subject, Meier is forced to complicate the Manifest Destiny ethos of *Civilization.* The Native American nations are differentiated, and behave in different ways. You can't win through simple genocide, but must trade and collaborate with at least some Native Americans some of the time. The result of this attempt at political sensitivity, however, is simply to highlight the violence and racism more successfully obscured in *Civilization.* There's no getting around the goal of *Colonization:* to colonize the New World. And while you have a choice of which European power to play, you can't choose to play a Native American nation. (This ethnocentrism reflects the demographics of computer game players, who, like computer users, remain disproportionately white.)[45]

Civilization's level of abstraction also leads to oversimplification. The immense timespan of *Civilization* reifies historically specific, continually changing practices into transhistorical categories like "science," "religion," and "nation." Art and religion in *Civilization* serve a purely functional role: to keep the people pacified. If you pursue faith and beauty at the expense of economic development, you're bound to get run over by less cultivated nations. Scientific research follows a path of rigid determinism; you always know in advance what you're going to discover next, and it pays to plan two or three inventions ahead. And you can't play "The Jews" in *Civilization,* or other diasporic peoples. The game assumes that a "civilization" equals a distinct political nation. There's no creolization in *Civilization,* no hybridity, no forms of geopolitical organization before (or after) the rise of nationalism. Either you conquer your enemy, or your enemy conquers you. You can trade supplies and technology with your neighbors, but it's presumed that your national identities will remain distinct. Playing a single, unchanging entity from the Stone Age to space colonization turns the often-slippery formation of nationhood into a kind of immutable racial destiny.

From the Forest to the Trees: The Sims

If *Civilization* rests on ideological premises we may choose to question, the distinct dynamics of computer gaming give the player the chance to transcend those assumptions. Computer games are designed to be played until they are mastered. You succeed by learning how the software is put together. You win the game by deconstructing it. Unlike a book or film that is engaged only once or twice, a computer game is played over and over until every subtlety is exposed, every hidden choice obvious to the savvy player. The moment the game loses its interest is when all its secrets have been discovered, its boundaries revealed. That's when the game can no longer suck you in. No game feels fresh forever; eventually, you run up against the limits of its perspective, and move on to other games.

In the years after its debut in 1987, *SimCity* inspired numerous sequels and spin-offs. These games for the most part built on the original's gameplay rather than reinventing it. In 2000, however, *SimCity* creator Will Wright released a game that would transform the simulation genre. *The Sims* is a "people simulator." You control a household of characters, who can be roommates, lovers, or combinations of parents and children. You are responsible for each character's every activity—sleeping, eating, working, socializing, even using the toilet. The result is like a dollhouse come to life, and it's a truly engrossing experience. *The Sims* is the inverse of *SimCity*. While *SimCity* is about the big picture, *The Sims* allows you to drill down to the level of individual "Sims." The latest version of *SimCity*, in fact, *SimCity 4*, links the two levels, allowing you to import characters from *The Sims* into *SimCity*.

The Sims quickly became the top-selling computer game in the United States. In 2003 four of the top six best-selling computer games were *Sims* products, including *The Sims Deluxe* and three expansion packs. (*SimCity 4* was number seven.)[46] *The Sims 2*, released in September 2004, was an even bigger hit. It sold more than one million copies in just its first ten days of release, marking the biggest videogame launch in the history of Electronic Arts, the game's publisher. Combined cumulative sales of all *Sims* games topped 41 million units by October 2004. This discussion will concentrate on the original *Sims* game, while keeping in mind subsequent developments.[47]

Part of the success of *The Sims* can be explained by how it has reached a deeply underserved audience: women gamers. While most computer games, from *Doom* to *Civilization*, prioritize violence and conflict,[48] *The*

From *The Sims* (Maxis Software, 2000).

Sims emphasizes interpersonal relationships. It also presents female characters of less outsized proportions than *Tomb Raider*'s Lara Croft. Women make up 56 percent of *Sims* players, compared to 43 percent of gamers overall.[49]

Prior to *The Sims,* there had been some American computer games with a focus on character, such as games in the role-playing genre. But these characters were almost always heroic archetypes thrust into larger-than-life fantasy and science fiction scenarios. There is also a tradition of romance-oriented "relationship simulation" computer games in Japan, but none of these games had been successfully imported into the American market. *The Sims* was the first American game to allow you to explore a character not through the modalities of fantasy or adventure, but of drama—the everyday.

So, how does *The Sims* construct this imaginary everyday world? The game is designed to be flexible and open-ended, but it does set some core rules. The primary measure of your moment-to-moment success is each character's "Mood" bar. When the Mood bar is full, the Sim is happy, and is more responsive, energetic, and productive. When the bar runs low, the Sim is sad, and grows lethargic and unresponsive. The key to your long-term goals for the Sim—whether they center on career, family, or whatever you choose to value—is making sure that the Sim stays happy as she or he goes about her or his daily tasks.

The Sim's mood, in turn, is a reflection of the state of satisfaction of eight basic "Needs": Hunger, Comfort, Hygiene, Bladder, Energy, Fun, Social, and Room. (*The Sims 2* adds more existential needs, called "Aspirations.") Each one of these needs is tracked on a separate bar. A filled bar means the need is totally fulfilled at the moment; an empty bar means the need is totally unfulfilled. Various actions satisfy a Sim's needs. Eating satisfies hunger, washing satisfies hygiene, and so on. As time goes by, each bar runs down, until the need is again satisfied.

In order to satisfy many of these needs, you need to buy products. To buy products, you need money. You start the game with a set amount of money, then get a job and go to work to earn more. (Kids go to school instead of work, and "earn" grades instead of money.) Work and school are represented in the game only through their absence. The Sims take off for their jobs and classes, but the game interface stays at the house. If nobody's left at home, the hours rush by at accelerated speed, until the Sims return.

So, to get ahead in the game, you need to buy stuff. Much of the gameplay is spent in "Buy Mode." The game clock pauses, and a menu of consumer options pops up: appliances, furniture, decorations, and so on. Each item has a game function. A stove is needed to cook food, for example. The more expensive the stove, the more satisfying the food, filling the "Hunger" meter more fully.

The economics of *The Sims* has inspired one easy criticism: that it's a consumerist fantasy that turns life into one big shopping spree. A review of the game in the *New York Times,* for example, was titled "The Sims Who Die with the Most Toys Win."[50] Given the large number of women who play *The Sims,* this critique fits snugly with familiar gender stereotypes about women as shopping-obsessed overconsumers. But this analysis misses a complicating factor: the critical currency in *The Sims* is not money, but *time.* The gameplay is a continuous balancing act, a race to juggle multiple needs before time runs out and the day is over. Misallocate time, and the results are disastrous. If you miss too much work, you're fired. If you skip too much school, a truant officer hauls you off to military school. If you go too long without using the bathroom, you pee your pants. If you don't eat, you die.

The Sims, then, is a reflection not only of consumerism, but also of what sociologist Arlie Russell Hochschild calls "the time bind"—the constant pressure on Americans today, particularly working mothers, to juggle the competing demands of work and home.[51] The game is even grittily pessimistic about the possibilities of raising children in a two-income family. A Sim couple can make a child (the sex is chastely blurred out— the game is rated T by the Entertainment Software Ratings Board, for "content that may be suitable for persons ages 13 and older").[52] But with the new responsibilities a baby brings, if both Sim parents work outside the home, inevitably either one of the characters will miss work and get fired, or the baby will wind up so neglected that a social worker shows up and takes it away. (In *Sims 2,* you can hire a nanny, but as in real life, this requires substantial funds.)

A third economy in *The Sims* is personal relationships. In order for a Sim to advance in her or his job and make more money, the Sim needs to collect friends. Sims make friends by interacting with other Sims, both within the household (controlled by the player) and in the neighborhood (controlled by the computer). Sims talk to each other, but they don't speak English; rather, they speak "SimSpeak," gibberish that conveys emotion through intonation, but not precise meaning. They can also engage in a wide range of social behaviors, such as dancing, back rubbing, tickling, and kissing. A group of bars just like the eight Mood bars track how well the Sim is liked by each of her/his acquaintances. Another challenge of the game, then, is to orchestrate relationships to build up each Sim's number of friends, as well as find romantic partners for each Sim. (Taking a progressive stand, the game includes the possibility of gay and lesbian as well as straight romances. Gay couples can't make babies, but may adopt.)[53]

Given these themes, the appeal of the game to girls and women struggling to define their roles in contemporary America makes sense. *The Sims* is not simply an escapist fantasy, but a model with which to experiment with different sets of personal priorities, as reflected in different game strategies.

There's plenty of room to experiment, since you control not just one member of the household, but all of them, commanding them individually while coordinating their interactions with each other. Gameplay is not just a constant juggling act from one task to the next, but from one character to another. The currently "active" character in any moment of gameplay is represented by a diamond over the character's head. (In a twist on that *Tetris* commercial, recent commercials for *The Sims* represent everyday real-life situations as if they were taking place in the world of the game, complete with diamonds floating overhead. Like the *Tetris* ad, the commercials highlight how playing the game restructures your perception of the world outside the game.)

Identification in *The Sims*, then, is multiple and shifting. You can bounce from one side of a flirtation to the other, conducting a romance. Unlike *SimCity*, however, the identification remains personalized, even through the shifts. The game interface may present a god's-eye perspective—it's a third-person overhead view, never POV—but the game never disengages to the Olympian heights of the main map screens in *SimCity* and *Civilization*. More than any adventure game, *The Sims* allows you to develop characters you can really care about.

MMORPGs: From Personal Computer Gaming to Interpersonal Computer Gaming

The Sims may be a game that values interpersonal interaction, but as originally designed, it was a solitary experience. Concurrent with the success of *The Sims*, however, was the second major gaming phenomenon of the turn of the millennium: the rise of multiplayer online gaming.

Online game environments had been around for many years. In the 1980s and 1990s, many players participated in MUDs, or "Multi-User Domains," also known as "Multi-User Dungeons," since the majority of the spaces were organized around fantasy themes.[54] Nonetheless, MUD-ding remained a largely subcultural activity, text based, far removed from the flashy world of cutting-edge computer gaming. In 1997, however, *Ultima Online* debuted as the first MMORPG—"Massively Multiplayer Online Role Playing Game." The even-more successful *Everquest* followed in 1998. These slick, 3D games capitalized on the rise of the internet to transform personal computer gaming into interpersonal computer gaming. In these games, a player controls a character within a giant fantasy world, interacting with thousands of other online players.

The world of MMORPGs is now a massive business. *Everquest* has 420,000 subscribers, each of whom pays a monthly fee on top of the original purchase price of the game. *Star Wars Galaxies,* the online version of the venerable franchise, boasts 470,000 subscribers. *Final Fantasy Online,* played through the Playstation 2 network adapter, has 500,000 subscribers worldwide.[55] Other online games include the superhero-themed *City of Heroes,* the Tolkien adaptation *Middle-Earth Online,* and *The Matrix Online.*

Online games have become rich, engrossing fantasy spaces, complex societies with their own newspapers, social events, and economies. This last aspect has become particularly interesting to many economists, who have begun to study the emergence of complex economic systems among players.[56] Many successful veteran players sell game artifacts online, through eBay, to less advanced players—for real-world money. Some players have managed to make livings by arbitraging game items: buying low off eBay, then reselling at higher prices. Julian Dibbell recounts his experience as a professional *Ultima Online* arbitrageur in a fascinating weblog, *Play Money.*[57]

Seeing the success of the MMORPGs, Maxis brought out *The Sims Online* in 2002 to great publicity, including a *Newsweek* cover story.[58] Surprisingly, the game has been a bust, with only 80,000 players.[59] It appears players preferred the simulated social engagement of *The Sims* to the online "real thing." The game has been marred by large numbers of "griefers" who harass other players. The game also received negative publicity when Peter Ludlow, a philosopher of language who was participating in the game while studying it, was booted off the system. He had been publishing an online newspaper, *The Alphaville Herald,* about the game, including candid discussion of problems with the game. Maxis asserted its ultimate right to control its collective fantasy space. But the subsequent hue and cry demonstrated the growing public awareness that online game worlds are significant public spaces. Stories on the controversy appeared in the *New York Times* and on CNN, the BBC, and *The Daily Show.* Ludlow has now moved to another MMORPG with a more flexible philosophy, *Second Life,* and publishes *The Second Life Herald.*

The New Lively Art

This discussion of a few influential games can only scratch the surface of a multibillion-dollar entertainment industry. Henry Jenkins has suggested that we think of computer games as "the new lively art,"[60] an emergent form joining the other popular arts surveyed by Gilbert Seldes in his 1924 classic, *The Seven Lively Arts.*[61] In the last few years, a community of scholars have emerged to interrogate the aesthetics, ideology, and economics of computer games.[62] In 2001 the first peer-reviewed journal in the field, *Game Studies,* was launched.

As game studies has struggled to move beyond the interactive-cinema paradigm, it has turned to the analysis of what is distinctive about games as games. To that end, Espen Aarseth and others have proposed a new term to label the field: "ludology," from the Latin word *ludus,* for game.[63] Their work parallels my own efforts to distinguish the distinct properties of computer games. However, in their desire to claim new disciplinary territory against poachers from English and film departments eager to claim games as just another form of storytelling, some ludologists reject the concept of narrative altogether as a useful tool for interpreting computer games.[64] As this chapter has demonstrated, while computer games cannot simply be described as narrative, even fluid, open-ended games like *SimCity* and *The Sims* have many story-like aspects.

Henry Jenkins in a recent essay proposes a sensible middle ground between the narratologists and the ludologists. Expanding the concept of "spatial stories," Jenkins suggests that we understand game design as "narrative architecture," and designers as "world builders" rather than storytellers.[65] The phrase "world building" comes from the genres of science fiction and fantasy. It describes the projects of creators such as L. Frank Baum, J. R. R. Tolkien, and Gene Roddenberry, each of whom developed an elaborate fictional universe that spread beyond the bounds of individual stories. The focus on world building clarifies the utopian dimensions of game design: the designer's role is not merely to tell a story, but to imagine an entire new world.

One useful extension to this world-building model is to consider Fredric Jameson's argument in "World Reduction in Le Guin: The Emergence of Utopian Narrative."[66] Jameson examines the surprising barrenness of the landscape in Ursula Le Guin's classic science fiction novels *The Left Hand of Darkness* and *The Dispossessed,* compared to our usual presumption that world building is a process of excess. (Think of Tolkien's many volumes of appendices and histories, fleshing out the world of Middle Earth.) Jameson concludes that another way to think of the SF spatial story is as a process of "world reduction"—boiling down a universe to uncover its most essential aspects. In a sense, this is what all games must do: decide which aspects of a universe are important to gameplay, and which are peripheral. In this sense, we can understand games such as *SimCity, Civilization, The Sims,* and *Everquest* as projects both of world building and world reduction. Simulation games give the player the opportunity to create elaborate fantasy universes. But they necessarily limit the parameters of play. *Civilization* reduces its world to expansion and war; *The Sims* to time, money, and friends.

The power of world reduction may also help explain the challenges faced by the sequels and expansions to these original simulation games. The original *SimCity* and *Civilization* were forced to reduce their worlds to basic abstractions because the computers of 1987 and 1991, respectively, didn't have the capacity for greater complexity. The games used bold, chunky graphics because of the limits of monitor resolutions and graphic cards. Their algorithms for modeling economic growth were limited because of the processing power available to calculate them. These restrictions were frustrating, but also imposed discipline: designers were forced to carefully chose their models, reducing their worlds to a bare minimum. Subsequent games have been liberated from these restrictions as Moore's Law has zoomed onward. But as a result, they can grow so complex and detailed that their underlying premises are swamped in excess detail.

This irony—that simplicity may convey information more powerfully than detail—is developed in Scott McCloud's wonderful *Understanding Comics,* a theorization of comic book art presented in the form of a comic book starring McCloud himself.[67] One of McCloud's key points is that in comic art, simplicity evokes universality. We can think of comic drawing as a continuum, from the almost pure abstraction of a stick figure or smiley face on one end, to photo-realism on the other end. One might assume that the greater detail of photo-realism would inherently be a more effective artistic technique. But McCloud points out that many of the most powerful, evocative comic characters are the most abstracted. Think of Charlie Brown, Pogo, or Nancy. Their very simplicity encourages identification, empowering the reader to fill in the details. Similarly, the early computer games, out of technological necessity, embraced an aesthetic of abstraction, starting with the simple dots and lines of Pong. As computer games have grown more technologically advanced, this abstraction has been replaced with a quest for "realism" through the most detailed rendering of 3D spaces and textures. But this so-called progress comes with a cost.

I have to admit that as of this writing, my favorite computer game stars a group of stick figures. *Kingdom of Loathing* is an online role-playing game. In the tradition of simple text-based adventure games like *Adventure* and *Zork,* you control a character who explores a world full of quests, battles, and treasures. But while almost all contemporary computer games update these classics by buffing them to a 3D, megapixel sheen, *Kingdom of Loathing* has a sketchy, hand-drawn look. The interface is simple, as well: almost all options are just a mouse click or two away. There's no motion, either, just a static series of web pages. In place of the text-based commands, the interface is a streamlined process of pointing and clicking. The style perfectly fits the game's silly, *Monty Python*-esque sensibility, in which the kingdom's currency is "meat," wizards are known as "Pastamancers" and "Saucerors," heroes battle enemies such as "The Procrastination Giant" and "Ninja Snowmen," and locations include "The Obligatory Pirate's Cove" and "The Naughty Sorceress's Lair." But the game's world is rich and compelling—there are hundreds of monsters to fight and treasures to discover. And a community of thousands of players has built up a vibrant economy, in which players trade meat for valued objects such as hell ramen, supermartinis, and hippopotamus pants. *Kingdom of Loathing* demonstrates one elegant balancing point between the giddy pleasures of world building and the bracing focus of world reduction.

From Scott McCloud, *Understanding Comics* (Perennial Currents, 1994).

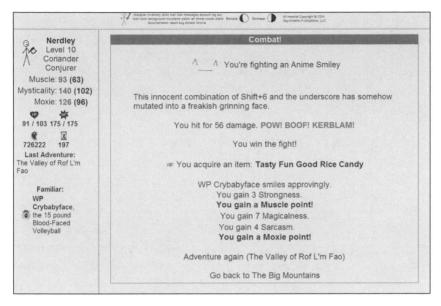

Kingdom of Loathing. From http://www.kingdomofloathing.com.

PART III

The Interpersonal Computer

7

Imagining Cyberspace

In the 1990s the personal computer became an interpersonal computer. Increasingly, computer users employed the PC not just a tool for individual information processing, but as a medium for communication.

PC users of the 1970s and 1980s were able to communicate with each other by using modems to transmit information via phone lines to hobbyist-run bulletin board systems (known as BBSes), larger commercial online services such as Prodigy (backed by IBM and Sears), CompuServe, Delphi, and America Online, and some academic networks. Some BBSes, such as The Well in San Francisco, developed large, strong "virtual communities."[1] But the development of the PC as a communication medium was limited by the incompatibility of the various networks. Each network was a localized, bounded space. Computer users who logged on to one BBS or online service couldn't easily communicate with any others. Modems were add-on items (rather than being standard equipment on new PCs, as they are today), and many users didn't see much point in buying one.

The development of the protocols for the World Wide Web (WWW) by Tim Berners-Lee in 1990 began to break down the walls between networks.[2] The WWW built upon the internet, a network that was first developed by the U.S. Department of Defense in the 1960s, and which had become a global network for the exchange of academic information.[3] The formatting language of the web, Hypertext Markup Language (HTML), provided a simple system to link millions of disparate "pages" into an interconnected network of information. The development of the first graphical web browser, Mosaic, by Marc Andreessen in 1993 made the WWW simple and easy to use. Responding to increasing consumer demand, first the Prodigy online service, then other online services made the web and internet email available to their users. What economists call "network effects" accelerated this expansion: each new user made the network a more comprehensive and valuable communication tool, making it easier to add the next user, and so on, and so on.[4] Email and web surfing became the next killer applications, driving new computer sales. As computer sales went up, competition among manufacturers intensified and prices fell, making computers affordable for millions of new users. Today, the internet is a mass medium used by 57% of the American population, although a "digital divide" persists.[5]

So, who invented the internet we know today? One might say it was the scientists at ARPANET, who designed the original network in the 1960s. Or perhaps Berners-Lee. Or maybe Andreessen. All of these technologists helped make the contemporary internet possible. But the explosion of computer-mediated communication in the 1990s is not simply the result of technological advancement. Specialists had been emailing each other for over twenty years before the rest of the world began to notice. America Online had been kicking around for most of a decade before it became the darling of Wall Street. Even the World Wide Web began as a curiosity before taking off. All these developments couldn't come together—the critical mass that turned these technologies into a mass medium couldn't be reached—until a framework was available through which a large number of users could begin to accept and understand this new medium. The internet represents not just a technological shift, but a cultural shift. Developing ways for users to make sense of and talk about computer-mediated communication was as important to the making of the internet as inventing the TCP/IP protocol or codifying HTML.

Which brings us to William Gibson, a science fiction writer. No concept has been as critical to our contemporary understanding of computer-mediated communication as the notion of "cyberspace." Coined by Gibson in the 1982 story "Burning Chrome," elaborated in his 1984 novel *Neuromancer,* the concept of cyberspace has become a framework for thinking about a global network of communications that seems to exist outside of ordinary time and space. By envisioning this network as a kind of parallel universe, it offers the possibility of cognitive mapping, of developing a sense of location and perspective within this daunting array. Without the notion of cyberspace, I don't think we could make sense of the internet. Or, if we did, we'd think of it in very different ways.

One might argue that although the term cyberspace was only coined twenty years ago, the concept has been around much longer. Certainly, the notion of cyberspace builds on our earlier conceptions of imaginary spaces. Science fiction novelist and journalist Bruce Sterling, in his nonfiction *The Hacker Crackdown,* retroactively declares cyberspace to be over a hundred years old. "Cyberspace," he famously writes, "is the 'place' where a telephone conversation appears to occur. . . . *The place between* the phones. The indefinite place *out there.*"[6]

But this generalization misses the new social practices opened up by the concept of cyberspace. A further look at the telephone example might be helpful here. The telephone is a powerful communications technology that can be used in very different ways from the one-on-one model we're most familiar with today. The "party line" framework, for example, envisioned a phone conversation as something quite like a contemporary online chat room—a link between the individual and a broader community, rather than a connection between isolated individuals. But alternate models of telephony such as the party line fell away as a reified notion of the telephone as a one-to-one communication device took hold.[7] The telephone could have produced cyberspace, but it didn't. Instead, cyberspace on a broad scale did not emerge until the 1990s.

My emphasis here on "invention" is somewhat simplistic. The internet today is the product not just of its originators, but of the many users who have taken those inventions in new and unpredictable directions. Likewise, what we think of as cyberspace today isn't exactly what William Gibson had in mind two decades ago. As the word has circulated through American culture, its meaning has changed. Different users, occupying different levels of cultural influence, have appropriated the term to respond to new circumstances. This chapter traces the conceptual development of the term cyberspace. By looking more closely at how the term was first introduced, how it worked its way into mainstream discourse, and what it means today, we can develop a better sense of how we have ended up thinking what we think about the internet today—and also, perhaps, how we might think differently about cyberspace in the future.

From the Utopian Sphere to the Public Sphere

For the most part, science fiction writers are pretty marginal to mainstream American discourse. SF novels hardly ever make best-seller lists. Even those writers most lauded by the science fiction community are rarely given more than passing notice in the mainstream press. But if SF literature seems to have little direct effect on how most Americans look at the world, it does have its moments of influence, its sliver of the American public sphere. It is one slice of the utopian sphere.[8] And on occasion, ideas can amass the cultural capital to cross over from the utopian sphere to the public sphere. This is what happened to the concept of cyberspace.

The cyberspace we know today—the World Wide Web—didn't exist in 1982 when Gibson coined the term. Gibson, in fact, knew very little at all about computers. He didn't even own one when he wrote *Neuromancer*.[9] But Gibson recognized that a new form of interaction between people and computers was emerging, one that didn't yet have a name. His inspiration was watching kids at the local video arcade. He told one interviewer,

> I could see in the physical intensity of their postures how *rapt* the kids inside were. It was like one of those closed systems out of a Pynchon novel: a feedback loop with photons coming off the screens into the kids' eyes, neurons moving through their bodies, and electrons moving through the video game. These kids clearly *believed* in the space games projected.[10]

As a science fiction writer, Gibson did more than just identify an emerging trend. The SF device of extrapolation allowed him to allegorize this new experience, highlighting its most compelling aspects by making literal what today is only metaphor. Thus, the informational link that seems to bind together player and video game into one feedback loop becomes, in *Neuromancer,* a physical link. When the characters in *Neuromancer* log on to cyberspace, they literally "jack in," attaching electrodes to directly connect their brains to the computer. (This device has since been borrowed by the film *The Matrix* and its sequels, which have finally translated a version of Gibson's sensibility for a mass audience.)

So, what does cyberspace look like in *Neuromancer?* Returning to the book recently for the first time in a few years, I was struck by something that had slipped my mind as I'd grown used to equating cyberspace with the internet: in the original text itself, cyberspace includes not only what we would think of today as the internet, but also what we would call virtual reality. Writing before the popularization of either of these words, Gibson used the terms "simstim" and "the matrix" to refer to his extrapolated versions of what we'd now call VR and the internet, respectively. Simstim, short for simulated stimulation, is a full sensory hookup that allows the user to see, hear, and feel the experiences of another person. The matrix is the disembodied realm where hackers can glide through abstract, three-dimensional representations of data—"bright lat-

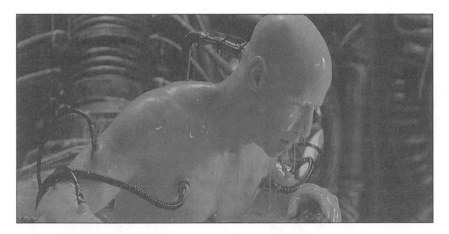

From *The Matrix* (Warner, 1999).

tices of logic unfolding across that colorless void,"[11] as Gibson puts it. Cyberspace, in *Neuromancer,* encompasses *both* of these forms of virtual space.

The climactic chapters of the novel play these two visions of cyberspace off each other. Case, the hero, is connected to a computer on board a starship. His job is to supervise the robbery of the starbase below, the home of the powerful Tessier-Ashpool clan. This robbery involves breaking and entering on both the physical and virtual planes. On the surface of the starbase, Molly, Case's partner, is penetrating the physical defenses of the Tessier-Ashpool stronghold. Meanwhile, within the starbase's computer network, a sophisticated computer virus unleashed by Case is slowly hacking through the system's security software. Jacked into cyberspace, Case follows both break-ins. Via a simstim connection, he sees, hears, and feels everything that Molly does. Then, with a flick of a switch, Case's consciousness shifts to the matrix, where, disembodied, he directs the progress of the computer virus. As the action climaxes, Case flips back and forth between these two versions of cyberspace, simstim and the matrix.

Today, the term cyberspace almost always refers to our current analogue to *Neuromancer*'s matrix, the internet. The most contemporary-sounding passages in *Neuromancer* are those that celebrate the disembodied, floating pleasures of the matrix—what Case calls "the bodiless exultation of cyberspace." But as we shall see, this has not always been the case. In the 1980s, it was simstim, rather than the matrix, that seemed the most compelling vision of cyberspace.

Neuromancer was an immediate success in the world of science fiction. It won all the major SF awards for 1984, including both the Nebula (voted by critics) and the Hugo (voted by fans). This success in itself did not mean the broader public would necessarily take notice. Many of the most celebrated science fiction authors of the last two decades have received little attention outside the SF community. To reach a broader audience, *Neuromancer* needed to be identified with a movement beyond the mainstream of science fiction.

That movement was "cyberpunk." First coined by SF writer Bruce Bethke, the term was picked up by SF magazine editor Gardner Dozois as a way to characterize the work of Gibson and several similar writers. In the hands of leading ideologue Bruce Sterling, the term quickly became a way to define this new generation of writers against the SF mainstream. Cyberpunk was supposed to do for science fiction what punk rock did for rock and roll—shake up an ossified institution and return it to the streets. The cyberpunk label allowed Gibson to be pitched to the readers of magazines like *Rolling Stone* and *Spin* as hip SF, SF for bohemians who think of mainstream SF as embarrassingly geeky. The irony, as reluctant cyberpunk fellow traveler Greg Bear put it, was that "we had a movement that was posing as if it were out on the edge when in fact it was firmly embraced and at the center."[12] The regrettable by-product of this pose was to hype cyberpunk at the expense of the rest of science fiction, further marginalizing those SF authors whom the cyberpunks denigrated as "humanists," such as Orson Scott Card and John Varley—many of whom had interesting things to say about new technologies themselves, if in a less flashy style. In any case, the move worked, and Gibson successfully passed from the science fiction subculture into bohemia and youth culture.

A second avenue into the public sphere for *Neuromancer* was via high culture. Cyberpunk propagandists played up Gibson's literary lineage at the expense of his science fiction forebears. By connecting itself with the work of postmodern fabulists like Thomas Pynchon and William Burroughs, cyberpunk legitimated itself in academia. Today, *Neuromancer* sits fairly comfortably in the canon of contemporary American literature.

To try to trace the history of the diffusion of the term cyberspace, I entered the word into that ultimate embodiment of the postmodern public sphere: the Nexis database. The results show an almost perfect geometric progression. In 1988 cyberspace appeared 11 times, always in stories about Gibson. In 1989 the number shot up to 31, including the first use of the term away from Gibson. The numbers approximately doubled in 1990, and again in 1991. By 1992 the number of stories was up to 236— including a mention in that arbiter of linguistic acceptance, William Safire's "On Language" column.[13] Finally, in 1993, cyberspace entered standard American vocabulary, appearing in over 1,000 Nexis articles— at which point the database stops counting. Today, cyberspace sits comfortably in the pages of *Webster's Dictionary, The American Heritage Dictionary,* and *The Oxford English Dictionary.*

From Simstim to the Matrix

What was striking, in going through these Nexis articles, was not just the rise in numbers, but also the change of emphasis as cyberspace made its way to the public sphere: from cyberspace as a three-dimensional, immersive experience, to cyberspace as a transglobal communications network. In other words, from simstim to the matrix. The early understanding of cyberspace reflected a cultural moment that's been all but forgotten in the wake of the subsequent internet mania: the VR fad of the late 1980s and early 1990s. The Safire column on cyberspace, for example, is titled "Virtual Reality." This was the era when overpriced VR games began to show up at every arcade, the Nintendo Power Glove made a big splash, and movies like *The Lawnmower Man* titillated with the promise of virtual sex. Remember, in 1992, the internet was not yet a mass medium. Mosaic, the first graphical web browser, had not yet debuted. The text-based gopher and ftp systems were the state of the art for online interface. At this point, cyberspace meant where you were when you strapped on goggles, hooked up motion sensors, and dove into a computer-generated 3D landscape.

What happened? VR fizzled as the technology failed to live up to the hopes invested in it. VR arcade games made players nauseous. Parents worried that Nintendo's proposed VR goggles would permanently damage children's visual perception. *Lawnmower Man II* bombed. What emerged in place of the VR hype was the internet. Pundits who had been promising full sensory interfaces began to notice that now you could download websites made up of old-fashioned words and pictures from any corner of the globe. Trend-spotting technopundit Howard Rheingold, for example, followed up 1991's *Virtual Reality* with 1994's *The Virtual Community: Homesteading on the Electronic Frontier.* The former book was about simstim technologies such as goggles and gloves. The latter is about the matrix, as constructed through words on a computer screen. In place of the fantasy of a fully embodied, immersive experience, the internet offered the prospect of a new medium of communication, via some very familiar physical interfaces: eyes viewing a screen, fingers on a keyboard. The less fantastic, but perhaps more powerful, promise of the matrix replaced the fantasies of simstim.

So, why this shift in the imaginative properties of cyberspace? How do we make sense of this odd transition—from VR's crash and burn to the internet's liftoff? I don't think we can simply write the VR craze off as a passing fad, a speed bump on the road to the internet. The extrapolated promises of VR established the metaphors with which we now make sense of the internet. VR literalized the idea of complete, physical immersion in a computer-created world. It allowed for some kind of materialist conception of what the disembodied realm of cyberspace felt like. The vision of VR allowed users to fantasize transcending the body—but through the exchange of bodies, the habitation of a new body. In *Neuromancer,* it quite literally means walking in another person's shoes, as Case sees and feels everything Molly does.[14] As the possibility of the internet emerged, the demand for this materialist account of the experience of cyberspace faded. The fantasy of exchanging bodies—of walking in Molly's shoes—was replaced by the fantasy of escaping the body altogether, floating in the disembodied world of the internet.

This vision of an existence where all the limitations of the physical world disappear and consciousness can roam free has become almost a cliché about cyberspace today. Technohype envisions the internet as a utopia where you can transcend race, transcend gender, transcend the boundaries of the flesh. As critics such as Langdon Winner[15] and Ann Balsamo[16] have pointed out, though, the problem is that this eagerness to proclaim the transcendence of the body can lead to the repression of the bodies that cyberspace can't simply get rid of. The return of the repressed hit home for me recently in a most direct way: carpal tunnel syndrome, the result of too many hours sitting at my computer typing without paying attention to the impact of the experience on my physical being. On a broader scale, a failure to recognize the materiality of cyberspace helps keep the physical labor it takes to build and maintain cyberspace invisible.

Whole-body Interfaces

Perhaps one way out of this dangerous fantasy is to bring some simstim back into the matrix, by expanding our interface with cyberspace. Today, what almost all computer activities have in common with reading, writing, watching TV, or going to the movies are the channels of input and output. Information is sent from the hands to the text via a keyboard, mouse, joypad, or remote control, or simply by turning a page. And information is circulated back to the user through the eyes and ears, via monitor, TV, movie screen, or page. Computer games, as we've seen, speed up the circuit between text and user, tightening the feedback loop. But they don't actually expand the range of inputs and outputs.

As a result, what all these pursuits hold in common is the temptation to abstract the body from the mind—or, more specifically, from the circuit of eyes, ears, and hands. Computer games, with their even more intense cybernetic circuits, make the temptation to tune out everything beyond the circuit even greater. This is the kernel of truth behind the phobic discourse of "computer game addiction." But if video and computer games offer this dangerously solipsistic temptation, they can also provide us with the tools for more holistic alternatives. For me, the most exciting new development in the world of video and computer games is the rise of experiments in interface design beyond the eyes-ears-hands circuit. The new genre of what I'd call "whole-body" games got its start with arcade dance games such as *Dance Dance Revolution,* or *DDR* for short. These games turn the floor into a giant gamepad. You have to match the arrows and symbols flashing on the screen with the corresponding spots on the floorpad, while keeping in time with the music. A huge hit in arcades, *DDR* has now made the transition to home games, while spawning numerous sequels and imitators, such as *Britney's Dance Beat.*

Even more exciting is a new game accessory introduced by Sony in 2003, the Eye Toy. This is a small camera that perches on top of a Playstation 2 game console. The camera inserts your image onto the game screen. You then must control your movements as your game image interacts with the game world. Motion-recognition technology can tell when you're waving your arms to the left, right, up, or down.

The original Eye Toy came packaged with a group of games that let you battle ninjas, fight boxers, and bounce soccer balls. One expansion disc adds dance games, while another retrofits old Sega games for whole-body play.

So far the Eye Toy games, like *DDR,* are simple action games. But by expanding the palette of interactivity, they open up great new opportunities for interface designers to merge the bifurcated worlds of simstim and the matrix.

8

Dot-com Politics

The exponential growth in the number of internet users in the 1990s fueled a gold rush in "dot-com" stocks, up until the tech crash of 2000. This boom was paralleled by an explosion in technotopian rhetoric, as dreams of technologically driven social transformation conveniently meshed with get-rich-quick fantasies. A bevy of new magazines, bursting to overflow with dot-com advertising, arose to spread the cybertopian gospel, including *Red Herring, Industry Standard, Fast Company, Upside,* and *Business 2.0.* The bible of this cybertopianism was undoubtedly *Wired* magazine, which both reported on the technology industry and attempted to place the boom in a broader social context. To better understand the ideology of the dot-com boom, this chapter will take a closer look at the cyber-libertarian politics of *Wired* during the Silicon Valley gold rush.

Wired as first conceived was an odd amalgam, a high-tech business magazine with a cyberpunk edge. The magazine was founded in 1993 by veterans of the *Whole Earth Review,* the bible of the West Coast–based, left-wing "appropriate technology" movement. By the 1990s, these ex-bohemians, including Louis Rosetto, Stuart Brand, and Howard Rheingold, had embraced Silicon Valley–style capitalism as a force of positive social change, grafting 1960s-style utopian rhetoric onto their business coverage.[1] *Wired* quickly established itself as cyberspace's paper of record. It veered from sections like "Deductible Junkets," which listed upcoming computer-industry conventions, to "Idées Fortes," which published manifestos from hackers, phone phreaks, and other cybercultural fringe dwellers.

Unlike many of its imitators, *Wired* remains in publication today, having been sold by its original founders to the Condé Nast magazine empire in 1998. However, since the dot-com crash, it's become a much more conventional—and chastened—business-and-culture magazine. My discussion will focus on the *Wired* of the boom years. Many of the ideological conflicts of the dot-com era, however, remain with us today.

The Hacker Mystique

The ambiguous figure of the hacker was central to the mythology of *Wired*. The term hacker can mean several different things, depending on its context of use. While hacker is a term of honor for many computer users, it is also used disparagingly by some, to identify programmers as "nerdy social outcasts."[2] Like "queer" and "nigger," hacker is today a term worn as a subcultural badge of pride by many computer programmers and users. Who gets to count as a true hacker, however, is a subject of much contestation.

Steven Levy's 1984 history of computing, *Hackers: Heroes of the Computer Revolution,* is about the "original hackers," the young programmers and designers who rebelled against the bureaucracy and hierarchy of 1950s-style mainframe computing, leading what Levy calls "The Computing Revolution"—the development of small, (relatively) cheap, (relatively) easy-to-use computers accessible to the general public. Levy defines hackers as "those computer programmers and designers who regard computing as the most important thing in the world."[3] Levy is most interested in how these experimenters' enthusiasm and creativity inspired them to break all the supposed rules of computing, opening up a new, more "empowering" way to use computers. Levy identifies the original hackers as the undergraduate members of MIT's Tech Model Railroad Club (TMRC) in the 1950s, who began experimenting with MIT's powerful PDP-10 miniframe computer and developed a new way to work with computers—not simply designing programs offline and feeding them to the computer on punch cards, but *interacting* with the computer, exploiting the computer's ability to give quick feedback to develop sophisticated games and simulations. Levy traces the etymology of the term "hacker" from the term a "hack," which "had long been used to describe the elaborate college pranks that MIT students would regularly devise, such as covering the dome that overlooked the campus with reflecting foil." Among the TMRC members, a "hack" came to mean any

> project undertaken or a product built not solely to fulfill some constructive goal, but with some wild pleasure taken in the mere involvement. . . .

As the TMRC people used the word, there was serious respect implied. While someone might call a clever connection between relays a "mere hack," it would be understood that, to qualify as a hack, the feat must be imbued with innovation, style, and technical virtuosity. Even though one might self-deprecatingly say he was "hacking away at The System" (much as an ax-wielder hacks at logs), the artistry with which one hacked was recognized to be considerable.[4]

TMRC members began to call themselves "hackers," to emphasize that they were not conventional programmers, but idealists absorbed in the pleasure of computing for its own sake. Hackers would be expected to work through the day and night for weeks at a time to finish their programs, to subsist on junk food and little sleep, to ignore the regular necessities of life in their obsession to get their programs right. As the innovations pioneered at MIT began to be more widely appreciated, the term hacker came to be a label of honor for committed computer programmers and designers.

Another use of the term hacker developed in the 1970s. As computer networks became more complex, some users began to experiment with ways to break into these networks, usually just for the sake of exploration, sometimes with more mischievous or malevolent motives. The 1983 movie *Wargames* popularized the image of the teenage hacker bringing the world to the brink of nuclear war from his bedroom. Through the 1980s and 1990s, a "hacker underground" developed, whose members, influenced by cyberpunk fiction, tended to see themselves as an anarchistic elite. Groups of hackers with names like Master of Deception and Legion of Doom have broken into the networks of telephone companies, credit-card bureaus, and even the military.[5] In 1994 the pursuit and capture of the infamous hacker Kevin Mitnick by programmer Tsutomu Shimomura became a national news story, inspiring three books.[6]

The meaning of the term hacker today is in dispute. Many members of the hacker underground see themselves as following in the footsteps of the TMRC, exploring and experimenting on the internet the way the first innovators did with the PDP-10. Some of these hackers hold to a code of honor that distinguishes "hacking" (exploring a system to learn more about it) from "cracking" (breaking into a system for personal gain). (This distinction, however, can get fuzzy as well. Is it stealing to appropriate telephone lines for free long-distance calls, when otherwise the lines would simply go unused? This is what one group of hackers, known as "phone phreaks," does.) Many more mainstream computer programmers who call themselves hackers in the old sense resent the term's appropriation by what they see as a group of adolescent lawbreakers. But other mainstream hackers enjoy the implication of a continuity between what they do and what groups like the Legion of Doom do—it lets a bit of the outlaw mystique rub off on them, even if they're working on perfectly legitimate computer tasks. This last perspective, as we will see, is part of the complex ideological work *Wired* did to reconcile corporate profits and bohemian anarchism.[7]

Information and Freedom

Wired featured writing by the likes of Bruce Sterling, William Gibson, and Neal Stephenson, cyberpunk authors known for their dystopian critiques of multinational capital. But *Wired* folded that sensibility into a corporate-friendly, giddily optimistic, and wildly hyperbolic tone as it chronicled, as Rosetto's founding editorial put it, "social changes so profound their only parallel is the discovery of fire."[8] Typical of *Wired*'s cyberpunk-recuperated-for-capitalism sensibility were stories that portrayed industry figures as countercultural rebels-with-a-cause. An interview with TCI Cable CEO John Malone, for example, was titled "Infobahn Warrior." The cover of the issue pictured a doctored image of the middle-aged multimillionaire in full *Road Warrior* regalia, complete with a leather jacket with one arm ripped off, leather pants bristling with ammunition, a gun in his hand, and a mangy dog at his side.[9]

Underlying the magazine's two very different-seeming perspectives was a fundamental libertarian ethic embodied in the slogan "Information wants to be free," first coined by *Whole Earth Catalog* editor and *Wired* contributor Stewart Brand in his 1987 book, *The Media Lab: Inventing the Future at MIT*.[10] The phrase became a touchstone for much cybercultural discourse; it's sometimes referred to as the Hacker Ethic.[11]

"Information wants to be free" is a classic example of essentializing techno-determinism, implying that information itself is analogous to a sentient creature with its own desires, intentionally struggling against censorship, regulation, and all other attempts to impede its circulation. This anthropomorphization reifies information, abstracting it from any recognition of its means of production—the labor, infrastructure, and so-

Cover of *Wired*, July 1994.

cial context that produce any piece of information, and make it meaningful. Granted, Brand's attribution of desire to an inanimate force isn't meant to be taken literally—it's intentionally excessive. The phrase "Information wants to be free" is perhaps a kind of strategic essentialism—a self-conscious attempt to clarify and codify a set of values by locating them not in people and social structures, but in something that seems more fundamental. Nonetheless, once that reification takes place, it begins to exert an explanatory power of its own. Thus, predictions for the future and value judgments about the present end up based on a presumption of what information itself is said to "want."

But in any case, what exactly does it mean for information to be free? Here's where *Wired*'s libertarian ethic bound the cyberpunks to the capitalists, leading to such bizarre amalgams as Electronic Frontier Foundation[12] founder John Perry Barlow: prominent cyberspeech advocate, Grateful Dead lyricist, and staunch Republican.

For cyberpunks, the freedom in question is civil liberty—the freedom to explore cyberspace without limitation. *Wired,* along with its sister online service HotWired, became a critical rallying point for opponents of government measures to limit online civil liberties. These threats included most prominently the Communications Decency Act, a sweeping measure designed to shield minors from online pornography that could potentially have outlawed a broad range of internet discourse, from cursing to participating in cybersex to distributing information on birth control. (The act passed and was signed into federal law as a part of the Communications Reform Act in 1996, but First Amendment challenges in federal court quickly struck it down.)

The computer industry shares hackers' concerns over the government's role in cyberspace. However, for the industry, the concern isn't primarily about free speech, but about the free market—not about John Stuart Mill, but Adam Smith. The freedom in question is the principle of laissez-faire, the freedom to make as much money as possible without government regulation.

What makes the elision between the two notions of freedom possible is the difficulty of determining where the marketplace of ideas ends and the marketplace of things begins when the product in question is information. Liberal free-speech theory is built on the presumption that there are two worlds, one of ideas, the other of material things, which can be easily distinguished. The distinction might be summed up by the childhood chant "Sticks and stones may break my bones, but names will never hurt me."[13] But in an "information economy," when the ownership of noncorporeal commodities such as copyrights, trademarks, and patents is as economically critical as the control of more traditional means of production, the simple distinction between ideas and things is no longer so transparent. Often, a company's most valuable asset is not its factories or its raw materials, but its "brand."[14]

I would suggest that recent debates over issues such as hate speech have their roots in the changing relationship of ideas to things in an information economy. The insistence of pro-censorship feminists such as Catharine MacKinnon that speech must be understood as a material practice—as "speech acts"—testifies to the breakdown of the liberal consensus that "names will never hurt me."[15]

Julian Dibbell offered a provocative investigation of these questions in his influential essay "A Rape in Cyberspace." Originally published in the *Village Voice* in 1993, widely distributed online, and now expanded into the book *My Tiny Life: Crime and Passion in a Virtual World,* the work describes a disturbing incident in a Multi-User Dungeon called LambdaMOO. The sense of community and personal commitment on a MUD can be intense—dedicated users can spend as many as 60 or 70 hours a week online. As Dibbell writes, "What happens inside a MUD-made world is neither exactly real nor exactly make-believe, but profoundly, compellingly, and emotionally *true.*"[16]

MUD users have at their disposal various "commands"—akin to a simple computer programming language—that allow them to control how they are represented to the rest of the community. What happened in this case was that one user, "Mr. Bungle," hacked his way into LambdaMOO's operating system and changed the way the commands worked so that he could control the onscreen representations of other users' characters. With this power, he input commands that caused another user's female character to appear to accompany him to LambdaMOO's central meeting space against her will. He then input commands that displayed to the room's audience descriptions of his male character subjecting the other user's female character to a violent sexual assault. Given the level of emotional engagement in a MUD, the woman behind the female character felt deeply violated, the victim of a kind of "virtual rape."

Dibbell's essay describes the way in which the community of LambdaMOO attempted to address this violation of its civic order, ultimately leading in the banishment of the offending character—and the anonymous user behind him—from the online community. What is most important for my discussion here is what this episode says about the distinction between ideas and things—or, in this case, the slightly different categories of words and actions—in cyberspace. As Dibbell writes,

> the more seriously I took the notion of virtual rape, the less seriously I was able to take the tidy division of the world into the symbolic and the real that underlies the very notion of freedom of speech.
>
> Let me assure you, though, that I did not at the time adopt these thoughts as full-fledged arguments, nor am I now presenting them as such. I offer them, rather, as a picture of the sort of mind-set that my initial encounters with a virtual world inspired in me. I offer them also, therefore, as a kind of prophecy. For whatever else these thoughts were telling me, I have come to hear in them an announcement of the final stages of our decades-long passage into the Information Age, a paradigm shift that the classic liberal firewall between word and deed (itself a product of an earlier paradigm shift commonly known as the Enlightenment) is not likely to survive intact. After all, anyone the least bit familiar with the workings of the new era's definitive technology, the computer, knows that it operates on a principle impracticably difficult to distinguish from the pre-Enlightenment principle of the magic word: the commands you type into a computer are a kind of speech that doesn't so much communicate as make things happen, directly and ineluctably, the same way pulling a trigger does. They are incantations, in other words, and anyone at all attuned to the technosocial megatrends of the moment—from the growing dependence of economies on the global flow of intensely fetishized words and numbers to the burgeoning ability of bioengineers to speak the spells written in the four-letter text of DNA—knows that the logic of the incantation is rapidly permeating the fabric of our lives.
>
> And it was precisely this logic, I was beginning to understand, that provided whatever real magic LambdaMOO had to offer . . . the conflation of speech and act that's inevitable in any computer-mediated world, be it Lambda or the increasingly wired world at large.[17]

Corporate Libertarianism

Where one chooses to draw the line between *ideas* and *things* involves trade-offs. A broad definition of ideas drastically limits a society's ability to regulate its economy, when that economy is founded on the exchange of information. On the other hand, a broad definition of things opens the door for the kind of intrusive censorship the cyberpunks are so worried about. *Wired* chose the first of these paths, the broad definition of ideas. The ideal of free speech expands to encompass the economics of laissez-faire, satisfying both the cyberpunks and the corporations.

This bargain was mutually beneficial to the magazine's two constituencies, allowing each to acquire some of the other's cultural capital. *Wired* allowed capitalists to appropriate the bohemian edge of cyberpunk and pretend they were "Infobahn Warriors" rather than conventional businessmen. Cyberpunks agreed to accept the inequities of the free market as inevitable forces of creative destruction, and in return receive a big, shiny, well-reported magazine.

The downside of this bargain was its distortion of cyberpunk's critique of power. Governments, after all, are not the only institutions that infringe individuals' liberties. As James Brook and Iain A. Boal write,

> While it is of course true that government bureaucracies routinely monitor people through checking and matching, for example, Internal Revenue Service and driver license records, only rare individuals—political dissidents or particularly unlucky criminals—find themselves targeted for direct electronic surveillance. On the other hand, the average person is subject to intense scrutiny by business: their work is monitored and controlled by machinery, their leisure activities are closely examined and programmed, and their purchases and financial transactions are tracked and analyzed.[18]

In cyberpunk novels such as *Neuromancer* and Neal Stephenson's *Snowcrash,* the true global powers are multinational corporations. Governments, when they exist at all, are simply hollow shells, laughable in their attempts to compete with the influence of the multinationals. As we saw in chapter 5, recognition of the power of multinational capital in the face of individual states' claims to sovereignty is cyberpunk's most radical and compelling theme—and an example of how science fiction functions not just as a prediction of the future, but as a critique of the present. But as appropriated by *Wired,* cyberpunk's critique of corporate power devolved into a more familiar nightmare of Big Brother. The many institutions that threaten individual liberty collapsed into the simple specter of government control.

Wired did have one corporate enemy: Bill Gates, CEO of Microsoft. Rather than a generalized critique of capital, *Wired*'s libertarian ethic led to an individualist attack on a single monopoly. According to *Wired*'s vision of late capitalism—what it often called "the virtual economy"—new information technologies rendered bureaucracies obsolete and economies of scale unnecessary. Individual entrepreneurs had all the tools they needed to compete head-to-head with corporate behemoths. Cyberspace finally made possible real equality of opportunity, and fulfilled the American Dream. Microsoft was the lone exception clogging up an otherwise ideal market that naturally wanted to be free. *Wired*'s faith in the free market was a kind of neo–Social Darwinism, a cyber-fitted revision of Gilded Age rhetoric. Not surprisingly, evolutionary theorists who skirt the edge of Social Darwinism, such as Richard Dawkins and Daniel Dennett, were often cited in the pages of *Wired*.[19]

Wired's faith in the can-do spirit of plucky entrepreneurs was rooted in a very specific reading of the history of the personal-computer industry. The archetype for the cyberpreneurial narrative is the start-up computer company. Companies like Hewlett-Packard, Apple, and Microsoft each began as "a couple of guys in the garage." (Don Hewlett's old garage in Palo Alto, in fact, is now a Silicon Valley tourist attraction.) Each company took on much larger competition, and, thanks to its technical skills, business savvy, and superior products (along with heavy investments of venture capital), won. Eventually, yesterday's start-ups became today's behemoths, and the process starts all over again. Dozens of histories of the computer industry tell versions of this Horatio-Alger-in-cyberspace story.

The narrative of these stories isn't completely inaccurate. The computer industry, as the technological cutting edge of late capitalism, is subject to the kind of continual flux and change that gives innovative new companies the chance to trip up complacent giants, as all sprint madly to keep up with Moore's Law. As we've seen, IBM, happy with its mainframe computer business, didn't see any reason to pay attention to the growing personal-computer market in the 1970s, and paid the price. IBM slipped again when the clones overtook the IBM PC in the 1980s, allowing upstart manufacturers like Dell and Compaq to beat it at its own game, while Microsoft, run by two Harvard dropouts barely in their twenties, cornered the operating-system market. (Microsoft, of course, eventually turned from David into Goliath.)

But these inspiring underdog stories—pimply Bill Gates outfoxing Big Blue—are only one part of the story of the computer industry. Left out of the *Wired* account of rugged cyberpreneurship was the role of the federal government in bankrolling the computer industry—from the military sponsorship of ENIAC during World War II to the original construction of the Internet as ARPAnet, a flexible military communications network designed so that if some cities were bombed, critical messages could be rerouted and still delivered. It's no surprise that the hotbed of computer industry development for the past fifty years has been California, also home of the U.S. defense industry.[20]

Wired pundits hyped the growth of the internet as a prime example of the virtues of free enterprise over regulated development. But the internet from the start has been the result of collaboration among the military, academia, and the federal government. Only recently has private enterprise stepped in to capitalize on decades of publicly funded development. It's hard to imagine that the decentralized, democratic, anarchic spirit of internet culture would have turned out the same way if from day one the bankrollers had been concerned to turn a profit. In fact, it's hard to imagine that without sustained public funding, the internet could have happened at all.

It's not even clear that the computer industry ever functions the way *Wired* idealized it—as a place where technology allows the best ideas to win out over brute corporate muscle. Software professionals are almost unanimous in agreeing that the Apple's Macintosh Operating System is a more elegant user interface than Microsoft Windows. (Some would argue that the failed Amiga system was even better.) As we've seen, the Mac took the computing world by storm, introducing an innovative, easy to use point-and-click graphical user interface. Microsoft spent the next eleven years trying to catch up. Early versions of the Windows interface were clunky and unsuccessful; with the 1992 release of Windows 3.1, Microsoft finally achieved something still clearly inferior, but at least in the ballpark. Nonetheless, the superior marketing muscle of Microsoft, combined with the low costs of the PC clones, succeeded in making Windows the standard for computer operating systems. And with Windows 95, Microsoft finally achieved approximately what Apple had accomplished over a decade earlier. Meanwhile, Apple, after developing a cult following in the 1980s, failed to win over a majority of users, and for years has struggled to retain enough market share to survive. Microsoft has pursued the same strategy with product after product: taking on a successful rival (*Lotus 1-2-3, WordPerfect, Borland C++, Netscape Navigator*), creating a comparable if clunkier competitor (*Excel, Word, Visual C++, In-*

ternet Explorer), then using its size and power to crush its competition. Finally, in 2000, U.S. District Court Judge Thomas Penfield Jackson declared Microsoft in violation of the Sherman Antitrust Act. But even this ruling has barely slowed Microsoft down, as a 2001 settlement left the company intact and its power unchecked.

Also ignored in the Wired account of the "virtual economy" were the workers who manufacture chips at such an astronomical rate. Labor as imagined by the "virtual economy" fantasy encompasses only information work: software design, microprocessor engineering, business management. But cyberspace demands plenty of hands-on labor, too. The women working brutal hours in chip-construction plants in Malaysia, the electronics assemblers in Silicon Valley exposed to a variety of toxic elements, the janitorial staffs cleaning up after all those "symbolic analysts": for these workers, the difference between Wired's utopian entrepreneurial capitalism and old-fashioned bureaucratic multinationalism is just an increase in the pressure to produce.

Certainly, the cutthroat pace of Moore's Law does generate more product innovation than would a less competitive system. But at what cost? And for what purpose? The value system of engineering presumes that the best-designed product is the most worthy product. That's why the victory of Windows over the Mac is so galling to industry observers; it's often narrated as a struggle between good and evil, and evil's winning. (We'll get to the hackers' new hope, Linux, in chapter 10.) There's a further presumption that the victory of the better product signals a more general social gain—the success of excellence, the defeat of mediocrity. But the pursuit of excellence may come at a steep price. And the rhetoric of excellence can become an excuse to justify some very familiar forms of exploitation.

The Neo-Luddites: A Failed Critique

The most visible critique of Wired's corporate-libertarian techno-utopianism in the 1990s came from self-identified reactionaries. Many looked specifically back to Luddism, a nineteenth-century British labor movement that resisted the rise of the factory system by attempting to destroy industrial machines. These writers labeled themselves Neo-Luddites. Others preferred to avoid the negative connotations of the "Luddite" label, but offered similar critiques.

The most prominent of these ideologues couched their critiques within the familiar high-culture rhetoric of danger from the middlebrow. Just as American intellectuals of the 1950s attacked the emerging mass medium of television as a threat to traditional literary values, Sven Birkerts, in *The Gutenberg Elegies: The Fate of Reading in an Electronic Age,* complained that hypertext, CD-ROMs, and even audio books endangered the survival of old-fashioned reading.[21] Like the mass-culture critics' war on TV, Birkerts' critique of new information technologies may have been vaguely from the left, but its elitism made it easily assimilable into familiar conservative critiques of the decadence of mass culture.

Some neo-Luddites were more class-conscious than Birkerts, addressing issues of unequal access, the homogenization of global culture, the exploitation of information-technology workers, and multinational corporations' control over information. The terms of this critique, however, for the most part echoed Birkerts' nostalgia. Typical was the collection *Resisting the Virtual Life,* edited by James Brook and Iain A. Boal. In their introduction, Brook and Boal made a compelling case for a form of Neo-Luddism that is not simply antitechnology, but concerned with resisting exploitative uses of technology:

> Like the Luddites of the first industrial revolution, we refuse to cede to capital the right to design and implement the sort of automation that deskills workers, extends managerial control over their work, intensifies their labor, and undermines their solidarity. Automation in the name of progress and "inevitable" technological change is primarily to the benefit of that same class that not so long ago forced people off the land and into factories, destroying whole ways of life in the process: "labor-saving" devices have not so much reduced labor as they have increased profits and refined class domination.[22]

Here, Brook and Boal thoughtfully attack assumptions about the inevitability of technological change, insisting that we ask, progress *for whom?* But which specific uses of technology are genuinely progressive, and which exploitative? For Brook and Boal, the bias was clearly in favor of a less "virtual" era in the past:

> Virtual technologies are pernicious when their simulacra of relationships are deployed society-wide as substitutes for face-to-face interactions, which are inherently richer than mediated interaction. Nowadays, the

monosyllabic couch potato is joined by the information junkie in passive admiration of the little screen; this passivity is only refined and intensified by programmed "interactivity."[23]

Brook and Boal's critique of virtual technologies specifically equated cyberculture with that familiar bugaboo, television. But their valorization of face-to-face interactions, if taken at face value, actually suggested something far more radical: that even *literacy* has been a bad idea for the human race. Wouldn't it be better for stories to be told around a campfire, rather than written down through the mediation of words on paper? In fact, isn't a medium like television at least closer than reading in replicating the experience of face-to-face communication?

The fundamental problem here is the presumption that face-to-face communication is inherently "richer than mediated interaction." This is the perspective that Jacques Derrida in *Of Grammatology* labels "logocentrism."[24] It rests on a "metaphysics of presence" that fantasizes that face-to-face conversation can offer an unmediated, direct form of communication outside of the prison house of language. Writing is an example of a technology in which the mediating process—turning words into physical marks, reordering them, laboring over them sentence by sentence—allows for the creation of cultural documents of a complexity and richness impossible in simple conversation. Equally questionable is the idea that face-to-face interaction is ever unmediated. Conversation occurs via language, an always slippery tool.

Brook and Boal's omission of reading in their examples of "passive," "mediated" technology suggests that they don't really think face-to-face communication is always preferable to mediation. Rather, their presumption is that new forms of communication are inherently suspect, and liable to be quickly appropriated as tools of exploitation. In their own critique of *Wired*-style cyber-hype, Brook and Boal write, "The rhetoric of liberation attached to the information industry is, in our perspective, just one more obstacle to understanding and reshaping the world in more desirable directions."[25]

Against this perspective, I've argued in this book that it's exactly the utopian sphere opened up by the promise of new technologies that makes political change possible. Yes, *Wired*'s version of that utopia is something to argue with and fight against. But it's not the only vision of liberation available in cyberspace. Even within the information industry itself, the impulse to view one's work as liberating—the grandiosity with which

Steve Jobs promised that the Macintosh would "make the world a better place"—is inspiring, and something to work with rather than against in an era in which all too few endeavors ever claim such ambitions. To simply give up on utopia, to dismiss all the hope and inspiration generated by these amazing new tools, to see it all, in fact, as an obstacle, is to throw away any claim on the future.

Even after the dot-com crash, *Wired* and its descendants remain amused and mystified by its enemies' choice to affiliate themselves with such prominent historical *losers*. From the *Wired* perspective, it's just more proof that technological "progress" is inevitable. The Neo-Luddites were right to challenge the presumptions of technological determinism. But to insist on going backwards (a favorite neo-Luddite role model is the Amish) is to confound most Americans' sense of the possible, and to demand that people do away with many tools they have found useful and enriching to their lives. I don't think this politics can win over more than a small elite playing with the new luxury of "living simply." The virtual future may not be optimal, but it's the only one we have, and it's got plenty of room to go wherever we choose to take it.

9

Beyond Napster

To this point, our discussion has concentrated specifically on computers and the computer industry. As the United States has become more and more thoroughly computerized, however, the line between computers and the rest of American life has grown increasingly blurry. In the media world, this phenomenon is called "convergence." When culture is digitized into sequences of zeroes and ones, the realms of music, film, and television converge with software. Where once each of these other forms was tied to a distinct analog format—vinyl, celluloid, videotape—now they can be interchangeably stored on hard drives and optical discs, and they can all be duplicated and transferred over the internet. Likewise, the distinctions among computers, music players, and home video systems grow hazy, when computers are used to record, transfer, and play music, while the Apple iPod music player and the TiVo digital video recorder contain hard drives and sophisticated microprocessors.

No medium has been more affected by the digitization of culture than music. In the mid-1980s, digitization was the music industry's salvation. The compact disc was introduced and vinyl phased out amid declining sales. The format inspired millions of consumers to repurchase their old vinyl records at new, higher prices, spurring a decade-long boom in back-catalog sales.

At the turn of the millennium, however, the industry faced the other side of digitization. In May 1999 Shawn Fanning, a freshman at Northeastern University, founded the Napster online music service. Napster was a peer-to-peer file-sharing system. It networked the hard drives of internet users around the globe, so that they could share any music they'd copied onto their computers for free, beyond the costs of hardware and bandwidth. By January 2000 Napster had grown so popular with college students (who often have broadband connections through their dorms) that its traffic was slowing many academic computer networks. By July

2000 Napster had 20 million registered users. By February 2001 that number was 58 million. Computer industry tracker Media Metrix labeled Napster the fastest-growing software application in history.[1]

At the same time as Napster's rise, the music industry began a multiyear decline in sales.[2] The industry blamed Napster and other file-swapping services for the decline. With so much music available for free online, the argument went, no wonder consumers weren't buying CDs the way they used to. Michael Greene, President and CEO of the National Academy of Recording Arts and Sciences, even took time out during the 2002 Grammy ceremony to scold music downloaders. He told viewers,

> This illegal file-sharing and ripping of music files is pervasive, out of control and oh so criminal. Many of the nominees here tonight, especially the new, less-established artists, are in immediate danger of being marginalized out of our business. Ripping is stealing their livelihood one digital file at a time, leaving their musical dreams haplessly snared in this World Wide Web of theft and indifference.[3]

The record industry's claims of harm from Napster are subject to debate. Some studies have demonstrated that file swappers are actually more likely to purchase CDs—they use the systems to check out records they're considering purchasing.[4] And there are other credible explanations for the industry slump, including the recession, the consolidation of the radio industry, the collapse of the teen-pop boom of the late 1990s, and rising competition from DVDs and videogame sales.[5] Another reason for the decline of profits was the end of a multiyear price-fixing scam among the major record labels. The industry recently settled a class-action lawsuit making any purchaser of a CD between 1995 and 2000 eligible for a refund of up to $20.[6]

Nonetheless, in December 1999, the Recording Industry Association of America (RIAA) filed suit against Napster, claiming that the system infringed on its members' copyrights. In July 2000 U.S. District Judge Marilyn Hall Patel issued a preliminary injunction against Napster. After months of appeals and unsuccessful attempts to rid the service of all unauthorized material, in July 2001 Judge Patel ordered the site offline. As other file swapping systems emerged in Napster's place, such as Morpheus and Kazaa, the industry in 2003 began suing not only online services, but individual users, even minors, who had shared "pirated" music, as well. Napster ultimately filed for Chapter 11 bankruptcy protection, then was bought out by the global media conglomerate Bertelsmann AG. In 2003 the brand name "Napster" reappeared as the label for a completely new program, an online service which sold downloadable music for 99 cents per song.

The crisis of the record industry has caused economic pain for many laid-off label employees. But it has also opened up the music industry as a utopian sphere, a space in which computerization has forced listeners, artists, and executives to rethink how popular music might be produced, distributed, and consumed.

The record industry as it is currently structured is famously exploitative of artists and listeners.[7] Most major label acts live in a state of constant indebtedness to their labels, rarely seeing any royalty money beyond their advances—which explains why many aren't as worried about losing sales to file sharing as one might think. Metallica famously attacked their fans as selfish ingrates for downloading songs from Napster rather than paying for albums. But for most artists, albums are simply publicity tools for the real profit centers: concert tickets and merchandise. Longtime recording artist Janis Ian writes, "Who gets hurt by free downloads? Save for a handful of super-successes like Celine Dion, none of us. We only get helped."[8] Even international superstar Robbie Williams recently shocked attendees of a music industry convention by declaring of online file sharing, "I think it's great, really I do."[9]

The industry has also done an awful job of sharing the breadth of the American musical tradition with a mass audience. Following the same blockbuster logic as their corporate cousins in the movies, record executives have concluded that it's easier to sell 3 million copies of one record than 300,000 of 10 different records, or 30,000 of 100, or 3,000 of 1,000.

Now this whole model is coming apart. In its place has emerged a range of alternate visions of the relationship between culture and commerce. This chapter will look at the differing values and assumptions behind the range of responses to the record industry crisis in the wake of Napster. I'll look at four paradigms: First, the current, waning CD-oriented model, which conceives of music as a tangible physical commodity. Second, the pay-per-download model followed by online services such as iTunes and the new Napster, which conceives of music as an intangible bundle of rights. Third, the subscription model of the competing online service Rhapsody, which conceives of music as a utility. Fourth, the file-sharing model of Napster and its descendants, which conceives of music as electronic folk culture.

The structure of this chapter, and the rest of this book, is somewhat different from what has preceded it. So far, the focus of each chapter has been on a moment in the past. Starting from that historical discussion, each chapter has carried the story forward into the present. With this chapter, however, our narrative has become a history of the present. While I will continue to put contemporary debates in historical context, the focus in the next two chapters will necessarily be on the present, rather than the past. The conclusion, in turn, will look toward the future.

Music as Physical Commodity

The music industry's business model for much of its existence has been organized around the creation, distribution, and sales of round objects that, when inserted in the right devices, reproduce recorded sound. Before the CD was the 33 1/3 rpm vinyl record; before that, the 45; before that, the 78. Prerecorded cassettes and 8-tracks used audiotape in a similar system. All of these objects are part of a system organized around commodifying music. (Before the advent of recording technologies, sheet music served the role of the ownable part of music.)[10] We take this process so much for granted that it's worth noting just how strange it is. Music itself is intangible—it's sound waves. You can't "own" music in the same way that you can own a car, or a table, or a shirt. You can only own an object upon which music has been recorded.

The music industry has responded to this awkward fit between intangible music and the world of consumer objects by successfully fetishizing the record album as as an object—or even more, as part of a set of objects, the record collection. This fetishization reached new heights with the dawn of the CD era. The labels managed to convince millions of consumers to replace their vinyl records with CD versions of the exact same music—to pay again for the same music in a new package. This physical model of music as commodity helps explain the public acceptance of file swapping. The music industry has taught listeners that the commodity value of music comes from the way it's packaged. No wonder, then, that consumers felt that without that package, the music itself should be free.

What were the cultural consequences of chopping the universe of music into 45 to 60 minute chunks and selling it on round discs? What it did was to create artificial scarcity. Hundreds of thousands of records are out there to be listened to, but who can afford them all at $18.99 each, the current list price for most new CD releases? The expense of each record encourages a specific kind of listening practice: what we could call "intensive" listening, rather than "extensive" listening.

I'm borrowing these terms from the history of the novel. Before the mass-culture explosion of the twentieth century, it was common for households to own only a small number of books. It was expected that each of these books would be read over and over again—the way the Bible still is today. Readers sacrificed breadth for depth—they studied a few books very closely, rather than reading more books a single time each.

Different media may be consumed in greater depth or breadth, depending on the distribution practices available at a given time. Video games, for example, have long been individually expensive, designed for repeat play. Game magazines even rate games for the number of hours of play they afford—the more hours, the better the deal. But new systems of distribution, such as the Blockbuster video chain's addition of rental games to its inventory, are changing gamers' practices, making it practical for gamers to rent a larger number of games, and play each for a shorter amount of time. Movies, on the other hand, appear to be going in the opposite direction. The rise of DVD sales, at the expense of video rentals, suggests viewers are choosing to watch a smaller number of movies intensively, rather than renting extensively.

This change in distribution and consumption practices influences the content of culture itself. Deep videogaming demands lengthy, difficult games, like *Myst* and the *Final Fantasy* series. The rise of broad videogaming has encouraged the creation of shorter, more linear games, like the recent games based on the films *The Lord of the Rings* and *The Matrix*. On the other hand, deep movie viewing demands movies worth watching over and over again—either because of visually complex special effects, as in the *Star Wars* movies, or multilayered narrative, as in puzzle movies like *Memento,* or ideally both, as in *The Matrix*.

The packaging and distribution of music has long encouraged intensive rather than extensive listening. The homogenization of radio playlists in recent years has only accelerated this development. Deep listening has its advantages. It fosters intense attachment to specific records and artists, and so it helps to explain the culture of music fandom. It encourages close study of individual records, and so encourages musicians to create rich, multi-layered records that reward repeated listenings, musically and lyrically.

But there's been a loss, as well, in the choice of depth over breadth. America has a rich, diverse musical tradition. But there's only so much of that tradition you can afford at $18.99 per record. Deep listening discourages experimentation and discovery—if you try a new artist and you don't like the record, you're out a substantial sum of money.

American popular music has long thrived on hybridity: the intermixture of cultures to create something new. At the turn of the last century in the port city of New Orleans, out of the mixture of African spirituals, Latin dances, and British ballads, emerged a new cultural form, jazz. American popular music has continued to refresh itself by mixing and reworking genres, from blues to rock and roll to heavy metal to hip-hop. There's a set of values implicit in this hybridity as well. It's a politics of inclusiveness—of both appreciating difference and finding new common ground. But deep listening discourages this hybridity. It reinforces generic boundaries by raising the costs of exploration.

People who really love music, and want to get to know more than a sliver of what's available, get around these barriers in different ways. When I was growing up, I borrowed from friends' collections. I scoured every library within reach to develop a better grounding in country, jazz, and blues. When I reached college and worked at a radio station, I started receiving free promotional copies of new releases. After college, I worked for a while as a magazine rock critic, and put myself on the labels' mailing lists to continue receiving free promo copies. Without the kind of breadth I found outside the normal channels, I never could have become a critic. It would have been impossible to learn what I needed to know at full price. But most listeners don't have access to promo copies. Most libraries don't consider a well-rounded musical collection worth the price. And so most Americans never hear what they're missing.

Music as Contract

The second model, the download system, is the record industry's attempt to train consumers to treat individual intangible musical files as consumer products. Early attempts in this vein, such as PressPlay, were big flops, constrained by monthly fees, limited catalogs, and the competition of the file-sharing services. Apple's iTunes store, however, has been much more successful, selling over 100 million downloads between April 2003 and July 2004.

Downloading systems face the question of what it means to sell music with no object attached. Before iTunes, most systems had responded by considering the download as a bundle of limited rights: the right to play music in certain contexts, in certain ways. The early PressPlay service, for example, offered a tiered system of music purchases. For a monthly fee, the user received the right to a certain number of "streams," a certain number of "downloads," and the option to purchase individual "burns." "Streams" were songs that resided on PressPlay's servers, and could only be played on the user's PC, while the user was connected to PressPlay. "Downloads" were copied from PressPlay's server and stored on the user's own hard drive, but couldn't be transferred from the hard drive to other media such as CDs or MP3 players. In addition, downloads were only available as long as the user's subscription remained current—if it lapsed, the songs were no longer playable. Finally, a limited portion of the PressPlay catalog were available as "burns"—songs that, for an extra price (typically 99 cents), could be copied onto blank CDs.

All of these restrictions followed from a model under which music is not treated as a commodity, but as a licensing arrangement between producer and consumer. This model makes sense to the developers of these downloading systems, because it's how the software industry itself works. Few consumers realize it, but you don't actually "buy" software—rather, you pay a license to use software. The details of that license are buried in the small print of the box that pops up when you first install a new piece of software, asking you to click "Agree." The license contains many more restrictions than most users realize. Regulatory battles are currently being fought, for example, to determine whether an "End User License Agreement" can require that any review of a piece of software be preapproved by the software company before it can be published. And Microsoft insists that users purchasing *MS Office* buy one copy for each household computer—defining even intra-family sharing as IP theft.

But while Microsoft, as a monopoly, has been able to get away with foisting this redefinition of the rules of ownership upon consumers, this model continues to conflict with everyday assumptions of what it means to purchase a product. Clearly, most music consumers assume that if you "buy" music, you own it, and can use it whenever and wherever you like—just like a book, or a television.

The iTunes model doesn't explicitly challenge the vision of music as a bundle of rights. But it loosens that bundle enough to make a download seem more like the purchase of a commodity. Every song costs 99 cents, with no additional monthly fees. Any song downloaded from iTunes can be immediately transferred to an iPod, Apple's portable music player. In addition, songs can be burned onto CD up to 10 times—enough to make copies for multiple friends while discouraging mass reproduction. While not quite as flexible as MP3, Apple's digital rights management is much more flexible than that of previous systems.

The breadth of the iTunes model is greater than that of the CD model, because listeners can choose to download individual songs. In the era of the 45 rpm single, individual hit songs were widely available to record consumers. But since the 1980s, the record industry has been maximizing profits by refusing to release most successful singles in any form other than on full-length albums. Listeners end up buying entire records just to get one song. (The first big hit to take this approach was MC Hammer's "U Can't Touch This," which was only available on the album *Please Hammer, Don't Hurt 'Em.*) Thus, consumers' available money goes for just a few, overpriced records, rather than a broader number of singles. With iTunes, listeners have a much greater opportunity to shop around, experiment, and explore. It's not as cheap as file swapping, but it is just a buck a song.

With the breakdown of the CD into individual tracks may come the loss of some of the advantages of deep listening. If the single rather than the CD becomes the commodity, there's less incentive to produce a more rich, challenging work that encourages repeated listenings. The modern notion of the record album as artistic statement is a by-product of the technological changes in the 1950s that made it possible to distribute music on 33 1/3 rpm records holding 45 minutes or so of music. Artists like Frank Sinatra responded by putting together records such as *Songs for Swinging Lovers,* in which each individual song contributed to a larger theme. In the 1960s and 1970s rock bands with artistic ambitions took to the album as a way to express more complex themes than could be developed on one single—whether through "concept albums" like the Beatles' *Sgt. Pepper's Lonely Hearts Club Band,* "rock operas" like the Who's *Tommy,* or simply coherent artistic projects like Van Morrison's *Astral Weeks.* The MP3's challenge to the CD threatens this tradition. Even users who purchase CDs may rip them onto portable players or compilations, rearranging tracks in the process. On the liner notes to the album *18,* electronica artist Moby politely requests, as is true of a lot of my records, I think that they make the most sense if you listen to the whole thing. so my arrogant request is that you listen to this record in its entirety at least once. when i make a record i try to craft something that's a cohesive whole created from a bunch of different songs.[11]

But if digital distribution threatens the dissolution of the traditional album, it also offers new alternatives. Rather than taking years between grand statements, artists can distribute individual new songs as they're recorded, developing a more engaged, ongoing dialogue with their listeners. An early example of this opportunity occurred in response to the 2003 Iraq war: artists such as the Beastie Boys, R.E.M., John Mellencamp, and Lenny Kravitz were able to quickly record antiwar singles and distribute them online, bypassing both radio censorship and the cumbersome CD distribution process.

Music as Utility

The third model is the music subscription service. The most successful of these has been Rhapsody. Rhapsody has a vast, though far from complete, catalog of records from every major label. For $10 a month, listeners can listen to an audio stream of any record in the catalog. You can listen for as long as you want, to as many songs as you want, for the same $10 price.

Rhapsody, in other words, treats music less like a commodity than a utility. You aren't paying $10 for a particular song or group of songs, but for access to all the songs. Suddenly, the economics of listening change: there's no difference in cost between listening to one record twenty times versus twenty records once. And so, Rhapsody encourages the broadest possible listening practice.

The downside of Rhapsody as it's currently configured is that you only have access to the music from your computer. There's no way to download the music to a portable device, and burning permanent copies costs extra. It currently appears to be losing out to iTunes. Its best long-term business hope appears to involve selling itself not to individual users, but to broadband access systems. Several internet access providers give their users Rhapsody subscriptions as part of a package of services—a lure to justify the extra expense of broadband over dial-up. This arrangement distances music on Rhapsody even further from any status as a commodity, and turns music into an information service.

Music as Folk Culture

The fourth model is file swapping. Most discussions of file-swapping systems have centered on questions of legality.[12] Napster has been shut down by federal courts. Other systems of slightly different design (they don't use central servers) are still battling the record industry in court. But what's most intriguing for our purposes is the widespread public embrace of file sharing, regardless of what the record industry and even the courts have had to say. What this suggests, whatever the legal outcomes, is a breakdown in common-sense assumptions about the status of music as property.

The industry may complain that listeners use Napster because it's so easy and consequence-less to "steal" music. But this logic presumes that all that ever stops any of us from shoplifting, or hot-wiring cars, is simply the fear of getting caught. Actually it's ideology, not the threat of force, that is primarily responsible for keeping physical property safe: a social consensus that stealing is wrong. Whatever the law ends up saying, Napster has broken that social consensus when it comes to intellectual property. Survey after survey says that most computer users don't consider file swapping a crime.

So why don't they? The answer is that Napster has helped establish a fourth model for thinking about music, one which reaches back to an era before the rise of mass media: music as folk culture, communally owned and shared. It recognizes that every song is not simply the sole product of an individual artist, but one drop in a much broader stream—that the fiction of intellectual property blinds us to the way we all share culture.

The phrase "electronic folk culture" was coined by the documentary filmmaker Craig Baldwin to describe the work of Negativland, the Emergency Broadcast Network, the Barbie Liberation Organization, and other artists of appropriation profiled in his 1995 film, *Sonic Outlaws*.[13] These artists all borrow copyrighted texts—songs, video clips, Barbie dolls—then rework them into collages of meta-cultural commentary. All of the artists argue that their work should be covered by the "fair use" doctrine of copyright law, which allows some room for reproduction of copyrighted works "for purposes such as criticism, comment, news reporting, teaching (including multiple copies for classroom use), scholarship, or research."[14] But more broadly, we could see the rise of Napster as a broad cultural movement for a definition of *all* use as fair use: a public insistence that in a postmodern media culture, the institution of copyright, as currently applied, strangles creativity and hampers the public's ability to interpret and engage the media.

The American legal system has gone in the other direction. The U.S. Constitution enshrines the idea of copyright within clear limitations, specifying that its purpose is not simply to protect intellectual property, but to promote creativity: "The Congress shall have the power to . . . promote the Progress of Science and useful Arts, by securing for limited Times to Authors and Inventors the exclusive Right to their respective Writings and Discoveries."[15] But Congress, in regulating copyright, has gradually expanded the rights of copyright owners while shrinking the public domain. Congress originally set the term of copyright at a mere fourteen years. The United States now grants copyrights for 70 years past the death of the author, thanks to the 1998 Sonny Bono Copyright Terms Extension Act. A 2003 challenge to the act, *Eldred v. Ashcroft*, lost in a 7-2 decision by the Supreme Court. The prime beneficiary of the victory was the Walt Disney Corporation, as a loss would have sent the first Mickey Mouse cartoon, 1928's "Steamboat Willie," into public domain.

As Siva Vaidhyanathan puts it in *Copyrights and Copywrongs: The Rise of Intellectual Property and How It Threatens Creativity,*

> Gradually the law has lost sight of its original charge: to encourage creativity, science, and democracy. Instead, the law now protects the producers and taxes consumers. It rewards works already created and limits works yet to be created. The law has lost its mission, and the American people have lost control of it.[16]

The law doesn't even do a very good job of protecting the actual creators of culture. As Tom McCourt and Patrick Burkart explain,

> Although copyright protections are universally justified as incentives for individuals to create, recordings (particularly those of new artists) are often contractually defined as "work for hire," or collective works akin to films, on grounds that they involve producers, engineers and other personnel in addition to the featured artist. Therefore, these recordings

are owned by the companies that finance and market them, not by the artist whose name appears on them.[17]

The folk model is a rejection of contemporary copyright law's constricted vision of culture, and file sharing is a kind of civil disobedience.

The folk model is the ultimate form of broad listening, but it's also surprisingly deep, because what it allows is for each artist to appropriate, rework, and rethink the culture that came before. Hip-hop sampling, dance remixes, and the recent trend of "bastard pop," which takes two or more very different songs and mashes them together to create something new—all these practices are part of this new, postmodern folk aesthetic.

If this folk model prevails, the music industry as we know it may indeed collapse. It may not be possible to maintain the current industrial infrastructure in the face of so much sharing. But with or without the music industry as we know it, people will still make and listen to music. Artists will still be able to earn money by performing—as we've seen, that's how most of them make their livings now anyway. And what may rise out of the ashes of the music industry is something new: a different kind of mass culture. The utopian dream of postmodern folk culture is a vision of a fully democratized mass culture. A vision in which every consumer is also a producer. Where everyone has equal, universal access to their cultural inheritance. And where everyone has equal, universal access to the means of cultural production and distribution. It's a vision of a culture that finally transcends the violence done to a society when art is turned into a commodity.

10

Linux and Utopia

On March 10, 2000, the NASDAQ stock index, which tracked many of the companies riding the dot-com boom, stood at an all-time high of 5,133. By April 14 the NASDAQ had fallen to 3,321, a loss of more than 35%. The dot-com boom was over.[1]

In the aftermath of the crash, many of the promises of the cybertopians have begun to ring hollow. A new wave of public skepticism toward the official rhetoric of cyberlibertarianism and technological determinism has emerged. Relying on Moore's Law, the unhampered free market, and the logic of the stock exchanges hadn't turned out to be a guarantee of the "twenty-five years of prosperity, freedom and a better environment for the whole world" predicted in "The Long Boom," an infamous *Wired* cover story of 1997.[2] The rise of the internet hadn't repealed the business cycle after all.

Having passed through the hothouse environment of the late 1990s, in which any new internet-based business model could quickly command ludicrous levels of financing and hype, we are in a position to take stock of what computers have come to mean to us, and to evaluate the promise they still hold. The danger of this moment is that it may easily turn to pessimism; many of the hopes for new technology died in the spring of 2000. But the failure of overhyped attempts to exploit irrational investment does not discredit those plans and projects that were more than get-rich-quick schemes. Out of the ashes of the dot-com boom are emerging new cybercultural visions, new models for economic life in the twenty-first century.

Of these visions, one of the most compelling and influential is the open-source movement, an attempt to develop cheap, freely distributed, easily adaptable alternatives to the Microsoft Windows operating system. The open-source alternative to Windows is known as Linux. Linux had its moment in the dot-com sun, when developers Red Hat Systems went

Cover of *Wired*, July 1997.

public and produced many instant open-source millionaires. But now that the hype has passed, we're in a position to more clearly see the promises—and limitations—of open source as an alternate model for software development, intellectual property, and perhaps more general distribution of wealth in an information society.

What Is Linux?

Linux is a computer operating system, like Microsoft's Windows and Apple's Macintosh OS. An operating system is more than just another program. It's the software beneath the software—the underlying code that turns a piece of hardware into a functioning computer.

What makes Linux different from other operating systems is that it's "open source." This means that it can't be "copyrighted" in the traditional sense—rather, it is distributed under a General Public License, which "allows free use, modification and distribution of the software and any changes to it, restricted only by the stipulation that those who received the software pass it with identical freedoms to obtain the source code, modify it, and redistribute it."[3] Rather than a copyright, the GPL is often referred to as a "copyleft," and open-source software is sometimes called "freeware." Linux software is developed collaboratively, among a large group of volunteer hackers around the world, communicating via the internet. Several for-profit companies, such as Red Hat and Caldera, sell packaged versions of Linux along with documentation and product support, but the same software is also available for free online.

What interests me about Linux, and open source in general, isn't the technical specifics, but how it's emerged as a space in which to experiment with economic and social relations outside the bounds of what we normally think of as capitalism. The development of open-source software, of course, is specialized work, which has emerged in the context of a specific, distinct community. But what has captured the imaginations of so many developers and users of Linux is its broader utopian promise—the way it seems to point to a future organized around a very different set of social relations than those of late capitalism. I don't assume that open-source development, as a distinct practice, could necessarily serve as a template for a broad range of economic relations. Not every product needs to be debugged; not every worker has the skills of a Linux programmer. But I do think that the open-source vision of unalienated, uncommodified labor can serve as a model for what we might want work to look like in the twenty-first century.

Of course, as Fredric Jameson tells us, the flip side of utopia is reification.[4] Capitalism omnivorously absorbs dissent through the process of commodification. Radical ideas are appropriated, packaged, and sold through the very system they sought to criticize. As we have seen, early radical visions of the PC as a tool for the democratization of technology were successfully packaged and sold, first by Apple, then by Microsoft. The PC certainly did change the world—hegemony is always a process of negotiation—and certainly many more people have access to the power of computing technology than ever before. But the mass proliferation of the PC failed to fundamentally alter structures of power. This is a familiar story—think of the dilemma of independent rock bands wary of "selling out" to major labels. To reach the public sphere, you need to get your product out into the marketplace. But once you do, you're a part of the system you're trying to oppose.

Tiziana Terranova makes a version of this argument in "Free Labor: Producing Culture for the Digital Economy."[5] Terranova argues that rather than being a resistant alternative to capitalist production, the free labor donated by open-source programmers, amateur web designers, chat-room moderators, and the other unpaid volunteers who populate cyberspace is best understood as an integral part of capitalism in a digital economy. These intellectual workers provide much of the "content" that makes the web so lucrative for AOL, Microsoft, and the other organizations that have no compunctions about making money off volunteers' work.

Similarly, Andrew Ross in "The Mental Labor Problem"[6] describes the submission of so many software developers to exploitative conditions (80-hour workweeks, temporary contracts, lack of health benefits)—and even the glamorization of those conditions (e.g., the cult of the caffeine-fueled "all-nighter")—as an example of the spread of the "cultural discount" to an ever-increasing portion of the postmodern workforce. The "cultural discount" describes the phenomenon of creative professionals who are willing to accept wages lower than they could receive in other professions, in return for the opportunity to perform more personally satisfying labor. Ross's point is that this system—rooted in the bohemian's Romantic rejection of the market—is now a structural component of the capitalist knowledge economy, allowing, for example, universities to get away with paying minuscule wages to teaching assistants and adjuncts, overproduced by the graduate system and desperate to retain a foothold in the life of the mind.

Linux developers might be seen as the quintessential victims of the creative discount, donating the intellectual capital that enriches corporations like Red Hat and IBM. But what's so distinctive about open source is how it structurally short-circuits the process of appropriation and commodification. Linux developers donate their labor, but with a particularly resilient set of strings attached in the form of the GPL. What the strings require, ironically, is that no *other* strings be attached—that the developers' work must remain freely available and modifiable. Thus, while the cultural discount often entails ceding control of one's work in exchange for access to an audience—think of all the musicians forced to cede ownership rights of their master recordings to their record labels—Linux developers forego remuneration in return for ongoing assurance of creative control.

Corporations such as Microsoft recognize the fundamental threat this system offers to their current regime of intellectual property. Microsoft has even begun red-baiting the open source community. Microsoft CEO Steve Ballmer has described Linux as "communism,"[7] and told one reporter, "Linux is a cancer that attaches itself in an intellectual property sense to everything it touches."[8] Windows chief Jim Allchin likewise stated, "I'm an American. I believe in the American Way. I worry if the government encourages open source, and I don't think we've done enough education of policy makers to understand the threat."[9]

The Microsoft monopoly has stifled innovation, squashed competition, and raised the cost of computing beyond the reach of many. While the cost for most computer hardware has dropped significantly in the last decade, the cost of Microsoft Windows hasn't. Today, a substantial part of the purchase price of almost every computer sold goes to the "Microsoft tax," since it's automatically installed on your computer whether you ask for it or not, and the licensing fees are figured into the price of the computer.

Increasingly, individual users, organizations, and governments around the world are rejecting the Microsoft tax, turning to Linux as a cheap, flexible alternative. Many Third World countries have discovered that installing Linux operating systems on bare-bones computers can create huge savings, making it practical to bring computers to schools, libraries, and government agencies.

The Politics of Open Source

So, if Linux offers a utopian alternative to capitalist relations as we know them today, what does this model consist of? What are the politics of open-source development?

That's not an easy question to answer, because the meanings of Linux—the narratives that attempt to explain and draw lessons from this inspiring project—are themselves a subject of conflict. Scouring the net for different perspectives on Linux, I've encountered an astounding range of competing explanations. I've seen open source described as communism, socialism, anarchism, a form of academic research, a gift economy, an e-lance economy, and the triumph of the free market. Granted, not all the descriptions are incompatible. But, as we'll see, I think some concurrently held ideas are more incompatible than their holders admit.

There's a struggle going on right now to define the significance of Linux, this startling, inspiring success story. In the rest of this chapter, I'd like to look at the two most influential conceptions of Linux: the visions put forward by Eric Raymond and Richard Stallman. Raymond and Stallman have much in common: both are computer programmers whose work has been critical for the development of Linux. Stallman developed the GNU operating system, which was the antecedent for Linux; Raymond has helped put together many critical pieces of open source software, including the program *fetchmail*. Both have become advocates for and theorists of Linux, winning converts with influential essays—Stallman's "GNU Manifesto," Raymond's "The Cathedral and the Bazaar." Both are what we could call, using Antonio Gramsci's term, "organic intellectuals"—not academics studying a community from outside that community, but intellectuals who have emerged from within the community they write about, who are attempting to help their own community define itself, both internally and for the world outside.

While Raymond and Stallman speak from within the same community of Linux programmers, they represent almost diametrically opposed views about the politics and ultimate significance of their projects. Raymond celebrates open source as the triumph of the free market, and is most interested in open source as an efficient tool for software development. Stallman anchors his vision for free software in a broader critique of the system of intellectual property. Raymond's and Stallman's visions are often labeled "libertarian" and "communist," respectively. But I don't think that's quite right. Both Raymond and Stallman start from the libertarian values so endemic in hacker culture—they just end up in different places. Raymond is better characterized as a corporate libertarian, and Stallman as a left-libertarian.

I'm firmly in the Stallman camp. In the rest of this chapter, I want to look at what I see as the limitations of Raymond's approach, and the virtues of Stallman's.

Eric Raymond: Open Source as Corporate Libertarianism

First, a little background on Raymond. Eric Raymond is a software developer who's been very active for almost twenty years in the development of open-source software tools. He's also become a kind of hacker linguist and anthropologist, compiling the *New Hacker's Dictionary*[10] and writing a widely read "Brief History of Hackerdom."[11] In the last few years, Raymond has become perhaps the most influential ideologue of open source. Raymond's self-appointed role has been to explain open source to skeptical businesspeople, as part of the attempt to widen the influence of Linux and win the war against Microsoft. His essay "The Cathedral and the Bazaar" helped convince Netscape to make Navigator, its flagship internet browser program, open source. And his exposure and analysis of leaked internal memoranda from Microsoft, dubbed the "Halloween Documents," inspired hackers with the news that the Behemoth itself is taking Linux very seriously indeed. "The Cathedral and the Bazaar" is now included in a collection of essays of the same name, published by open-source publisher O'Reilly & Associates.[12]

Raymond's politics are a familiar form of hacker libertarianism—what Richard Barbrook and Andy Cameron have described as "the Californian Ideology,"[13] and Paula Barsook[14] labels "cyberselfishness." Hacker libertarianism values the free flow of information above all else, and typically celebrates the unfettered capitalist marketplace as the great maximizer of liberty. Libertarianism is of course skeptical of all concentrations of power, but tends to worry much more about the government than about corporate power—other than perhaps, Microsoft, which as a monopoly impedes the free market. As we saw in chapter 8, hacker libertarianism has turned out to fit comfortably into the net economy, providing an ideological justification for the vast amounts of wealth accumulated by a fortunate few.

But what's particularly striking is how much work Raymond has to do to fit the open-source development process into the comfortable framework of the free market. Raymond's organizing metaphor contrasts the hierarchal command structure of cathedral-building with the decentralized competitive world of a bazaar. But merchants at a bazaar are trying to sell their products for a profit. Open-source developers, on the other hand, are volunteers contributing their time.

To get around this seeming contradiction, Raymond develops an account of open-source development as a "gift economy." Now, the notion of open-source development as a gift economy is an intriguing one, developed most fully in Richard Barbrook's essay "The High-Tech Gift Economy":

> Within the developed world, most politicians and corporate leaders believe that the future of capitalism lies in the commodification of information. . . . Yet, at the "cutting edge" of the emerging information society, money-commodity relations play a secondary role to those created by a really existing form of anarcho-communism. For most of its users, the Net is somewhere to work, play, love, learn and discuss with other people. Unrestricted by physical distance, they collaborate with each other without direct mediation of money or politics. Unconcerned about copyright, they give and receive information without thought of payment. In the absence of state or markets to mediate social bonds, network communities are instead formed through the mutual obligations created by gifts of time and ideas.[15]

The problem with Raymond's account of the open-source community as gift economy is that it shunts aside the very aspects of the gift economy that distinguish it from commodified relations. Raymond sees the gift economy as the free market extended by other means. In what he calls a "post-scarcity" environment, hackers no longer feel the need to compete for money, so instead compete for prestige—or "egoboo," as he calls it (short for "ego boosting"),[16] borrowing a term from science fiction fandom. Drawing on the assumptions of evolutionary psychology, he writes, "One may call [hackers'] motivation 'altruistic,' but this ignores the fact that altruism is itself a form of ego satisfaction for the altruist."[17] But this line of argument is tautological; if one defines in advance every choice a person makes as inevitably a maximization of personal utility, then even seemingly selfless behavior can be explained in selfish terms—thus, the old freshman philosophy saw that even Mother Teresa really acted with the goal of maximizing her own self-interest, rather than helping others for the sake of it.

To get outside this tautology, we need to ask under what circumstances altruism reigns over other forms of perceived self-interest. To Raymond, the answer is the "post-scarcity" economy, in which money no longer matters, and so other markers of status take its place. It's here that Raymond reveals the solipsism and ahistoricism endemic to corporate libertarianism. By post-scarcity, Raymond claims to mean something very specific: "disk space, network bandwidth, computing power." But what this list takes for granted is the much vaster social infrastructure open-source research rests on: its long-term subsidization by state-sponsored research universities, and of course the development of the internet by the Defense Advanced Research Projects Agency. Raymond likewise doesn't pause to consider the vast portions of the United States, to say nothing of the rest of the world, in which not only is computing power scarce, but so are the necessary conditions of survival—and which aren't moving any closer to post-scarcity under the present regime of capital.

Richard Stallman: Open Source as Left-Libertarianism

While Raymond obliviously takes a post-scarcity economy for granted, Richard Stallman sees post-scarcity as a goal that must be struggled for, and which demands structural economic changes if it's to be achieved.

Stallman was one of the great programmers of the MIT Artificial Intelligence Lab immortalized in Steven Levy's *Hackers*.[18] In the early 1980s Stallman left MIT, upset by the privatization of software that Stallman had always viewed as community property. Stallman founded the Free Software Foundation, and began the project of developing an open-source version of the UNIX operating system, which he dubbed GNU, for "GNU's Not Unix." (In a typical example of hacker humor, the name is a "recursive acronym" that defines itself only by itself in an endless loop.) GNU, in turn, became much of the basis for the subsequent development of Linux. Stallman developed the concept of "copyleft" as an alternative to copyright—a way to ensure that the free software he developed could not subsequently be appropriated and privatized.

As noted above, Stallman starts out with the same libertarian framework as Raymond. The difference is that Stallman pushes it further. His investment in the free flow of ideas leads him to a more fundamental interrogation of the right to own information. While Raymond anchors his analysis in the essay "Homesteading on the Noosphere"[19] in a kind of para-Lockean theory of property rights, Stallman rejects intellectual property altogether. As Stallman told *Byte* magazine,

> I'm trying to change the way people approach knowledge and information in general. I think that to try to own knowledge, to try to control whether people are allowed to use it, or to try to stop other people from sharing it, is sabotage. It is an activity that benefits the person that does it at the cost of impoverishing all of society.[20]

Stallman contrasts a piece of software to a loaf of bread. If somebody takes my loaf of bread, I don't have it anymore; it's a limited resource. But software is like an infinitely replicable loaf of bread. To not share your loaf with me, when you'd still have your loaf, is what Stallman calls "software hoarding."

What I find inspiring about Stallman's line of reasoning is how it embraces the best parts of the hacker ethic—its respect for the free flow of information, and its idealistic desire to change the world—and, by pushing it to its logical conclusions, reaches a more egalitarian, communitarian vision that begins to question the capitalist sanctity of private property. As such, it offers a way out of cyberselfishness, an alternate cybertopian vision. In fact, it's this vision that is largely responsible for the sense of mission among so many open-source developers and users.

It's not surprising that Eric Raymond's version of free software is more popular with the new Linux entrepreneurs like Red Hat's Bob Young. It fits much more comfortably into conventional capitalism, even if it takes some getting used to and perhaps offers lower profit margins. But thanks to the genius of the copyleft system, Stallman's ideas can't fade away so easily; even in its capital-friendly form, open-source software still challenges the regime of intellectual property, and offers a compelling utopian alternative. The power of that alternative can be seen in the explosion of interest in similar challenges, such as Napster.

In his GNU manifesto, Stallman offers his own image of the future, a familiar vision of technological utopianism that draws on the tradition of Edward Bellamy, Buckminster Fuller, and Isaac Asimov. Utopian projections can be ideological fantasies, blinding us to life as it is actually being lived. But at their best, they point us to a set of future goals—and suggest some tools for getting there. Bellamy's *Looking Backward* may not have come true, but it nonetheless inflected progressive reform in the early twentieth century; likewise, Fuller helped inspire the New Left of the 1960s. Similarly, I take heart from Stallman's vision of the future:

> In the long run, making programs free is a step toward the post-scarcity world, where nobody will have to work very hard just to make a living. People will be free to devote themselves to activities that are fun, such as programming, after spending the necessary ten hours a week on required tasks such as legislation, family counseling, robot repair, and asteroid prospecting.[21]

Conclusion
Cybertopia Today

This book began with the introduction of two related concepts: the utopian sphere and the dialectic of technological determination. Through the subsequent chapters, we've seen how discourse about computers has functioned as a space to explore alternative visions of the future. This space within the public sphere was made possible by the curious logic of technological inevitability, which shuts down critical engagement with the social causes of technological change, while opening up room to imagine the future that "inevitable" technological changes might deliver. In part 1, "Mainframe Culture," we saw the early struggles over the meanings of computers—between analog holism and digital atomization, between technophilia and technophobia, and between patriarchy and gender instability. In part 2, "The Personal Computer," we saw how the introduction of the PC extended and transformed these debates, establishing a new vision of the computer as a tool for personal liberation. And in part 3, "The Interpersonal Computer," we saw how the rise of the internet opened up further spaces for new technotopian visions, for better or worse: cyberspace's fantasy of transcending the body, *Wired*'s dream of friction-free capitalism, Napster's postmodern rejection of commodification, and Linux's gift-based alternative to capitalism.

With the dot-com boom receding in memory, one might think cyberculture no longer holds the same power to inspire electric dreams. Certainly computers aren't quite as hip as they were a few years ago. But the technological cutting edge continues to be the place where the shackles of doxa can be escaped, and new visions may emerge. In this conclusion, I'll look at three final examples of contemporary cybertopianism to map the topography of the utopian sphere in the twenty-first century: blogging, hydrogen energy, and ubiquitous computing.

The Blogosphere

"Weblog," or "blog" for short, is a broad term than can be used to describe any frequently updated personal web page, from a teenager's diary to an armchair pundit's political commentary to a journalist's freelance reporting. The technology to publish a weblog has been available since the beginning of the World Wide Web, but the original common-sense notion of a website was static—it was also called a "home page," after all. Web-design software encouraged this static model, offering no easy system for regularly refreshing content and archiving old posts.

In the late 1990s, however, a new model emerged that conceived of a website as an ongoing space for personal reflection and commentary. Soon, software was developed to facilitate this new kind of online publishing, including Blogger, Movable Type, and Radio Userland. More recently, a new markup language, RSS (short for Really Simple Syndication), has been developed. RSS allows bloggers to format their blogs so that they can be read by "aggregators"—programs that allow users to "subscribe" to blogs, so they can be regularly notified of new postings, and scan multiple blogs from a single interface.[1]

Blogs first reached widespread political recognition shortly after the 2002 election, through the Trent Lott controversy. On Thursday, December 5, 2002, Lott, the Senate Republican leader from Mississippi, gave a toast at Senator Strom Thurmond's 100th birthday party. Lott said, "I want to say this about my state: When Strom Thurmond ran for president, we voted for him. We're proud of it. And if the rest of the country had followed our lead, we wouldn't have had all these problems over all these years, either."[2] Thurmond had run in 1948 on the segregationist Dixiecrat ticket. Lott's comments, then, seemed to endorse segregation and repudiate the civil rights movement.

This was not the first time that Lott had shown nostalgia for segregation. In the 1990s he spoke several times at meetings of the Council of Conservative Citizens, the successor to the racist Citizens' Councils of the 1950s and 1960s. These earlier incidents, however, had caused only minor comment, as major news organizations chose not to follow up on the story. Similarly, it appeared that Lott's comments at Thurmond's party would cause little commotion. The event was covered by many reporters and broadcast live on C-SPAN. The next day's papers and top news shows, however, contained no mention of the story. Arianna Huffington writes,

No fewer than a dozen reporters were present when Lott waxed nostalgic about Jim Crow . . . but only one, ABC News producer Ed O'Keefe, thought it newsworthy. His bosses didn't share his enthusiasm however, and, after running the story on a 4:30 AM broadcast, didn't use it on either "Good Morning America" or "World News Tonight."[3]

Interviewing Lott the day after the speech on CNN's *Inside Politics*, Jonathan Karl didn't even mention the incident. The *Washington Post* reported on the incident on Saturday, December 7, but the paper buried Thomas Edsall's story on page A6. Edsall later told Howard Kurtz, the *Post*'s media critic, that he had to fight for the space he got—his editor wanted to treat it as just another brief item in a political column.[4] On Sunday's *Meet the Press*, Tim Russert's bipartisan panel were universally dismissive of the issue.[5] The media gatekeepers had decided the story wasn't big news.

What made this story different from previous Lott slips, however, was a new media element: what bloggers call the blogosphere. In the days after the speech, commentary on the incident appeared on a number of popular sites. Joshua Michael Marshall's *Talking Points Memo* and Atrios's *Eschaton* became clearinghouses for information about Lott's comments, the media's lack of response, and Lott's history of racism. Independent-minded conservative bloggers such as Glenn Reynolds of *Instapundit* and Andrew Sullivan were equally outraged. Sullivan wrote, "We may be about to ask thousands of young African-Americans to risk their lives for this country. And the leader of the Senate publicly wishes they were still living under Jim Crow. It's repulsive."[6] Hundreds of other blogs picked up on the story, linking back to and expanding the coverage by Marshall, Atrios, Sullivan, and others. As Huffington writes,

It's important to note that these cyber-pundits—the vast majority of whom are unpaid amateurs—didn't just rail against the repulsiveness of Lott's comments and the lameness of his subsequent kinda-sorta apologies. They also were instrumental in helping connect the dots of the majority leader's long history of racist stances, including his college-era fight to keep blacks out of his University of Mississippi fraternity, his resistance to honoring the memories of slain civil rights heroes Martin Luther King and Chaney, Goodman, and Schwerner, his ringing support of Confederate icon Jefferson Davis, and his too-cozy-for-comfort relationship with the racist Council of Conservative Citizens. The blizzard of damning information left little doubt that Lott's comments had not been, as he first claimed, merely "a poor choice of words."[7]

A comment that seemed destined to die on the vine instead found a second life. After several days of escalating online outrage, the mass media finally acknowledged the controversy. By Tuesday, December 10, the story had finally appeared in the *New York Times* and on the major networks. In the following days, as media pressure built, it became a real Washington scandal. Politicians who had hoped to ignore the story were forced to address it. As Michael Kinsley writes,

> The President's deliberations were exceptionally deliberate. On Days 5 and 6 after Lott's remarks, the White House shrugged the matter off. On Day 7, Bush declared that Lott's remarks were "offensive." It is hard to understand how anyone can take a week to take offense at a racist remark.[8]

Lott issued a first awkward half-apology on Monday, December 9, then when that didn't work, a series of ever more extensive apologies. Finally, in desperation, he took his case directly to an African American audience, appearing on Black Entertainment Television claiming to support affirmative action. Finally, he was forced to step down as Senate majority leader. It seemed to be, as right-wing columnist John Podhoretz put it in the *New York Post,* "The Internet's First Scalp." As Marshall wrote, "I'm certain that the web generally—and particularly a lot of different weblogs—kept this story in front of people and forced attention to it long enough that it became impossible to ignore."[9] The blogosphere, it appeared, had infiltrated the public sphere, bypassing the media gatekeepers to turn a nonstory into a story.

Blogs became an even bigger news story in 2003 when they were credited with the early success of Howard Dean's campaign for the Democratic presidential nomination. Dean began his campaign as a long shot, far behind in name recognition and fundraising compared to front-runners John Kerry and Richard Gephardt. Dean's campaign manager, Joe Trippi, a veteran of both presidential campaigns and Silicon Valley, devised a pioneering new strategy to raise Dean's profile: a web-centric, open-source campaign. Dean's *Blog for America* featured frequent updates from the candidate and staff. The site facilitated the creation of blogs among Dean supporters, as well, and encouraged "Deaniacs" to share their enthusiasm in the comments sections of other political blogs.[10]

Trippi also exploited another new web-based communication tool: Meetup.com, a site designed as a clearinghouse for groups of people with shared interests, from needlework to poker to politics. The Dean Meetup group soon had tens of thousands of members who met on the first Tuesday of every month to plan local campaigns and contribute to the national campaign through projects such as writing letters to Iowa Democratic primary voters.

The Dean/Trippi blog strategy appeared to be one of the factors that catapulted Dean into the lead in polls of Democratic voters in Iowa and New Hampshire by late 2003. The strategy meshed smoothly with Dean's image as a rebel against politics as usual—a fiery progressive who stood up against the war in Iraq and Bush's tax cuts, at a time when other Democrats appeared meek and conciliatory.

The Deaniacs were inspired not just by the candidate himself, but by the campaign as a whole, which seemed to challenge the top-down, mass-media-driven model of modern campaigning with a new merger of grass-roots activism and high-tech tools. To many, the egalitarian virtual community created by the campaign was Dean's true message. Zephyr Teachout, who orchestrated *Blog for America,* celebrated how the development of many independent pro-Dean blogs spread "ownership of the campaign."[11]

Dean's web strategy also turned out to be a financial gold mine. Dean supporters not only read pro-Dean blogs, but clicked on links that led to fundraising pages, from which they could easily donate to the campaign through online transactions. Dean's online fundraising was the biggest innovation in political fundraising since the developing of direct mail in the early 1970s. The Dean blogs pushed the fundraising as a participatory project, setting deadlines and continually tracking their progress. Dean ended up outraising all the other Democratic candidates in 2003.

The Dean boom of late 2003, however, crashed in January 2004 in the Iowa and New Hampshire primaries, where Dean finished third in both races. After struggling for a few more weeks, Dean pulled out of the race. Many commentators likened the Dean campaign's failure to the dot-com crash of 2000. As Philip Gourevich wrote in the *New Yorker,*

> Dean likes to call his grass-roots support base a movement to change American politics, and he clearly considers it to be something bigger and grander than a mere Presidential campaign. . . . His following, forged largely in cyberspace through online communities, had the quality of a

political Internet bubble: insular and sustained by collective belief rather than any objective external reality.[12]

Along the lines of Gourevich's criticism, many writers in the wake of the Dean crash likened the campaign to an "echo chamber." Rather than the blogosphere expanding the public sphere, it appeared that the blogosphere was just a self-contained crowd of idealists preaching to the converted. But David Weinberger makes the point that it's the public sphere that's the real echo chamber: "No, if you want to see a real echo chamber, open up your daily newspaper or turn on your TV. There you'll find a narrow, self-reinforcing set of views."[13]

The Dean debacle illustrates the difficulties of translating the blogosphere to the mass media's public sphere. Online fundraising gave Dean a major financial advantage. What Dean used that money for, though, was primarily to buy conventional, uninspiring television ads. Dean's campaign failed to find a televisual equivalent to Dean's online message. Indeed, since the very point of the online campaign was how it differed from the mass-market style of modern campaigns, it's hard to imagine how it could have. But television remains the primary American public sphere, and Dean had no choice but to try to go where the viewers were.

The stories of Lott and Dean show the current possibilities and limitations of weblogs. Blogs embody the hopes of so many cybertopians that computers might democratize the distribution of information. As A. J. Liebling put it, "Freedom of the press is guaranteed only to those who own one." Today, it really is possible for any citizen with web access to publish and distribute her views instantly around the world. The question remains, however, to what extent individual voices can build audiences to rival the distribution power of the mass media.

The blogosphere itself is a utopian sphere—a space where the idealism of the Dean campaign could grow and expand, unchecked by the gatekeepers of the mass media. The utopian hope of the blogging world is that the blogosphere might become the public sphere—not just an adjunct or echo chamber, but a forum where a large portion of Americans get their news and share their views. Then, next time, the blogosphere wouldn't have to turn to the mass media to get its message out. The blogosphere would *be* the mass media.

In a sense, the Dean campaign really was a bubble. A bubble is exactly what the dialectic of technological determinism creates: a safe space insulated from the immediate demands of pragmatic calculation. The Deaniacs had the enthusiasm of believers convinced that they'd caught the tide of history, exploiting the unstoppable power of this new technology to change the world. As many Deaniacs self-mockingly put it, they'd "drunk the Kool-Aid." Every new movement needs its bubble, to avoid collapsing into the pessimism of everyday "common sense." The question is whether, once that movement's been incubated in its bubble, it can withstand contact with the harsh world outside. The Deaniacs have vowed to blog on; Dean has turned his campaign organization, Dean for America, into a new political advocacy organization, Democracy for America. The dialectic of technological determinism helped carve out a space where Howard Dean's campaign could reimagine American progressivism. It's up for grabs whether that utopian impulse can be transformed into a mass movement.

Hydrogen Hype

The Dean movement demonstrates the power of the dialectic of technological determinism to inspire movements for political change. But the rhetoric of technotopianism can also be exploited to justify complacency by replacing real-world solutions with pie-in-the-sky fantasies. A recent example of this process in action is the Bush administration's embrace of hydrogen energy technology. (Hydrogen isn't exactly a computing technology. But relentless hype in *Wired* and other cybercultural outlets has made it a key element of contemporary technotopianism.[14] And of course, any contemporary technology inevitably relies on computers for research and implementation.)

After the oil crisis of the 1970s, federal regulations substantially improved the average American car's fuel efficiency. But the rise of gas-guzzling SUVs in the 1990s reversed this trend. SUVs are treated by regulators as light trucks rather than cars, and fuel-economy regulations are far more lax for trucks than cars. Automakers successfully blocked every effort to revise the CAFE (Corporate Average Fuel Economy) standards to close the SUV loophole. Following 9/11, Bush and the Detroit automakers faced increasing pressure to do something. Environmentalist groups pushed the administration to raise fuel standards, which would force automakers to increase investments in fuel-efficient technologies such as hybrid gas-electric vehicles, and to trim sales of the profitable SUVs.

Instead of embracing these practical, immediately effective measures, Bush and the automakers took a different tack. They argued that haggling about hybrid electric vehicles was petty stuff, because the real breakthrough—hydrogen energy—is close at hand. Cars running on hydrogen will emit no pollution at all, and will run at much greater energy efficiency, they promised. While environmentalists worried only about the short term, the argument went, hydrogen backers were the real visionaries. This utopian fantasy of a clean alternative to gasoline was so appealing to the Bush administration that it was spotlighted in the 2003 State of the Union address:

> I ask you to take a crucial step, and protect our environment in ways that generations before us could not have imagined. In this century, the greatest environmental progress will come about, not through endless lawsuits or command and control regulations, but through technology and innovation. Tonight I am proposing 1.2 billion dollars in research funding so that America can lead the world in developing clean, hydrogen-powered automobiles.
>
> A simple chemical reaction between hydrogen and oxygen generates energy, which can be used to power a car—producing only water, not exhaust fumes. With a new national commitment, our scientists and engineers will overcome obstacles to take these cars from laboratory to showroom—so that the first car driven by a child born today could be powered by hydrogen, and pollution-free.[15]

The problem is that hydrogen fuel cells are still more than a decade away from commercial viability. We don't know if they'll work as well as promised. And the environmental consequences of generating so much hydrogen are still unclear. As Joseph Romm, a former Clinton energy official and author of *The Hype About Hydrogen*, puts it,

> People view hydrogen as this kind of . . . pollution-free elixir. That all you have to do is put hydrogen in something, and it's no longer an environmental problem, which is just absurd.
>
> [A] fuel cell . . . gets you a car that doesn't emit pollution right at the source of the car, the tailpipe. But global warming doesn't care where the emissions are emitted. That's why for those of us who care about global warming, the question is, where does the hydrogen come from?

I . . . think, General Motors, in particular, is hyping this because they don't like fuel-efficiency regulations for cars, and they've been holding out the promise that hydrogen will be this silver-bullet solution to all our automobile problems right around the corner, so don't force us into tighter fuel-economy standards.[16]

Unsurprisingly, a *Mother Jones* follow-up to Bush's 2003 promises found that "the budget that Bush submitted to Congress pays scant attention to renewable methods of producing hydrogen." Hydrogen research funding concentrated on methods using coal, nuclear power, and natural gas, while overall funding for research in renewable energy sources was actually cut.[17]

Hydrogen energy has been invoked to evade all manner of transportation reforms. In my own hometown of Atlanta, where the region has been under court orders for years to reduce toxic levels of air pollution, opponents of mass transit argue that long-term investment in flexible transportation solutions is unnecessary, since hydrogen cars will make all the smog disappear.

Investing in research on hydrogen energy from renewable sources is surely worthwhile, and hopefully one day it will transform the way America consumes power. But the hydrogen hype demonstrates how techno-topianism can be just a cynical cover for business as usual.

Flash Mobs and Beyond

At the same time as the rise of the internet in the 1990s, another transformation was happening to the American communications infrastructure: the proliferation of wireless phones. Portable phones grew increasingly smaller, cheaper, and more sophisticated with every year. By 2004 many included built-in digital cameras, internet access, and powerful microprocessors.

The rise of these new high-powered mobile communicators suggests that we may be entering a new stage in the history of the computer. Following the eras of the Mainframe, the Personal Computer, and the Interpersonal Computer, perhaps we are now entering the era of the Ubiquitous Computer. Or maybe, as microprocessors infuse tools from phones to cars to toasters, we can think of this as the era of the Invisible Computer[18]—the computer so ingrained into our daily lives that we don't even notice it anymore.

What might be the possibilities opened up by this new ubiquitous communication and computing environment? What utopian hopes and dystopian fears might it inspire? The dystopia is easy to imagine, actually: the panopticon, ubiquitous mobile technology enabling round-the-clock surveillance and the end of privacy. We can already see the beginnings of a new moral panic in such news items as gyms that have banned cell phones from locker rooms, out of fear of surreptitious photographs taken with undetectable digital cameras.

But the camera phones that can be snuck into a gym can also be snuck into a war zone, from which photos can be instantly sent without fear of confiscation. As "sean" writes in "Phonecams: Beyond the Hype," a thoughtful essay posted on the *cheesebikini?* website, "Networked cameras provide the ability to transmit photos to audiences without permission from the authorities. These devices rob government officials of their ability to detect and destroy photographic evidence at border crossings. This capability will be especially beneficial in war zones and in police states."[19]

Beyond these examples of how a phonecam could empower an individual user, mobile communications and computing technologies are also fascinating for how they might make possible new forms of collective action. Howard Rheingold, always quick to spot a technotrend, labels the new kinds of groups brought together by these technologies "smart mobs" in his 2002 book of the same name. He writes,

> Smart mobs consist of people who are able to act in concert even if they don't know each other. The people who make up smart mobs cooperate in ways never before possible because they carry devices that possess both communication and computing capabilities. Their mobile devices connect them with other information devices in the environment as well as with other people's telephones.
>
> Just as existing notions of community were challenged by the emergence of social networks in cyberspace, traditional ideas about the nature of place are being challenged as computing and communication devices begin to saturate the environment. As more people on city streets and on public transportation spend more time speaking to other people who are not physically co-present, the nature of public spaces and other aspects of social geography are changing before our eyes and

ears; some of these changes will benefit the public good and others will erode it.[20]

What could these new smart mobs accomplish? Rheingold identifies the protestors at the 1999 Seattle World Trade Organization meetings as an early example of a smart mob, using cell phones to effectively coordinate their actions. And he notes that "The 'People Power II' smart mobs in Manila who overthrew the presidency of President Estrada in 2001 organized demonstrations by forwarding text messages via cell phones."[21]

A less explicitly political, but more surreal and futuristic phenomenon emerged a year after the publication of Rheingold's prescient *Smart Mobs*: the flash mob. As *The Oxford English Dictionary* explains (the word was added in 2004), a flash mob is "a public gathering of complete strangers, organized via the Internet or mobile phone, who perform a pointless act and then disperse again."[22] Flash mobs appear to have started in June 2003 in New York. At one early mob, the group converged on Macy's. According to *cheesebikini*,

> New Yorkers used e-mail to coordinate a huge, instant gathering of people around a particular rug. Participants were instructed to tell questioning salesmen that they all lived together in a warehouse in Queens, and they were considering purchasing the item for use as a "Love Rug" back at the house. After precisely ten minutes the crowd dissipated.[23]

Subsequent, similarly surreal mobs convened in San Francisco, London, Rome, and the Mall of America in Minneapolis, Minnesota. Flash mobs continued in New York, as well: on July 24, 2003, a group joined to "make a bunch of increasingly surreal 'nature sounds' in Central Park."[24]

In September 2003 Garry Trudeau's comic *Doonesbury* gently mocked both the Dean and flash mob phenomena. Alex Doonesbury, a computer-savvy teenage Deaniac, explains, "I want to take the Flash mob to the next level, use it as a political tool, create more spontaneous meet-ups!"[25] Her plan is to organize hundred of people to simultaneously converge and chant, "Dean, Dean, Dean!"[26] Her stepmother Kim warns her, though, "That's a flash mob faux pas. You can't use it to promote something—it has to be absurdist." Alex is disappointed, then suggests the group instead chant, "Sharpton!" Kim agrees that would be appropriately absurd.

The flash mob's dedicated absurdism places it squarely in the tradition of 1920s Dadaism, 1960s happenings, and 1980s performance art. But its use of smart-mob technologies to blend planning with spontaneity holds out the promise of something truly new—so new that none of us really know yet what to make of it. Such is the case with all new technological practices. They're open, brimming with inchoate possibilities. Alex's utopian impulse is to bring together the Deaniacs and the flash mobbers, to create a new kind of political speech for a new kind of public sphere. She can't figure out exactly how to do it. But she's on the right track.

Resistance Is Never Futile

The rhetoric of technological determinism can be a galvanizing force for social change. But, as we have seen, the reality is that technological developments and their consequences are not inevitable, but rather are contingently shaped through cultural conflict. How computers will be used in the future will be the upshot of numerous struggles in multiple venues—courtrooms, boardrooms, legislative halls, artists' studios, classrooms, and individual desktops. The utopian sphere of cyberculture can be a beacon to a better world—a more just, egalitarian, democratic, creative society. But it won't happen unless we fight for it. The future is up to us.

Notes

Notes to the Introduction

1. Petroski, *The Pencil.*
2. See Lenhart et al., "The Ever-Shifting Internet Population"; Mossberger et al., *Virtual Inequality.*
3. See Latour, *Science in Action;* Pinch and Bijker, "The Social Construction of Fact and Artifacts"; Winner, "Upon Opening the Black Box and Finding It Empty."
4. See Williams, *Television;* Pool, *Technologies of Freedom.*
5. See, for example, McChesney, *The Problem of the Media.*
6. Negroponte, *Being Digital.*
7. See Bourdieu, *Outline of a Theory of Practice.*
8. See Aronowitz and DiFazio, *The Jobless Future.*
9. The quote, of course, is from Marx. For more on the economics of *Star Trek,* see Friedman, "Capitalism: The Final Frontier."
10. This dynamic is a particularly heightened version of the process described by Jameson in "Reification and Utopia in Mass Culture."
11. See Habermas, *The Structural Transformation of the Public Sphere.*
12. See also Jameson, *Marxism and Form.*
13. Kellner, "Ernst Bloch, Utopia and Ideology Critique." See also Kellner and O'Hara, "Utopia and Marxism in Ernst Bloch."
14. Morris, "Banality in Cultural Studies."
15. Whether contemporary American discourse contains anything like Habermas's vision of a public sphere, though, is an open question. See Robbins, ed., *The Phantom Public Sphere;* Schudson, *The Power of News.*
16. Jameson, *The Seeds of Time,* xii.
17. Jenkins and Thorburn, "Introduction," 9.
18. Morris, "Cultural Studies and Public Participation."
19. See Sloterkijk, *Critique of Cynical Reason;* Žižek, *The Sublime Object of Ideology.*
20. Richard Dyer eloquently makes this point in his examination of the utopian in Hollywood musicals, "Entertainment and Utopia."
21. Carey with Quirk, "The Mythos of the Electronic Revolution," 116.
22. For further demystifications of cyber-hype, see Pfaffenberger, "The Social Meaning of the Personal Computer"; Winner, *The Whale and the Reactor.*
23. Jacoby, review of *Looking Backward.*
24. Rosemont, "Edward Bellamy," 83.
25. Ross, *Strange Weather,* 132–133.
26. Ross, *Strange Weather,* 135.
27. Haraway, "Manifesto for Cyborgs," 181. Chapter 5 will more fully address Haraway's cyborg theory.

28. du Gay et al., 3. du Gay cites a similar approach developed by Richard Johnson in "The Story So Far."

NOTES TO CHAPTER 1

1. "Computer," *The Oxford English Dictionary,* 1989 ed.
2. This fact is remarked upon in most standard histories of computers, but rarely discussed further. More recently, feminist historians of technology and labor have begun to more deeply examine the role of human "computers." See Light, "When Computers Were Women"; Stanley, *Mothers and Daughters of Invention;* Tympas, "Perpetually Laborious."
3. Wilkes, "Babbage and the Colossus," 219. See also Cohen, "Babbage and Aiken."
4. Hyman, "Whiggism."
5. See Swade, *The Difference Engine.*
6. Eckert, "The Development of the ENIAC."
7. Bowden, *Faster Than Thought,* 7. Quoted in Cohen, "Babbage and Aiken," 174.
8. Cohen, "Babbage and Aiken," 183.
9. Cohen, "Babbage and Aiken," 172.
10. Augarten, *Bit by Bit,* 103. Quoted in Cohen, "Babbage and Aiken," 174. See also Campbell-Kelly and Aspray, *Computer,* 70–76.
11. Williams, *Television,* 7.
12. Barlow, "Declaration of Independence for Cyberspace."
13. Negroponte, *Being Digital,* 229.
14. See, for example, Goldstine, *The Computer from Pascal to von Neumann.*
15. Swade, email to the author, May 19, 1999. See also Swade, "Redeeming Charles Babbage's Mechanical Computer," 86–91; Swade, *The Difference Engine.*
16. Quote by Swade, from Highfield, "Machine May Prove History Books Wrong," 4.
17. Quote by Gibson, from Fischling, Hollinger, and Taylor, "'The Charisma Leak,'" 7.
18. Sussman, "Cyberpunk Meets Charles Babbage," 2. On *The Difference Engine,* see also Dyer-Witheford, *Cyber-Marx.*
19. Swade, *The Difference Engine,* 207.
20. Airy, "On Scheutz's Calculating Machine." Quoted in Swade, *The Difference Engine,* 201.
21. Airy, "On Scheutz's Calculating Machine." Quoted in Swade, *The Difference Engine,* 206.
22. Cowan, "The Consumption Junction," 263. Of course, in the case of computers before the PC, the consumers in question were for the most part institutions rather than individuals.
23. Swade, *The Difference Engine,* 169.
24. Plant, quoted in Kroll, "Technically Speaking."
25. Plant, *Zeroes and Ones,* 37.
26. Collier, *The Little Engines that Could've.* Cited in Swade, *The Difference Engine,* 168. See also Mattis, "Repurposing Ada."
27. Woolf, *A Room of One's Own.*
28. See Braverman, *Labor and Monopoly Capital,* 85.
29. Babbage, *On the Economy of Machinery and Manufactures,* 191. Quoted in Braverman, *Labor and Monopoly Capital,* 317.
30. Dyer-Witheford, *Cyber-Marx,* 3. See also Schaffer, "Babbage's Intelligence"
31. Beniger, *The Control Revolution,* 390.
32. Beniger, *The Control Revolution,* 391.

NOTES TO CHAPTER 2

1. Lubar, *InfoCulture*, 296.

2. Campbell-Kelly and Aspray, *Computer*, 63.

3. For an extreme example, see Kidwell and Ceruzzi, *Landmarks in Digital Computing*, which chooses to omit analog computers entirely. (There's no companion *Landmarks in Analog Computing*.)

4. Augarten, *Bit by Bit,* 13.

5. Goldstine, *The Computer from Pascal to von Neumann*, 39–40.

6. Owens, "Vannevar Bush and the Differential Analyzer," 72.

7. See Campbell-Kelly and Aspray, *Computer*, 63.

8. Bromley, "Analog Computing Devices."

9. Downey, "Virtual Webs, Physical Technologies, and Hidden Workers."

10. See Edwards, *The Closed World.*

11. ENIAC's place of honor is subject to some debate. In 1973 a U.S. patent judge declared Iowa State physics professor John V. Atanasoff and his graduate student Clifford Berry, who together built the Atanasoff-Berry Computer in the period from 1939 to 1942, to be the "inventors" of the computer. For a strong defense of Atanasoff and Berry, see Shurkin, *Engines of the Mind.* Most computing historians, however, argue that Atanasoff's machine was not flexible enough to count as a real computer. See Augarten, *Bit by Bit;* Campbell-Kelly and Aspray, *Computer;* Ceruzzi, *The History of Modern Computing.* Meanwhile, British history books often give the honor to ENIGMA, the powerful code-breaking machine developed by the British army during World War II.

12. Edwards, *The Closed World,* 43.

13. See Edwards, *The Closed World,* 66–70.

14. Edwards, *The Closed World,* 67.

15. See Edwards, *The Closed World,* 76–79.

16. Tympas, "From Digital to Analog and Back." See also Tympas, *The Computor and the Analyst.* Tympas argues that there's a politics behind the canonical historiography: historians of computing have considered only the labor of a technical elite of digital designers, rather than the large numbers of hands-on analog laborers.

> We know practically nothing of the computing labor of a great mass of men possessing computing skills because the computing machines with which they worked are rendered historically unimportant on the grounds that their *a posteriori* designation belongs to an inferior technical class—analog computers. (Tympas, "Perpetually Laborious," 78.)

17. Valley, "How the SAGE Development Began," 224. Quoted in Tympas, "From Digital to Analog and Back," 45–46.

18. Casaaza, *The Development of Electric Power Transmission.* Quoted in Tympas, "From Digital to Analog and Back," 47.

19. Weaver, correspondence to Samuel Caldwell. Quoted in Owens, "Vannevar Bush and the Differential Analyzer," 66.

20. Owens, "Vannevar Bush and the Differential Analyzer," 95.

21. See Friedman, "Vinyl"; Perlman, "Consuming Audio."

22. Negativland, "Shiny, Aluminum, Plastic, and Digital."

23. On the subject of synthesizers, a similar debate rages between partisans of analog and digital synths. While prized for their "unnatural" electronic sounds when first introduced, today analog synths are celebrated by aficionados for the "warmth" of their tone, compared to the "cold" tone of digital machines that attempt to replicate the old analog sound with samples. See Colbeck, *Keyfax.*

24. Rothenbuhler and Peters, "Defining Phonography," 246.

25. Rothenbuhler and Peters, "Defining Phonography," 245.

26. Rothenbuhler and Peters, "Defining Phonography," 258–259. On the other hand, Rothenbuhler and Peters do acknowledge the democratic potential in the increased manipulability of digital recordings, which can easy be sampled, chopped up, and recontextualized. Citing Walter Benjamin's "The Work of Art in the Age of Mechanical Production," they conclude, "The manipulability characteristic of digital recording and playback spells both the dream of democratic co-creation and the nightmare of lost nature. As in Benjamin's analysis of technical reproducibility, we here encounter both new possibilities for audience engagement and the loss of an aura" (252). We will return to the democratizing potential of digital music in chapter 9, when we discuss Napster and other digital music distribution systems.

27. Kidder, *The Soul of a New Machine,* 146. For more on the binary mindset of computer programmers, see also reporter Fred Moody's *I Sing the Body Electronic,* and programmer Ellen Ullman's searching memoir, *Close to the Machine.* For an even more critical perspective, see the neo-Luddite critiques discussed in chapter 8.

28. The distinction between index and symbol, drawing on the semiotic scheme of Charles Peirce, is suggested by Rothenbuhler and Peters, "Defining Phonography," 249.

29. Sterne, *The Audible Past,* 338.

30. Kosko, *Fuzzy Thinking,* 5.

31. Zadeh, "Fuzzy Sets."

32. McNeill and Freiberger, *Fuzzy Logic,* 37. Quoted in Gehr, "Fuzzy Inc."

33. Kosko, *Fuzzy Thinking,* 14.

34. See Ligorio, "Postmodernism and Fuzzy Systems"; Negoita, "Postmodernism, Cybernetics, and Fuzzy Set Theory."

35. Marshall and Zohar, *Who's Afraid of Schrodinger's Cat?* 162.

36. See Rezendes, "Keeping an Eye on the Scientists."

NOTES TO CHAPTER 3

1. Bakhtin, *The Dialogic Imagination.* On the application of Bakhtin's ideas to film studies, see Sklar, *Subversive Pleasures.*

2. See Akera, "IBM's Early Adaptation to Cold War Markets."

3. "Automation: Electronics for Plenty," 86.

4. Norbert Weiner, letter to Walter Reuther, August 13, 1949, quoted in Noble, *Progress without People,* 162–163. Weiner elaborated his concerns in *The Human Uses of Human Beings.* For a contemporaneous fictional exploration of these issues, see Kurt Vonnegut's *Player Piano.* On the history of automation, see Noble, *Forces of Production.*

5. Quoted in Dickens, *The Films of Katharine Hepburn,* 170.

6. Quoted in Dickens, *The Films of Katharine Hepburn,* 170.

7. The name Watson is a nod to the famous Watson family, who, in the form of father Tom and son Tom Junior, ran IBM for much of this century.

8. Summerhill, "Top Ten Reasons Why 'Bunny Watson' Was Right About Computers in Libraries."

9. Girls on Film, "Classic Movies of the Workplace."

10. "Automation: Electronics for Plenty," 86.

11. Aronowitz and DiFazio, *The Jobless Future,* 48.

12. Solow, "We'd Better Watch Out," 36.

13. Sichel, *The Computer Revolution,* 12.

14. Henwood, "Where's the Payoff?" 4.

15. McGovern, "The Technology Productivity Paradox."

16. Stephen Roach, "The Boom for Whom: Revisiting America's Technology Paradox," quoted in McGovern, "The Technology Productivity Paradox." See also Triplett, "The Solow Productivity Paradox."

17. "Solving the Paradox."

18. McKinsey Global Institute, "U.S. Productivity Growth, 1995–2000." See also Henwood, *After the New Economy,* 64–65.

19. Henwood, *After the New Economy,* 24–25.

20. Roach, "The Productivity Paradox," Section 4, Column 2, 9.

21. "Solving the Paradox."

22. McGovern, "The Technology Productivity Paradox."

23. Henwood, *After the New Economy,* 14.

24. Henwood, *After the New Economy,* 45–46.

25. Aronowitz and DiFazio, *The Jobless Future,* 27. See also Braverman, *Labor and Monopoly Capital;* Thompson, *The Making of the English Working Class;* Noble, *Forces of Production.*

26. Aronowitz and DiFazio, *The Jobless Future,* 33.

27. Flamm, *Creating the Computer,* 220–221.

28. Tympas, *The Computor and the Analyst,* 12.

29. For more on the history of robots in science fiction, see Telotte, *Replications.*

30. See Heims, *The Cybernetics Group.*

31. Cixous, *"Coming to Writing" and Other Essays.*

32. Soni, "The Promise."

33. See, for example, Kurzweil, *The Age of Spiritual Machines.* For an account of the state of the debate over the potential of AI, see Richards, ed., *Are We Spiritual Machines?*

34. Lubar, *InfoCulture,* 318; Augarten, *Bit by Bit,* 248.

35. Campbell-Kelly and Aspray, *Computer,* 140.

36. Lubar, *InfoCulture,* 318.

37. See Levy, *Hackers,* 130–133.

38. Sackett, *The Hollywood Reporter Book of Box Office Hits.*

39. Kubrick had HAL born five years earlier, in 1992, but many computer scientists find it hard to believe that such an important mission would be left to a nine-year-old computer, and prefer Clarke's version. See Stork, "The Best Informed Dream," 3–4.

40. Kestenbaum, "Cyberfest Celebrates HAL in Urbana."

41. Stork, "The Best Informed Dream," 11.

42. Stork, "The Best Informed Dream," 12.

43. Stork, "The Best Informed Dream," 1–2. I feel compelled to point out one presumption in *2001* that Kubrick and Clarke clearly never bothered to think through: that all space-flight service personnel in *2001* would be women, while all the astronauts would be men. Stork goes on to claim that "the film . . . doesn't look dated even though thirty years have passed since its release," (2) an astonishing claim to anyone with any fashion sense. The stewardesses' revealing, constraining outfits—bubble hats and all—look straight out of *Austin Powers,* and instantly place the film in its moment of late-1960s swinging sexism.

44. Garfinkel, "Happy Birthday, HAL," 188.

45. Bérubé, *Public Access,* 185.

46. Bérubé, *Public Access,* 188.

47. Paula Treichler, quoted in Pringle, "*2001:* 'You Are Free to Speculate.'"

48. Bérubé, *Public Access,* 185. Quotes from Kagan, *The Cinema of Stanley Kubrick,* 160; Nelson, *Kubrick,* 125; De Vries, *The Films of Stanley Kubrick,* 53; Ciment, *Kubrick,* 134.

49. Stevens, "'Sinister Fruitiness,'" 431. Italics in original.

50. Turing, "Computing Machinery and Intelligence."

51. The queer implications of the Turing Test are further explored in Stevens, "'Sinister Fruitiness.'"

52. For more on gender as performance, see Butler, *Gender Trouble.*

53. Stevens, "'Sinister Fruitiness,'" 431.

54. At the 1997 "birthday party" for HAL at Urbana-Champaign, Paula Treichler asked Arthur C. Clarke, appearing live via satellite, whether HAL was gay. *Inside Illinois* reports that "Clarke reared back his head in laughter, responding, 'I never asked him. That voice does sound rather ambiguous'" (Vicic, "HAL, HAL: The Gang Was All Here"). Kestenbaum also recounts the incident ("Cyberfest Celebrates HAL in Urbana.")

55. Gale, "Straight, Gay, or Binary."

56. See Russo, *The Celluloid Closet.*

NOTES TO CHAPTER 4

1. Pinch and Biker, "The Social Construction of Fact and Artifacts," 28.

2. My information on ECHO comes from Tomayko, "Electronic Computer for Home Operation." The ECHO doesn't appear in most accounts of the history of computers, although it does rate a paragraph in Veit, *Stan Veit's History of the Personal Computer,* 10.

3. Tomayko, "Electronic Computer for Home Operation," 61.

4. Even science fiction rarely raised this question, having been behind the curve on computerization. SF more typically imagined the technologization of the household through the widespread adoption of robot butlers.

5. See "Tech History Series: Failed Products"; "Pop Quiz: What Was the First Personal Computer?"

6. On the mechanization of the American home, see Cowan, *More Work for Mother.*

7. Lan, "Total Kitchen Information System."

8. See Lauderback, "A Network Computer—for your Kitchen."

9. See Spigel, *Make Room for TV.*

10. See Fatsis, "The Home Front: Executives Demand More of Home Offices"; "The Home Front: What's Hot, and Not, in Home Design."

11. See Spigel, *Welcome to the Dreamhouse,* 381–408.

12. See Gates with Myhrvold and Rinearson, *The Road Ahead,* 205–226. For an earlier version of the "smart house" fantasy, see Blankenship, *The Apple House.*

13. Although, demonstrating again the odd utopian allure of *2001,* one recent home-automation package was named HAL 2000, short for "home automated living."

14. Kemeny, quoted in Augarten, *Bit by Bit,* 253–254.

15. Levy, *Hackers,* 52.

16. Ceruzzi, "From Scientific Instrument to Everyday Appliance," 3.

17. Levy, *Hackers,* 168–197.

18. Though of course, networks would come to link PCs together, culminating in the rise of the internet in the 1990s. In the late 1990s partisans of the Java programming language argued that PCs would soon become obsolete, replaced by "networked computers" that could function as terminals displaying programs stored on centralized servers. While this change is still technically possible, as yet the privatized "personal computer" model still holds on—less out of technical necessity than ideological appeal.

19. See Malone, *The Microprocessor,* 33–47.

20. Moore, "Cramming More Components onto Integrated Circuits."

21. Yang, "On Moore's Law and Fishing." Quoted in Tumoi, "The Lives and Death of Moore's Law."

22. Hayes, "Terrabyte Territory."

23. Markoff, "Chip Progress May Soon Be Hitting Barrier," C1. For an economist's critique of this deterministic assumption, see Tuomi, "The Lives and Death of Moore's Law."

24. Alsdorf, "What Is Moore's Law?"

25. Malone, *The Microprocessor*, 14–15.

26. Malone, "Forget Moore's Law." See also Markoff, "Is There Life After Silicon Valey's Fast Lane?"

27. Boutin, "Stop the Clock."

28. Haddon, "The Home Computer," 10.

29. Haddon, "The Home Computer," 10–11.

30. Augarten, *Bit by Bit*, 266.

31. Augarten, *Bit by Bit*, 268.

32. Augarten, *Bit by Bit*, 268.

33. Hoff, quoted in Malone, *The Microprocessor*, 14.

34. Malone, *The Microprocessor*, 14.

35. Roberts and Yates, "Altair 8800."

36. *QST*, March 1974, 154. Cited in Ceruzzi, *The History of Modern Computing*.

37. Augarten, *Bit by Bit*, 269–270.

38. *Radio-Electronics*, July 1974, cover.

39. Augarten, *Bit by Bit*, 270.

40. Salsberg, "The Home Computer Is Here!" 4.

41. Haddon and Skinner, "The Enigma of the Micro," 444.

42. NRI Schools, advertisement, 8.

43. International Correspondence Schools, advertisement, 18–19.

44. Bell and Howell Schools, advertisement, insert.

45. Winkless, "Personal Technology," 4.

46. Campbell-Kelly and Aspray, *Computer*, 238–239.

47. See Levy, *Hackers*, 201–223.

48. For more on the roots of *Wired* in the *Whole Earth Catalog*, see Turner, *From Counterculture to Cyberculture*.

49. Brand, "Forward," in Nelson, *Computer Lib/Dream Machines*, iii. "Big Nurse" is a reference to the despotic character in *One Flew Over the Cuckoo's Nest*.

50. The Altair hobbyists did have a strong support network, built around magazines, user newsletters, conventions, and the first computer stores. MITS even sponsored "the MITS-MOBILE," a camper van which drove around the country "bringing the message of low-cost computing to thousands of people" ("Altair . . . on the Road," 1).

51. Roberts and Yates, "Altair 8800," 33.

52. Solomon, "Solomon's Memory," 37.

53. Veit, *Stan Veit's History of the Personal Computer*, 46–47.

54. Salsberg, "Jaded Memory," 7.

55. See, for example, Levy's influential *Hackers*, 190.

56. For some samples of the extensive discussion of "sense of wonder" in SF criticism, see Suvin, *Metamorphoses of Science Fiction;* Panshin and Panshin, *The World Beyond the Hill;* Hartwell, *Age of Wonders*. For a useful survey of the uses of the term, see Nicholls and Robu, "Sense of Wonder," 1083–1085.

57. Nye, *American Technological Sublime*.

NOTES TO CHAPTER 5

1. Linzmayer, *Apple Confidential*, 90.

2. Figures taken from Linzmayer, *Apple Confidential*, 7–8.

3. Veit, *Stan Veit's History of the Personal Computer*, 99–100.

4. Linzmayer, *Apple Confidential*, 13.

5. Veit, *Stan Veit's History of the Personal Computer*, 99.

6. Cringely, *Accidental Empires*, 65.

7. Augarten, *Bit by Bit*, 260.

8. Augarten, *Bit by Bit*, 261.

9. Cringely, *Accidental Empires*, 159–181.

10. Cringely, *Accidental Empires*, 119–138.

11. Campbell-Kelly and Aspray, *Computer*, 255.

12. Campbell-Kelly and Aspray, *Computer*, 255.

13. Cringely, *Accidental Empires*, 159–181. On IBM's troubles, see Ferguson and Morris, *Computer Wars*.

14. Cringely, *Accidental Empires*, 175.

15. Apple's representatives to software companies were known as "evangelists," and were charged with the mission of proselytizing for the company, convincing programmers to invest in the development of Apple software. See Kawasaki, *The Macintosh Way* and *Selling the Dream*.

16. Campbell-Kelly and Aspray, *Computer*, 256. Quotations from Chposky and Leonsis, *Blue Magic*.

17. Linzmayer, *Apple Confidential*, 42.

18. See Levy, *Insanely Great*; Smith and Alexander, *Fumbling the Future*; Hiltzik, *Dealers of Lightning*.

19. See Bardini, *Bootstrapping*; Levy, *Insanely Great*.

20. See Smith and Alexander, *Fumbling the Future*; Hiltzik, *Dealers of Lightning*.

21. Neilsen, "Voice Interfaces."

22. Linzmayer, *The Mac Bathroom Reader*, 117.

23. Sculley recounts this story in *Odyssey*, 154–182.

24. Millman, "Apple's '1984' Spot: A Love/Hate Story."

25. Horton, "TV Commercial of the Decade," 12.

26. See Johnson, "10 Years After 1984," 1; Conrad, *The One Hundred Best TV Commercials*.

27. Linzmayer, *The Mac Bathroom Reader*, 120; Bob Marich, "The Real Blitz Begins," 1.

28. Linzmayer, *The Mac Bathroom Reader*, 111.

29. Williams, *Television*, 20; Williams, *Towards 2000*, 187–189. See also du Gay et al., *Doing Cultural Studies*.

30. "20 Years of Macintosh 1984–2004."

31. "Lemmings," Apple Computer, advertisement, Chiat/Day, 1985.

32. Sculley, *Odyssey*, 228.

33. Kadetsky, "Silicon Valley Sweatshops."

NOTES TO CHAPTER 6

1. Portions of this chapter have appeared as Friedman, "Making Sense of Software"; and Friedman, "Civilization and Its Discontents."

2. At the time, it should be noted, Asimov was a paid spokesperson for Radio Shack, appearing in ads for the TRS-80. He later admitted that he continued to use his typewriter for rough drafts. (Asimov, *I. Asimov*, 471–476.)

3. See neo-Luddite works such as Birkerts, *The Gutenberg Elegies*; Slouka, *War of the Worlds*; Stoll, *Silicon Snake Oil*. For more on the neo-Luddites, see chapter 8.

4. See MAME website, http://www.mame.net.

5. Kasavin, *"Full Spectrum Warrior* Review."

6. The exponential rise in the processing power of home videogame systems parallels that of computer systems, since they're built on the same underlying microprocessor technology. However, since the product choices in videogame systems are so much more limited, the increase in processing power comes in stages, rather than the smooth curve of most charts of Moore's Law. Dell comes out with a new slate of computers running at slightly higher processor speeds every month. A videogame company's system, by contrast, typically lasts for 4 to 6 years, before being replaced with a new system with exponentially more processing power. The original Playstation, for example, appeared in 1995. The Playstation 2 appeared in 2000. The Playstation 3 is scheduled for release in early 2006.

7. See Levy, *Hackers;* Wilson, "A Brief History of Gaming, Part 1"; Laurel, *Computers as Theater.*

8. Laurel, *Computers as Theater,* 1.

9. See Levy, *Hackers;* Wilson, "A Brief History of Computer Gaming, Part 1."

10. This widely quoted phrase was coined by Electronic Arts executive Trip Hawkins in the early 1980s.

11. I'm certain the 1993 film *Groundhog Day* was made by computer game players—its plot perfectly captures the "oh no, not again" exasperation of playing the same sequence over and over, again and again, until you get everything right.

12. One intriguing current phenomenon in game design is a turn toward screenwriting techniques in an attempt to develop more emotionally engaging storylines. See Freeman, *Creating Emotion in Games.*

13. Will Wright, quoted in Reeder, "Designing Visions," 25.

14. Barol, "Big Fun in a Small Town," 64.

15. *Maxis Software Toys Catalog,* 4.

16. *Maxis Software Toys Catalog,* 10.

17. Card, "Gameplay," 58.

18. See Myers, "Time Symbol Transformations, and Computer Games."

19. Myers, "Computer Game Semiotics," 343.

20. Shelley, *Sid Meier's Civilization Player's Manual,* 7.

21. Latour, *Aramis,* viii.

22. Where, one may ask, in this confrontation between computer and player, is the author of the software? In some sense, one could describe playing a computer game as learning to think like the programmer, rather than the computer. On the basic level of strategy, this may mean trying to divine Sid Meier's choices and prejudices, to figure out how he put the game together so as to play it more successfully. More generally, one could describe simulation games as an aestheticization of the programming process: a way to interact with and direct the computer, but at a remove. Many aspects of computer gameplay resemble the work of programming; the play-die-and-start-over rhythm of adventure games, for example, can be seen as a kind of debugging process. Programming, in fact, can often be as absorbing a task as gaming; both suck you into the logic of the computer. The programmer must also learn to "think like the computer" at a more technical level, structuring code in the rigid logic of binary circuits.

23. See Weiner, *The Human Use of Human Beings.*

24. Heims, *The Cybernetics Group,* 15–16.

25. See Gibson, *Neuromancer.*

26. Actually, one might argue that the pleasure many get out of driving for its own sake, or the enjoyment of watching TV no matter what's on (what Raymond Williams in *Television* called "flow"), are examples of similar aestheticizations of the cybernetic connection

between person and machine. We might then say that just as these pleasures aestheticized previous cybernetic connections, simulation games do the same for our relationships with computers.

27. Geertz, *The Interpretation of Cultures*, 443.

28. Geertz, *The Interpretation of Cultures*, 449.

29. Harvey, *The Condition of Postmodernity*, 206.

30. Harvey, *The Condition of Postmodernity*, 206.

31. Jameson, *Postmodernism, or, the Cultural Logic of Late Capitalism*, 54.

32. Myers, "Chris Crawford," 27.

33. Fuller and Jenkins, "Nintendo and New World Travel Writing."

34. Fuller and Jenkins, "Nintendo and New World Travel Writing," 58.

35. See de Certeau, *Heterologies*; de Certeau, *Practice*.

36. Fuller and Jenkins cite de Certeau, *Practice*, 117–118.

37. Fuller and Jenkins, "Nintendo and New World Travel Writing," 66.

38. Fuller and Jenkins cites de Certeau, *Practice*, 118–122.

39. Fuller and Jenkins, "Nintendo and New World Travel Writing," 66.

40. Cronon, *Changes in the Land*.

41. One alternative might be to go ahead and treat an abstract object like a real protagonist, complete with an interior monologue. That's what Latour does in *Aramis*. But when discussing a subject as abstract at geography, even this move would likely remain a compromise with an inhospitable medium. In giving voice to geography, one risks anthropomorphization, falling back into the synecdochical trap of substituting the king for the land.

42. One might also think about how simulations narrate other abstractions, such as economic relationships. In addition to being maps-in-time, simulations are also charts-in-time. The player follows not only the central map in *Civilization*, but also the various charts, graphs, and status screens that document the current state of each city's trade balance, food supply, productivity, and scientific research. In this aspect, simulations share a common heritage with the Apple II's original killer application, the spreadsheet.

43. Wood, *The Power of Maps*.

44. See neo-Luddite critics such as Brook and Boal, "Preface"; Slouka, *War of the Worlds*.

45. See Kolko, Nakamura, and Rodman, *Race in Cyberspace*; Nakamura, *Cybertypes*.

46. Entertainment Software Association, "2004 Sales, Demographics and Usage Data."

47. "Electronic Arts Posts Record Sims 2 Sales."

48. On the gender politics of computer games, see Cassell and Jenkins, *From Barbie to Mortal Kombat*. For one designer's account of her own attempts to build games for girls, see Laurel, *Utopian Entrepreneur*.

49. "Women Get in the Game."

50. Herz, "Game Theory."

51. Hochschild, *The Time Bind*.

52. For more on sexuality in *The Sims*, see Consalvo, "Hot Dates and Fairy Tale Romances."

53. See Consalvo, "Hot Dates and Fairy Tale Romances."

54. On MUDs, see Turkle, *Life on the Screen*; Dibbell, "A Rape in Cyberspace."

55. Statistics from Meston, "The MMORPG Morass," 64.

56. See Shapiro, "Fantasy Economics."

57. Dibbell, *Play Money*; Dibbell, "The Unreal Estate Boom." See also Thompson, "Game Theories."

58. Croal, "*Sims* Family Values."

59. Meston, "The MMORPG Morass," 64.

60. Jenkins, "Games, the New Lively Art."

61. Seldes, *The Seven Lively Arts.*

62. For excellent surveys of the state of computer-game and videogame research, see Newman, *Videogames;* Wardrip-Fruin and Harrigan, eds., *First Person;* Wolf, ed., *The Medium of the Video Game;* Wolf and Perron, eds., *Video Game Theory Reader.* Interest in computer games has also spurred new theorization of the broader culture of games, including board games, card games, and role-playing games. See Salen and Zimmerman, *Rules of Play;* Sholder and Zimmerman, *Replay.*

63. See Wardrip-Fruin and Harrigan, "Ludology," 35; Frasca, "Simulation versus Narrative."

64. Henry Jenkins cites several examples of this perspective in "Game Design as Narrative Architecture," 118. These include Adams, "Three Problems for Interactive Storytellers"; Costikyan, "Where Stories End and Games Begin"; Juul, "A Clash Between Games and Narrative" and "Games Telling Stories?"; and Eskelinen, "The Gaming Situation." See also the responses by Jon McKenzie and Markku Eskalinen published side-by-side with Jenkins's article on pages 118–121.

65. Jenkins, "Game Design as Narrative Architecture."

66. Jameson, "World Reduction in Le Guin."

67. McCloud, *Understanding Comics.*

NOTES TO CHAPTER 7

1. For more on the early days of The Well, see Rheingold, *The Virtual Community.*

2. See Berners-Lee, *Weaving the Web.*

3. On the development of ARPANET, see Abbate, *Inventing the Internet;* Norberg et al., *Transforming Computer Technology;* Hafner and Lyon, *Where Wizards Stay Up Late;* Segaller, *Nerds 2.0.1.*

4. On network effects, see Shapiro and Varian, *Information Rules.*

5. Lenhart et al., "The Ever-Shifting Internet Population."

6. Sterling, *The Hacker Crackdown,* xi.

7. For more on the rise and fall of party lines, see Fischer, *America Calling.* For further examinations of alternate constructs of the telephone in its early years, see Marvin, *When Old Technologies Were New;* Sterne, *The Audible Past.*

8. *Neuromancer* is not exactly utopian. On the other hand, it's not really as dystopian as it's sometimes made out to be. The drab future of *1984* it's not. *Neuromancer*'s register is what I would call "rhapsodic dystopianism"—the future may be unpleasant for most people, but it still looks really cool and exciting, thanks to all those shiny toys. As an ambivalent fantasy of the future, then, *Neuromancer* certainly engages the ongoing debates over the shape of the future in the utopian sphere.

9. Gibson, interviewed in McCaffery, "An Interview with William Gibson," 270.

10. Gibson, interviewed in McCaffery, "An Interview with William Gibson," 271.

11. Gibson, *Neuromancer,* 5.

12. Bear, interviewed in "Interview with Greg Bear," 5.

13. Safire, "Virtual Reality," 6.18.

14. The exchange between Case and Molly is not an equal one. Case enjoys a voyeuristic pleasure in inhabiting Molly's female body, while Molly is offered no comparable opportunity. For more on the gendering of cyberspace in *Neuromancer,* see Balsamo, *Technologies of the Gendered Body;* Stevens, "'Sinister Fruitiness.'"

15. See Winner, "Silicon Valley Mystery House."

16. See Balsamo, *Technologies of the Gendered Body.*

NOTES TO CHAPTER 8

1. For more on the roots of *Wired* in the *Whole Earth Review,* see Turner, *From Counterculture to Cyberculture.*

2. Levy, *Hackers,* 7.

3. Levy, *Hackers,* 7.

4. Levy, *Hackers,* 23.

5. See Slatalla and Quittner, *Masters of Deception.*

6. See Goodell, *The Cyberthief and the Samurai;* Littman, *The Fugitive Game;* Shimomura, *Takedown.*

7. The literature on hackers, much of it in the "true crime" genre, is extensive. The most thoughtful discussions are Sterling, *The Hacker Crackdown;* and Ross, "Hacking Away at the Counterculture," in *Strange Weather,* 75–100.

8. Rosetto, "Why Wired?" 10.

9. Kline, "Infobahn Warrior."

10. Brand, *The Media Lab,* 202. Brand immediately continues, "Information also wants to be expensive." But this qualification has often been ignored in the slogan's subsequent appropriation.

11. Levy, writing in 1984, offers a more complete version of the Hacker Ethic, featuring several principles, one of which is "All information should be free" (*Hackers,* 40).

12. As a utopian discourse, cyberculture has often paralleled itself to that quintessential American fantasy, the myth of the frontier. Thus, with the Western frontier filled up and space exploration prohibitively costly, cyberspace becomes a kind of "electronic frontier." For a critique of this frontier rhetoric, see Lockard, "Progressive Politics, Electronic Individualism, and the Myth of Virtual Community." For more on the Electronic Frontier Foundation, see Ludlow, ed., *High Noon on the Electronic Frontier.*

13. The flip side of this sentiment is perhaps "The pen is mightier than the sword." But this claim, too, presumes that we can easily distinguish pens from swords.

14. See Klein, *No Logo.*

15. See MacKinnon, *Only Words.*

16. Dibbell, *My Tiny Life,* 17.

17. Dibbell, *My Tiny Life,* 27–28.

18. Brook and Boal, "Preface," xi. For more on corporate surveillance technologies, see Garson, *The Electronic Sweatshop. Processed World* was an acerbic magazine that chronicled corporate abuses of employees' liberty; much of its best writing is collected in Carlsson and Leger, eds., *Bad Attitude.* For more on corporate surveillance of consumers, see Larson, *The Naked Consumer.*

19. For a critique of the new Social Darwinism, see Ross, *The Chicago Gangster Theory of Life.*

20. For more on the military's role in the development of computer culture, see Edwards, *The Closed World;* also Flamm, *Creating the Computer.*

21. See Birkerts, *The Gutenberg Elegies.*

22. Brook and Boal, "Preface," vii–viii.

23. Brook and Boal, "Preface," vii.

24. Derrida, *Of Grammatology.* See also Chang, *Deconstructing Communication;* Peters, *Speaking into the Air;* Sterne, *The Audible Past.*

25. Brook and Boal, "Preface," xiv.

Notes to Chapter 9

1. "Napster Timeline."
2. See Mann, "The Year the Music Dies."
3. Greene, "The Insidious Virus of Music Downloading." Greene's speech was widely mocked online. (See, for example, michael, "Greene's Grammy Speech Debunked"; Silverman, "Greene's Speech Misses the Mark and Why You Shouldn't Use KaZaa.") Hilary Rosen, chair of the Recording Industry Association of America, also repeatedly blamed file sharing for the industry's downturn. See Bai, "Hating Hilary."
4. A 2002 study of 1,000 online consumers by Forrester Research found "no evidence of decreased CD buying among frequent digital music consumers" (Forrester Research Press Release, "Downloads Did Not Cause the Music Slump").
5. For a detailed critique of the record industry's economic analysis, see Bricklin, "The Recording Industry Is Trying to Kill the Goose That Lays the Golden Egg."
6. See Ordonez, "The Record Industry Owes You $20," D1.
7. For two candid takes from industry veterans, see Avalon, *Confessions of a Record Producer*; Albini, "The Problem with Music."
8. Ian, "The Internet Debacle—An Alternative View."
9. Adegoke, "Robbie Williams Says Music Piracy is 'Great.'"
10. See Chanan, *Musica Practica*.
11. Moby, liner notes to *18*.
12. For a survey of legal challenges to Napster and other online services, see Anestopoulou, "Challenging Intellectual Property Law in the Internet." The most prominent legal proponent of an expanded vision of fair use is the prolific Lawrence Lessig, founder of the Stanford Law School's Center for Internet and Society. See *Free Culture, The Future of Ideas*, and *Code*, as well as Lessig's blog at http://www.lessig.org. For an analysis of Napster from the perspective of political economy, see McCourt and Burkart, "When Creators, Corporations and Consumers Collide."
13. See also Henry Jenkins's similar formulation of "textual poaching" in Jenkins, *Textual Poachers*.
14. 17 U.S.C. 107.
15. U.S. Constitution, Article I, Section 8.
16. Vaidhyanathan, *Copyrights and Copywrongs*, 4. See also Vaidhyanathan, *The Anarchist in the Library*. For a similar critique, see McLeod, *Owning Culture*.
17. McCourt and Burkart, "When Creators, Corporations and Consumers Collide."

Notes to Chapter 10

1. On the dot-com crash, see Cassidy, *Dot.con*; Kaplan, *F'd Companies*.
2. Schwartz and Leyden, "The Long Boom: A History of the Future, 1980–2020."
3. Rosenberg, *Open Source*.
4. Jameson, "Reification and Utopia in Mass Culture."
5. Terranova, "Free Labor."
6. Ross, "The Mental Labor Problem."
7. Greene. "Ballmer."
8. Lea, "MS's Ballmer."
9. Bloomberg News, "Microsoft Executive Says Linux Threatens Innovation."
10. Raymond, ed., *The New Hacker's Dictionary*.
11. Originally published online, the essay was reprinted in Raymond, *The Cathedral and the Bazaar*.

12. Raymond, *The Cathedral and the Bazaar.*
13. Barbrook and Cameron, "The Californian Ideology."
14. See Borsook, *Cyberselfish.*
15. Barbrook, "The High-Tech Gift Economy."
16. Raymond, *The Cathedral and the Bazaar,* 65.
17. Raymond, *The Cathedral and the Bazaar,* 64.
18. Levy, *Hackers.*
19. Raymond, *The Cathedral and the Bazaar.*
20. Stallman, "Byte Interview with Richard Stallman."
21. Stallman, "The GNU Manifesto."

NOTES TO CONCLUSION

1. On the history of blogs, see Editors of Perseus Publishing, eds., *We've Got Blog.*
2. Lott, quoted in Edsall, "Lott Decried for Part of Salute to Thurmond," A6.
3. Huffington, "In Praise of Making a Stink."
4. Edsall, quoted in Kurtz, "A Hundred-Candle Story and How to Blow It."
5. FAIR, "Media Advisory: Media Play Catch-Up on Lott's Latest Endorsement of Racism."
6. Sullivan, quoted in Podhoretz, "The Internet's First Scalp."
7. Huffington, "In Praise of Making a Stink."
8. Kinsley, "Lott's Adventures in Gaffeland," 31.
9. Marshall, *Talking Points Memo.* December 13, 2002, 5:16 PM.
10. For early coverage of the Dean phenomenon, see Cummings, "The E-Team"; Shapiro, "The Dean Connection"; Manjoo, "Blogland's Man of the People." For one insider's account of the Dean campaign, see Trippi, *The Revolution Will Not Be Televised.*
11. Teachout, quoted in Cone, "The Marketing of a President."
12. Gourevitch, "The Shakeout." See also Manjoo, "Howard Dean's Fatal System Error."
13. Weinberger, "Is There an Echo in Here?"
14. Hydrogen power is a key player in *Wired*'s 1997 technotopian fantasy, "The Long Boom: A History of the Future, 1980–2020," by Schwartz and Leyden. See also Schwartz's 1999 follow-up, "Long Live the Long Boom"; Leslie, "Dawn of the Hydrogen Age"; Davis, "Fast Forward"; Offman, "Fuel Cell"; Silberman, "The Energy Web."
15. Bush, "2003 State of the Union Address."
16. Romm, quoted in Mieszkowski, "Just Say No, to Hydrogen."
17. Lynn, "Hydrogen's Dirty Secret."
18. The phrase is design expert Donald Norman's. See Norman, *The Invisible Computer.*
19. sean, "Phonecams."
20. Rheingold, *Smart Mobs,* xii, xxii.
21. Rheingold, *Smart Mobs,* xvii. Rheingold cites Bariuad, "Text Messaging Becomes a Menace in the Philippines."
22. The Oxford English Dictionary, quoted in AFP, "New Dictionary Makes Room for Baffling Va-Va-Voom."
23. sean, "Manhattan Flash Mob Photos."
24. sean, "Flash Mob in Central Park."
25. Trudeau, "Doonesbury," September 9, 2003.
26. Trudeau, "Doonesbury," September 10, 2003.

Bibliography

Abbate, Janet. *Inventing the Internet*. Cambridge, MA: MIT Press, 2000.

Adams, Ernest. "Three Problems for Interactive Storytellers." *Gamasutra*. December 29, 1999.

Adegoke, Yinka. "Robbie Williams Says Music Piracy Is 'Great.'" *Variety*. January 21, 2003.

AFP. "New Dictionary Makes Room for Baffling Va-Va-Voom." *Yahoo! News*. July 8, 2004. http://news.yahoo.com.

Airy, George Biddle. "On Scheutz's Calculating Machine." *Philosophical Magazine and Journal of Science XII* (July–December, 1856).

Akera, Atsushi. "IBM's Early Adaptation to Cold War Markets: Cuthbert Hurd and His Applied Science Field Men." *Business History Review* 76.4 (Winter 2002): 767–804.

Albini, Steve. "The Problem with Music." *Baffler* 5 (1993). http://www.thebaffler.com/albiniexcerpt.html.

Alsdorf, Matt. "What Is Moore's Law?" *Slate*. October 14, 1999.

"Altair . . . on the Road." *Computer Notes* 1.2 (July 1975): 1.

America's Army. Designed by U.S. Army. http://americasarmy.com.

Anderson, Benedict. *Imagined Community*. London: Verso, 1991.

Anestopoulou, Maria. "Challenging Intellectual Property Law in the Internet: An Overview of the Legal Implications of the MP3 Technology." *Information & Communication Technology Law* 10.3 (2001): 319–337.

Aronowitz, Stanley, and William DiFazio. *The Jobless Future: Sci-Tech and the Dogma of Work*. Minneapolis: University of Minnesota Press, 1994.

Asimov, Isaac. *I. Asimov*. New York: Bantam, 1994.

Augarten, Stan. *Bit by Bit: An Illustrated History of Computers*. New York: Ticknor and Fields, 1984.

"Automation: Electronics for Plenty." *Time*. March 28, 1955.

Avalon, Moses. *Confessions of a Record Producer*. San Francisco: Miller Freeman Books, 1998.

Babbage, Charles. *On the Economy of Machinery and Manufactures*. London: Charles Knight, 1832. Reprint, New York: Frank Cass & Co., 1963.

Bai, Matt. "Hating Hilary." *Wired*. February 2003.

Bakhtin, Mikhail. *The Dialogic Imagination: Four Essays.* Trans. Caryl Emerson and Michael Holquist. Austin: University of Texas Press, 1981.

Balsamo, Anne. *Technologies of the Gendered Body: Reading Cyborg Women.* Durham, NC: Duke University Press, 1996.

Barbrook, Richard. "The High-Tech Gift Economy." *First Monday* 3:12. (December 1998). http://www.firstmonday.org/issues/issue3_12/barbrook/index.html.

———, and Cameron, Andy. "The Californian Ideology." 1998. http://www.hrc.wmin.ac.uk/hrc/theory/californianideo/main/t.4.2.html.

Bardini, Thierry. *Bootstrapping: Douglas Engelbart, Coevolution, and the Origins of Personal Computing.* Stanford, CA: Stanford University Press, 2000.

Bariuad, Arturo. "Text Messaging Becomes a Menace in the Philippines." *Straits Times.* March 3, 2001.

Barlow, John Perry. "Declaration of Independence for Cyberspace." February 8, 1996. http://www.eff.org/~barlow/Declaration-Final.html.

Barol, Bill. "Big Fun in a Small Town." *Newsweek.* May 29, 1989.

Basic Books, Inc. v. Kinko's Graphics Corp. 758 F. Supp. 1522. S.D.N.Y. 1991.

Baym, Nancy. *Tune In, Log On.* Thousand Oaks, CA: Sage Publications, 1999.

Bell and Howell Schools. Advertisement insert. *Popular Electronics.* January 1975.

Beniger, James. *The Control Revolution.* Cambridge, MA: Harvard University Press, 1986.

Benjamin, Walter. "The Work of Art in the Age of Mechanical Reproduction." In *Illuminations.* Trans. Harry Zohn. New York: Schocken, 1968. 217–251.

Berners-Lee, Tim. *Weaving the Web.* New York: HarperBusiness, 2000.

Bérubé, Michael. *Public Access: Literary Theory and American Cultural Politics.* New York: Verso, 1994.

Bijker, Wiebe E., Thomas P. Hughes, and Trevor Pinch. *The Social Construction of Technological Systems: New Directions in the Sociology and History of Technology.* Cambridge, MA: MIT Press, 1987.

Birkerts, Sven. *The Gutenberg Elegies: The Fate of Reading in an Electronic Age.* New York: Fawcett Columbine, 1994.

Blankenship, John. *The Apple House.* New York: Prentice Hall, 1983.

Bloch, Enrst. *The Principle of Hope.* Cambridge, MA: MIT Press, 1995.

Bloomberg News. "Microsoft Executive Says Linux Threatens Innovation." *CNET News.* February 14, 2001. http://news.cnet.com.

Borsook, Paulina. *Cyberselfish.* New York: Public Affairs, 2000.

Bourdieu, Pierre. *Outline of a Theory of Practice.* Trans. Richard Nice. Cambridge: Cambridge University Press, 1977.

Boutin, Paul. "Stop the Clock." *Slate.* March 13, 2003.

Bowden, B. V. *Faster Than Thought: A Symposium on Digital Computing Machines.* New York: Pitman, 1953.

Brand, Stewart. *The Media Lab: Inventing the Future at MIT.* New York: Penguin, 1987.

Braverman, Harry. *Labor and Monopoly Capital.* New York: Monthly Review Press, 1974.

Bricklin, Dan. "The Recording Industry Is Trying to Kill the Goose That Lays the Golden Egg." *Dan Bricklin's Web Site.* September 9, 2002. http://www.bricklin.com/recordsales.htm.

Bromley, Alan G. "Analog Computing Devices." In *Computing Before Computers.* Ed. William Aspray. Ames: Iowa State University Press, 1990. http://ed-thelen.org/comp-hist/CBC.html.

Brook, James, and Iain A. Boal. "Preface." In *Resisting the Virtual Life: The Cultural Politics of Information.* Ed. James Brook and Iain A. Boal. San Francisco: City Lights, 1995. vii–xv.

Bush, George, "2003 State of the Union Address." Washington, D.C. January 28, 2003.

Butler, Judith. *Gender Trouble.* New York: Routledge, 1989.

Campbell-Kelly, Martin, and William Aspray. *Computer: A History of the Information Machine.* New York: Basic, 1996.

Card, Orson Scott. *Ender's Game.* New York: Tor Books, 1985.

———. "Gameplay: Games With No Limits." *Compute.* March 1991: 58.

Carey, James W., with John J. Quirk. "The Mythos of the Electronic Revolution." In *Communication and Culture: Essays on Media and Society.* Boston: Unwin Hyman, 1988. 113–141.

Carlsson, Chris, with Mark Leger, eds. *Bad Attitude: The Processed World Anthology.* New York: Verso, 1990.

Casaaza, J. A. *The Development of Electric Power Transmission: The Role Played by Technology, Institutions, and People.* New York: Institute of Electrical and Electronics Engineers, 1993.

Cassell, Justine, and Henry Jenkins. *From Barbie to Mortal Kombat: Gender and Computer Games.* Cambridge, MA: MIT University Press, 1998.

Cassidy, John. *Dot.con: How America Lost Its Mind and Money in the Internet Era.* New York: Perennial Currents, 2003.

Ceruzzi, Paul E. "From Scientific Instrument to Everyday Appliance: The Emergence of Personal Computers, 1970–77." *History and Technology* 13 (1996): 1–31.

———. *The History of Modern Computing.* Cambridge, MA: MIT Press, 1998.

Chanan, Michael. *Musica Practica.* New York: Verso, 1994.

Chang, Briankle. *Deconstructing Communication.* Minneapolis: University of Minnesota Press, 1996.

Chposky, James, and Ted Leonsis. *Blue Magic: The People, Power and Politics Behind the IBM Personal Computer.* New York: Facts on File, 1988.

Ciment, Michel. *Kubrick.* Trans. Gilbert Adair. New York: Holt, 1982.

Cixous, Hélène. *"Coming to Writing" and Other Essays.* Cambridge, MA: Harvard University Press, 1991.

Cohen, I. Bernard. "Babbage and Aiken." *Annals of the History of Computing* 10.3 (1988): 171–193.

Colbeck, Julian. *Keyfax: Omnibus Edition.* Emeryville, CA: MixBooks, 1996.

Collier, Bruce. *The Little Engines That Could've: The Calculating Machines of Charles Babbage.* New York: Garland, 1990.

Conceiving Ada. Dir. Lynn Hershman-Lesson. Screenplay by Lynn Hershman-Lesson, Eileen Jones, Sadie Plant, Betty A. Toole. Fox Lorber, 1999.

Cone, Edward. "The Marketing of a President." *Baseline.* November 13, 2003. http://www.baselinemag.com/print_article/0,3668,a=112601,00.asp.

Conrad, Michael. *The One Hundred Best TV Commercials.* New York: Times Books, 1999.

Consalvo, Mia. "Hot Dates and Fairy Tale Romances: Studying Sexuality in Video Games." In *The Video Game Theory Reader.* Eds. Mark J. P. Wolf and Bernard Perron. New York: Routledge, 2003. 171–194.

Costikyan, Greg. "Where Stories End and Games Begin." *Game Developer.* September 2000.

Cowan, Ruth Schwartz. "The Consumption Junction: A Proposal for Research Strategies in the Sociology of Technology." In *The Social Construction of Technological Systems.* Ed. Wiebe E. Bijker, Thomas P. Hughes, and Trevor Pinch. Cambridge, MA: MIT Press, 1987. 261–280.

———. *More Work for Mother: The Ironies of Household Technology from the Open Hearth to the Microwave.* New York: Basic, 1985.

Cringely, Robert X. *Accidental Empires.* New York: Addison-Wesley, 1992.

Croal, N'Gai. "*Sims* Family Values." *Newsweek.* November 25, 2002.

Cronon, William. *Changes in the Land.* New York: Hill and Wang, 1983.

Cummings, Jeanne. "The E-Team: Behind the Dean Surge: A Gang of Bloggers and Webmasters." *Wall Street Journal.* October 14, 2003.

Davis, Joshua. "Fast Forward." *Wired.* May 2004.

Davis, Mike. *City of Quartz: Excavating the Future in Los Angeles.* New York: Vintage, 1990.

de Certeau, Michel. *Heterologies: Discourse on the Other.* Trans. Brian Massumi. Minneapolis: University of Minnesota Press, 1984.

———. *The Practice of Everyday Life.* Berkeley: University of California Press, 1984.

De Vries, Daniel. *The Films of Stanley Kubrick.* Grand Rapids, MI: William B. Eerdmans, 1973.

Deleuze, Giles, and Felix Guattari. *Anti-Oedipus: Capitalism and Schizophrenia.* Trans. Robert Hurley, Mark Seem, and Helen R. Lane. New York: Viking, 1977.

Dennett, Daniel. "When HAL Kills, Who's to Blame? Computer Ethics." In *HAL's Legacy: 2001's Computer in Dream and Reality.* Ed. David G. Stork. Cambridge, MA: MIT Press, 1997. 351–365.

Derrida, Jacques. *Of Grammatology.* Trans. Gayatri Chakravorty Spivak. Baltimore: Johns Hopkins University Press, 1974.

Dery, Mark. *Escape Velocity: Cyberculture at the End of the Century.* New York: Grove Press, 1997.

Desk Set. Dir. Walter Lang. Screenplay by Henry and Phoebe Ephron. Fox, 1957.

Dibbell, Julian. *Play Money.* http://www.juliandibbell.com/playmoney/.

———. "A Rape in Cyberspace." *Village Voice.* December 23, 1993.

———. *My Tiny Life: Crime and Passion in a Virtual World.* New York: Holt, 1998.

———. "The Unreal Estate Boom." *Wired.* Jan 2003.

Dickens, Homer. *The Films of Katharine Hepburn.* New York: Citadel, 1990.

Downey, Greg. "Virtual Webs, Physical Technologies, and Hidden Workers: The Spaces of Labor in Information Internetworks." *Technology and Culture* 42.2 (2001): 209–235.

du Gay, Paul, Stuart Hall, Linda Janes, Hugh Mackay, and Keith Negus. *Doing Cultural Studies: The Story of the Sony Walkman.* Thousand Oaks, CA: Sage Publications, 1997.

Dyer, Richard. "Entertainment and Utopia." In *Only Entertainment.* New York: Routledge, 1992. 17–34.

Dyer-Witheford, Nick. *Cyber-Marx.* Urbana: University of Illinois Press, 1999.

Eckert, J. Presper. "Development of the ENIAC." Interview by David Allison. February 2, 1988. Video recording (RU 9537). Smithsonian Institution Archives.

Editors of Perseus Publishing, eds. *We've Got Blog: How Weblogs Are Changing Our Culture.* Cambridge, MA: Perseus Publishing, 2002.

Edsall, Thomas B. "Lott Decried for Part of Salute to Thurmond." *Washington Post.* December 7, 2002.

Edwards, Paul N. *The Closed World: Computers and the Politics of Discourse in Cold War America.* Cambridge, MA: MIT Press, 1996.

Electric Dreams. Dir. Steve Barron. Screenplay by Rusty Lemorande. MGM, 1984.

"Electronic Arts Posts Record Sims 2 Sales." Associated Press. September 29, 2004.

Ellison, David. "Streetfighter." *Polygraph* 8 (1996): 153–176.

Entertainment Software Association. "2004 Sales, Demographics and Usage Data: Essential Facts About the Computer and Video Game Industry." http://www.theesa.com/EFBrochure.pdf.

Eskelinen, Markku. "From Markku Eskelinen's Online Response." In *First Person: New Media as Story, Performance, and Game*. Eds. Noah Wardrip-Fruin and Pat Harrigan. Cambridge, MA: MIT Press, 2004: 120–121.

———. "The Gaming Situation." *Game Studies* 1 (July 2001). http://www.gamestudies.org/0101/eskelinen.

FAIR. "Media Advisory: Media Play Catch-Up on Lott's Latest Endorsement of Racism." December 11, 2002. http://www.fair.org/press-release/lott-advisory.html.

Fatsis, Stefan. "The Home Front: Executives Demand More of Home Offices." *Wall Street Journal*. September 22, 1995.

Ferguson, Charles H., and Charles R. Morris. *The Computer Wars: The Fall of IBM and the Future of Global Technology*. New York: Times, 1993.

Fischer, Claude S. *America Calling: The Social History of the Telephone to 1940*. Berkeley: University of California P, 1992.

Fischling, Daniel, Veronica Hollinger, and Andrew Taylor. "'The Charisma Leak': A Conversation with William Gibson and Bruce Sterling." *Science-Fiction Studies* 19.1 (March 1992): 1–16.

Flamm, Kenneth. *Creating the Computer: Government, Industry, and High Technology*. Washington, D.C.: Brookings Institution Press, 1988.

Forrester Research Press Release. "Downloads Did Not Cause the Music Slump, But They Can Cure It, Reports Forrester Research." August 13, 2002. http://www.forrester.com/ER/Press/Release/0,1769,741,00.html.

Frasca, Gonzalo. "Simulation versus Narrative: Introduction to Ludology." In *The Video Game Theory Reader*. Eds. Mark J. P. Wolf and Bernard Perron. New York: Routledge, 2003, 221–236.

Freeman, David. *Creating Emotion in Games: The Craft and Art of Emotioneering*. Indianapolis, IN: New Riders, 2004.

Friedman, Ted. "Capitalism: The Final Frontier." *Stim* 5.1. (September 1996). http://www.stim.com/Stim-x/0996September/Features/econ.html.

———. "*Civilization* and Its Discontents: Simulation, Subjectivity, and Space." In *On a Silver Platter: CD-ROMs and the Promises of a New Technology*. Ed. Greg M. Smith. New York: New York University Press, 1999. 132–150.

———. "Making Sense of Software: Computer Games and Interactive Textuality." In *CyberSociety: Computer-Mediated Communication and Community*. Ed. Steven G. Jones. Thousand Oaks, CA: Sage, 1995. 73–89. Reprinted as "The Semiotics of SimCity." *First Monday* 4.4 (April 1999). http://firstmonday.org/issues/issue4_4/friedman/index.html.

———. "Vinyl." In *alt.culture: An A-to-Z Guide to the '90s—Underground, Online, and Over-the-Counter*. Eds. Steven Daly and Nathaniel Wice. New York: Harper Perennial, 1995. 263.

Fuller, Mary, and Henry Jenkins. "Nintendo and New World Travel Writing: A

Dialogue." In *CyberSociety: Computer-MediatedCommunication and Community.* Ed. Steven G. Jones. Thousand Oaks, CA: Sage, 1995.

Gale, Wayne. "Straight, Gay, or Binary." *Suck.* May 2, 1997. http://www.suck.com/daily/97/05/02/daily.html.

Garfinkel, Simson. "Happy Birthday, HAL." *Wired.* January 1997.

Garson, Barbara. *The Electronic Sweatshop: How Computers Are Transforming the Office of the Future into the Factory of the Past.* New York: Penguin, 1988.

Gates, Bill, with Nathan Myhrvold and Peter Rinearson. *The Road Ahead.* New York: Viking, 1995.

Geertz, Clifford. *The Interpretation of Cultures.* New York: Basic, 1973.

Gehr, Richard. "Fuzzy, Inc." *Rubrics and Tendrils of Richard Gehr.* http://www.levity.com/rubric/fuzzy.html.

Gibson, William. "Burning Chrome." In *Burning Chrome.* New York: Ace, 1987. 168–191.

———. *Neuromancer.* New York: Ace, 1984.

———, and Bruce Sterling. *The Difference Engine.* New York: Bantam, 1991.

Girls on Film. "Classic Movies of the Workplace." *Electra.* 1998. http://web.archive.org/web/19990218174121/http://electra.com/gof11.html.

Goldstein, Paul. *Copyright's Highway: The Law and Lore of Copyright from Gutenberg to the Celestial Jukebox.* New York: Hill and Wang, 1994.

Goldstine, Herman H. *The Computer from Pascal to von Neumann.* Princeton, NJ: Princeton University Press, 1993.

Goodell, Jeff. *The Cyberthief and the Samurai.* New York: Dell, 1996.

Gourevitch, Philip. "The Shakeout." *New Yorker.* Feburary 9, 2004.

Gramsci, Antonio. *Selections from the Prison Notebooks.* Ed. and trans. Quintin Hoare and Geoffrey Nowell Smith. New York: International Publishers, 1971.

Greene, Michael. "The Insidious Virus of Music Downloading." *GRAMMY Magazine.* February 27, 2002.

Greene, T. "Ballmer: Linux Is a Cancer." *Register.* June 2, 2001. http://www.theregister.co.uk/content/4/19396.html.

Grossberg, Lawrence. "The Formation(s) of Cultural Studies: An American in Birmingham." *Strategies* 2 (Fall 1989): 114–149.

Groundhog Day. Directed by Harold Ramis. Screenplay by Danny Rubin and Harold Ramis. Columbia/TriStar Studios, 1993.

Grove, Andrew S. *Only the Paranoid Survive.* New York: Doubleday, 1999.

Habermas, Jürgen. *The Structural Transformation of the Public Sphere.* Trans. Thomas Burger with Frederick Lawrence. Cambridge, MA: MIT Press, 1991.

Haddon, Leslie. "The Home Computer: The Making of a Consumer Electronic." *Science as Culture* 2 (1988): 7–51.

———, and David Skinner. "The Enigma of the Micro: Lessons from the British Home Computer Boom." *Social Science Computer Review* 9.3 (Fall 1991): 435–447.

Hafner, Kate, and Matthew Lyon. *Where Wizards Stay Up Late*. New York: Simon & Schuster, 1996.

Hall, Stuart. "Encoding, Decoding." In *Culture, Media, Language: Working Papers in Cultural Studies, 1972–79*. Ed. Centre for Contemporary Cultural Studies. London: Hutchinson, 1980. 128–138.

Haraway, Donna. "Manifesto for Cyborgs: Science, Technology, and Socialist Feminism in the 1980s." *Socialist Review* 80 (1985): 65–108.

Hartwell, David G. *Age of Wonders*. New York: Tor, 1984.

Harvey, David. *The Condition of Postmodernity*. Cambridge, MA: Basil Blackwell, 1989.

Hayes, Brian. "Terabyte Territory." *Computing Science*. May–June 2002.

Heims, Steve J. *The Cybernetics Group*. Cambridge, MA: MIT Press, 1991.

Henwood, Doug. *After the New Economy*. New York: New Press, 2003.

———. "Where's the Payoff?" *Left Business Observer* 79 (October 1997): 2–3.

Herz, J. C. "Game Theory: The Sims Who Die With the Most Toys Win," *New York Times*. February 10, 2000.

Highfield, Roger. "Machine May Prove History Books Wrong." *Daily Telegraph*. August 17, 1989.

Hiltzik, Michael. *Dealers of Lightning: Xerox PARC and the Dawn of the Computer Age*. New York: Harper Collins, 1999.

Hochschild, Arlie Russell. *The Time Bind*. New York: Metropolitan Books, 1997.

"The Home Front: What's Hot, and Not, in Home Design." *Wall Street Journal*. December 6, 1996.

Horton, Cleveland. "TV Commercial of the Decade: Apple's Bold '1984' Scores on All Fronts." *Advertising Age*. January 1, 1990.

Huffington, Arianna. "In Praise of Making a Stink." *Salon*. December 20, 2002. http://www.salon.com/news/col/huff/2002/12/20/stink/print.html.

Hyman, R. Anthony. "Whiggism in the History of Science and the Study of the Life and Work of Charles Babbage." *The Babbage Pages*. http://www.ex.ac.uk/BABBAGE/whiggism.html.

Ian, Janis. "The Internet Debacle—An Alternative View." *Performing Songwriter*. May 2002. http://www.janisian.com/article-internet_debacle.html.

International Correspondence Schools. Advertisement. *Popular Electronics*. January 1975.

"Interview with Greg Bear." *Hailing Frequencies*. May–June 1995.

Jacoby, Russell. *The End of Utopia*. New York: Basic Books, 2000.

———. Review of *Looking Backward: From 2000 to 1887*. *Harper's Magazine*. December 2000.

Jameson, Fredric. *Marxism and Form*. Princeton, NJ: Princeton University Press, 1974.

———. *Postmodernism, or, the Cultural Logic of Late Capitalism*. Durham, NC: Duke University Press, 1991.

———. "Reification and Utopia in Mass Culture." *Social Text* 1 (1979): 130–148.

———. *The Seeds of Time*. New York: Columbia University Press, 1994.

———. "World Reduction in Le Guin: The Emergence of Utopian Narrative." *Science Fiction Studies* 7 (November 1975): 23–39.

Jenkins, Henry. "Game Design as Narrative Architecture." In *First Person: New Media as Story, Performance, and Game*. Eds. Noah Wardrip-Fruin and Pat Harrigan. Cambridge, MA: MIT Press, 2004: 118–130.

———. "Games, the New Lively Art." In *Handbook of Computer Game Studies*. Eds. Jeffrey Goldstein and Joost Raessens. Cambridge, MA: MIT Press, 2005. http://web.mit.edu/21fms/www/faculty/henry3/GamesNewLively.html.

———. *Textual Poachers*. New York: Routledge, 1992.

———, and David Thorburn, eds. *Democracy and New Media*. Cambridge, MA: MIT Press, 2003.

Johnson, Bradley. "10 Years After 1984." *Advertising Age*. January 10, 1994. Reprinted as "'1984' Revolutionized Ad Industry." *Business Marketing* February 1994.

Johnson, Richard. "The Story So Far: And for the Transformations." In *Introduction to Contemporary Cultural Studies*. Ed. David Punter. London: Longman, 1986. 277–313.

Juul, Jesper. "A Clash between Games and Narrative." Paper presented at the Digital Arts and Culture Conference, Bergen. November 1998. http://www.jesperjuul.dk/text/clash_between_game_and_narrative.html.

———. "Games Telling Stories?" *Game Studies* 1 (July 2001): http://www.gamestudies.org/0101/juul-gts.

Kadetsky, Elizabeth. "Silicon Valley Sweatshops: High-Tech's Dirty Little Secret." *The Nation*. April 19, 1993.

Kagan, Norman. *The Cinema of Stanley Kubrick*. New York: Continuum, 1989.

Kaplan, Philip J. *F'd Companies: Spectacular Dot-com Flameouts*. New York: Simon & Schuster, 2002.

Kasavin, Greg. "*Full Spectrum Warrior* Review." *Gamespot*. http://www.gamespot.com/xbox/strategy/fullspectrumwarrior/review.html.

Kawasaki, Guy. *The Macintosh Way*. New York: Harper Perennial, 1990.

———. *Selling the Dream*. New York: Harper Business, 1991.

Kellner, Douglas. "Ernst Bloch, Utopia and Ideology Critique." *Illuminations*. http://www.tau.edu/english/dab/illuminations/kell1.html.

———, and Harry O'Hara. "Utopia and Marxism in Ernst Bloch." *New German Critique* 9 (Fall 1976): 11–34.

Kelso, Brendan. *Being Fuzzy*. New York: Hyperion, 1993.

Kestenbaum, David S. "Cyberfest Celebrates HAL in Urbana." *Wired*. March 17, 1997.

Kidder, Tracy. *The Soul of a New Machine*. New York: Avon Books, 1981.

Kidwell, Peggy A., and Paul E. Ceruzzi. *Landmarks in Digital Computing: A Smithsonian Pictorial History*. Washington, D.C.: Smithsonian Institution Press, 1994.

Kingdom of Loathing. Designed by Jick. http://www.kingdomofloathing.com.

Kinsley, Michael. "Lott's Adventures in Gaffeland." *Time*. December 23, 2002.

Klein, Naomi. *No Logo: No Space, No Choice, No Jobs*. New York: Picador, 1999.

Kline, David. "Infobahn Warrior." *Wired*. July 1994.

Kolko, Beth, Lisa Nakamura, and Gilbert Rodman. *Race in Cyberspace*. New York: Routledge, 2000.

Kosko, Bart. *Fuzzy Thinking*. New York: Hyperion, 1993.

Kroll, Zoey. "Technically Speaking: An Interview with Sadie Plant by Zoey Kroll." June 1999. http://www.penelopes.org/archives/pages/ntic/newmed/sadie.htm.

Kurtz, Howard. "A Hundred-Candle Story and How to Blow It." *Washington Post*. December 16, 2004.

Kurzweil, Ray. *The Age of Spiritual Machines: When Computers Exceed Human Intelligence*. New York: Penguin, 2002.

Lan, Ted M. "Total Kitchen Information System." *Byte*. January 1976.

Larson, Eric. *The Naked Consumer: How Our Private Lives Become Public Commodities*. New York: Penguin, 1992.

Latour, Bruno. *Aramis, or the Love of Technology*. Trans. Catherine Porter. Cambridge, MA: Harvard University Press, 1996.

———. *Science in Action: How to Follow Scientists and Engineers Through Society*. Cambridge, MA: Harvard University Press, 1987.

Laurel, Brenda. *Computers as Theater*. New York: Addison-Wesley, 1993.

———. *Utopian Entrepreneur*. Cambridge, MA: MIT Press, 2001.

Lea, G. "MS' Ballmer: Linux Is Communism." *Register*. July 31, 2000. http://www.theregister.co.uk/content/1/12266.html.

"Lemmings." Apple Computer. Advertisement. Chiat/Day, 1985.

Lenhart, Amanda, with John Horrigan, Lee Rainie, Katherine Allen, Angie Boyce, Mary Madden, and Erin O'Grady. "The Ever-Shifting Internet Population." *The Pew Internet and American Life Project*. April 16, 2003. http://www.pewinternet.org/reports/pdfs/PIP_Shifting_Net_Pop_Report.pdf.

Leslie, Jacques. "Dawn of the Hydrogen Age." *Wired*. October 1997.

Lessig, Lawrence. *Code and Other Laws of Cyberspace*. New York: Basic Books, 2000.

———. *Free Culture: How Big Media Uses Technology to Lock Down Culture and Control Creativity.* New York: Penguin, 2004.

———. *The Future of Ideas: The Fate of the Commons in a Connected World.* New York: Vintage, 2002.

Levy, Steven. *Hackers: Heroes of the Computer Revolution.* New York: Dell, 1984.

———. *Insanely Great: The Life and Times of the Macintosh, the Computer That Changed Everything.* New York: Viking, 1994.

Light, Jennifer S. "When Computers Were Women." *Technology and Culture* 40.3 (1999): 455–483.

Ligorio, Tatiana. "Postmodernism and Fuzzy Systems." *Kybernetes* 33.8 (2004): 1312–1319.

Littman, Jonathan. *The Fugitive Game: Online with Kevin Mitnick.* New York: Little, Brown, 1997.

Linzmayer, Owen W. *Apple Confidential.* San Francisco: No Starch Press, 1999.

———. *The Mac Bathroom Reader.* San Francisco: Sybex, 1994, 219–232.

Lockard, Joseph. "Progressive Politics, Electronic Individualism, and the Myth of Virtual Community." In *Internet Culture.* Ed. David Porter. New York: Routledge, 1997.

Louderback, Jim. "A Network Computer—for your Kitchen." *ZDNet Anchordesk.* November 1, 1999. http://web.archive.org/web/19991127104629/http://www.zdnet.com/anchordesk/story/story_4036.html.

Lovelace, Ada. *Ada: Enchantress of Numbers: Prophet of the Computer Age.* Ed. Betty A. Toole. New York: Strawberry Press, 1998.

Lubar, Steven. *InfoCulture.* Boston: Houghton Mifflin, 1993.

Ludlow, Peter. *The Alphaville Herald.* http://www.alphavilleherald.com/.

———, ed. *High Noon on the Electronic Frontier: Conceptual Issues in Cyberspace.* Cambridge, MA: MIT Press, 1996.

Lynn, Barry C. "Hydrogen's Dirty Secret." *Mother Jones.* May/June 2003.

MacKinnon, Catharine. *Only Words.* Cambridge, MA: Harvard University Press, 1993.

Malone, Michael S. *The Microprocessor: A Biography.* New York: Springer-Verlag, 1995.

———. "Forget Moore's Law." *Red Herring.* February 2003. http://web.archive.rg/web/20030315195403/http://www.redherring.com/mag/issue122/5945.html.

Manjoo, Farhad. "Blogland's Man of the People." *Salon.* July 3, 2003. http://www.salon.com/tech/feature/2003/07/03/dean_web/print.html.

———. "Howard Dean's Fatal System Error." *Salon.* January 21, 2004. http://www.salon.com/tech/feature/2004/01/21/dean_internet/print.html.

Mann, Charles C. "The Year the Music Dies." *Wired.* February 2003.

Marich, Bob. "The Real Blitz Begins." *Advertising Age.* January 30, 1984.

Markoff, John. "Chip Progress May Soon Be Hitting Barrier." *New York Times.* October 9, 1999.

―――. "Is There Life after Silicon Valey's Fast Lane?" *New York Times.* April 9, 2003.

Marshall, Ian, and Danah Zohar. *Who's Afraid of Schrodinger's Cat?* New York: Quill, 1998.

Marshall, Joshua Micah. *Talking Points Memo.* December 13, 2002, 5:16 PM.

Martin, Brian. "Against Intellectual Property." http://www.eff.org/IP/?f=against _ip.article.txt.

Marvin, Carolyn. *When Old Technologies Were New.* Cambridge: Oxford University Press, 1990.

Mattis, Michael. "Repurposing Ada." *Salon.* March 16, 1999. http://archive .salon.com/21st/feature/1999/03/16feature.html.

Maxis Software Toys Catalog. Orinda, CA: Maxis, 1992.

McCaffery, Larry. "An Interview with William Gibson." *Storming the Reality Studio: A Casebook of Cyberpunk and Postmodern Fiction.* Ed. Larry McCaffery. Durham, NC: Duke University Press, 1991. 263–285.

McChesney, Robert W. *The Problem of the Media: U.S. Communiction Politics in the Twenty-First Century.* New York: Monthly Review Press, 2004.

McCloud, Scott. *Understanding Comics.* New York: Perennial Currents, 1994.

McCourt, Tom, and Patrick Burkart. "When Creators, Corporations and Consumers Collide: Napster and the Development of On-Line Music Distribution." *Media, Culture & Society* 25 (2003): 333–350.

McGovern, Gerry. "The Technology Productivity Paradox." *New Thinking.* Oct 29, 2001. http://www.gerrymcgovern.com/nt/2001/nt_2001_10_29_productivity.htm.

McKenzie, John. "Response by John McKenzie." In *First Person: New Media as Story, Performance, and Game.* Eds. Noah Wardrip-Fruin and Pat Harrigan. Cambridge, MA: MIT Press, 2004. 118–120.

McKinsey Global Institute. "U.S. Productivity Growth, 1995–2000." October 2001. http://www.mckinsey.com/knowledge/mgi/productivity/index.asp.

McLeod, Kembrew. *Owning Culture.* New York: Peter Lang, 2001.

McNeill, Daniel, and Paul Freiberger. *Fuzzy Logic.* New York: Simon & Schuster, 1993.

Meston, Zach. "The MMORPG Morass." *Surge* 3 (Summer 2004): 64.

michael. "Greene's Grammy Speech Debunked." *Slashdot.* March 7, 2002. http://slashdot.org/articles/02/03/07/2132243.shtml?tid=141

Mieszkowski, Katharine. "Just Say No, to Hydrogen." *Salon.* April 29, 2004. http://www.salon.com/tech/feature/2004/04/29/hydrogen_no/print.html.

Miller, James. *Flowers in the Dustbin: The Rise of Rock and Roll, 1947–1977.* New York: Simon & Schuster, 1999.

Millman, Nancy. "Apple's '1984' Spot: A Love/Hate Story." *Advertising Age.* January 30, 1984.

Moby. Liner notes to *18.* V2, 2002.

Moglen, Eben. "Anarchism Triumphant: Free Software and the Death of Copyright." *First Monday* 4.8 (August 1999). http://firstmonday.org/issues/issue4_8/moglen/.

Moody, Fred. *I Sing the Body Electronic: A Year with Microsoft on the Multimedia Frontier.* New York: Viking, 1995.

Moore, Gordon E. "Cramming More Components onto Integrated Circuits." *Electronics* 38.8 (April 19, 1965). ftp://download.intel.com/research/silicon/moorespaper.pdf.

Morris, Meaghan. "Banality in Cultural Studies." In *Logics of Television.* Ed. Patricia Mellencamp. Bloomington: Indiana University Press, 1990: 14–40.

———. "Cultural Studies and Public Participation." Talk sponsored by the University of North Carolina Program in Cultural Studies. November 10, 1999.

Mossberger, Karen, Caroline J. Talbert, and Mary Starsbury. *Virtual Inequality: Beyond the Digital Divide.* Washington, D.C.: Georgetown University Press, 2003.

Myers, David. "Chris Crawford and Computer Game Aesthetics." *Journal of Popular Culture* 24.2 (1990): 17–28.

———. "Computer Game Genres." *Play and Culture* 3 (1990): 286–301.

———. "Computer Game Semiotics." *Play and Culture* 4 (1991): 334–346.

———. "Time Symbol Transformations, and Computer Games." *Play and Culture* 5 (1992): 441–457.

Nakamura, Lisa. *Cybertypes: Race, Ethnicity and Identity on the Internet.* New York: Routledge, 2002.

"Napster Timeline." *CNN.com.* 2001. http://www.cnn.com/SPECIALS/2001/napster/timeline.html.

Negativland. "Shiny, Aluminum, Plastic, and Digital." *Negativ World Wide Webland.* http://www.negativland.com/minidis.html.

Negoita, Constantin. "Postmodernism, Cybernetics and Fuzzy Set Theory." *Kybernetes* 31.7/8 (2002): 1043–1049.

Negroponte, Nicholas. *Being Digital.* New York: Vintage Books, 1995.

Neilsen, Jacob. "Voice Interfaces: Assessing the Potential." *Jacob Neilsen's Alertbox.* January 27, 2003. http://www.useit.com/alertbox/20030127.html.

Nelson, Ted. *Computer Lib/Dream Machines.* Redmond, MA: Microsoft Press, 1987.

Nelson, Thomas Allen. *Kubrick: Inside a Film Artist's Maze.* Bloomington: Indiana University Press, 1982.

Newman, James. *Videogames*. New York: Routledge, 2004.

Nicholls, Peter, and Cornel Robu. "Sense of Wonder." In *The Encyclopedia of Science Fiction*. Eds. John Clute and Peter Nicholls. New York: St. Martin's, 1993. 1083–1085.

"1984." Apple Computer. Advertisement. Dir. Ridley Scott. Chiat/Day, 1984.

Noble, David. *Forces of Production: A Social History of Automation*. New York: Knopf, 1984.

———. *Progress without People: New Technology, Unemployment, and the Message of Resistance*. Toronto: Between the Lines, 1995.

Norberg, Arthur L., and Judy E. O'Neill, with contributions by Kelly J. Freedman. *Transforming Computer Technology: Information Processing for the Pentagon, 1962–1986*. Baltimore: Johns Hopkins University Press, 1996.

Norman, Donald. *The Invisible Computer*. Cambridge, MA: MIT Press, 1999.

NRI Schools. Advertisement. *Popular Electronics*. January 1975.

Nye, David E. *American Technological Sublime*. Cambridge, MA: MIT Press, 1994.

———. *Electrifying America: Social Meanings of a New Technology*. Cambridge, MA: MIT Press, 1990.

Offman, Craig. "Fuel Cell." *Wired*. July 2001.

Ordonez, Jennifer. "The Record Industry Owes You $20." *Wall Street Journal*. Feburary 5, 2003.

Owens, Larry. "Vannevar Bush and the Differential Analyzer: The Text and Context of an Early Computer." *Technology and Culture* 27.1 (January 1986): 63–95.

Panshin, Alexei, and Cory Panshin. *The World Beyond the Hill*. Los Angeles: J. P. Tarcher, 1989.

Perlman, Marc. "Consuming Audio: An Introduction to Tweak Theory." In *Music and Technoculture*. Ed. Rene T. A. Lysloff and Leslie C. Gay, Jr. Middletown, CT: Wesleyan University Press, 2003: 352–353.

Peters, John Durham. *Speaking into the Air*. Chicago: University of Chicago Press, 2000.

Petroski, Henry. *The Pencil: A History of Design and Circumstance*. New York: Knopf, 1992.

Pfaffenberger, Bryan. "The Social Meaning of the Personal Computer: Or, Why the Personal Computer Revolution Was No Revolution." *Anthropological Quarterly* 61.1 (January 1989): 39–47.

Pinch, Trevor, and Wiebe Bijker. "The Social Construction of Fact and Artifacts: Or How the Sociology of Science and the Sociology of Technology Might Benefit Each Other." In *The Social Construction of Technological Systems: New Directions in the Sociology and History of Technology*. Eds. Wiebe Bijker, Thomas Hughes, and Trevor Pinch. Cambridge, MA: MIT Press, 1987.

Plant, Sadie. *Zeroes and Ones: Digital Women and the New Technoculture.* New York: Doubleday, 1997.

Podhoretz, John. "The Internet's First Scalp." *New York Post.* December 13, 2002. http://web.archive.org/web/20021226070916/http://www.nypost.com/postopinion/opedcolumnists/51499.htm.

Pool, Ithiel de Sola. *Technologies of Freedom.* Cambridge, MA: Harvard University Press, 1983.

"Pop Quiz: What Was the First Personal Computer?" *Blinkenlights Archaeological Institute.* http://www.blinkenlights.com/pc.shtml.

Pringle, Kirby. "*2001:* 'You Are Free to Speculate.'" *Obelisk: The Cyberfest Newssite.* http://www.boraski.com/obelisk/cinema/s_2001speculate.html.

Ray, Robert. *A Certain Tendency of the Hollywood Cinema, 1930–1980.* Princeton, NJ: Princeton University Press, 1985.

Raymond, Eric. *The Cathedral and the Bazaar.* Sebastpol, CA: O'Reilly and Associates, 1999.

———, ed. *The New Hacker's Dictionary—3rd Edition.* Cambridge, MA: MIT Press, 1996.

Reeder, S. "Designing Visions." *Kids & Computers.* December 1992.

Reeves, Jimmie L., and Richard Campbell. *Cracked Coverage: Television News, The Anti-Cocaine Crusade, and the Reagan Legacy.* Durham, NC: Duke University Press, 1994.

Rezendes, Paul. "Keeping an Eye on the Scientists: Bart Kosko's Fuzzy Thinking Tries to Save Logical Positivism." *The Examined Life On-Line Philosophy Journal* 1.3 (Fall 2000). http://examinedlifejournal.com/articles/template.php?shorttitle=fuzzy&authorid=14.

Rheingold, Howard. *Smart Mobs: The Next Social Revolution.* New York: Basic Books, 2002.

———. *The Virtual Community: Homesteading on the Electronic Frontier.* New York: Addison-Wesley, 1993.

———. *Virtual Reality.* New York: Touchstone, 1991.

Richards, Jay W., ed. *Are We Spiritual Machines? Ray Kurzwel vs. the Critics of Strong A.I.* Seattle: Discover Institute, 2002.

Roach, Stephen S. "The Productivity Paradox." *New York Times.* November 30, 2003.

Robbins, Bruce, ed. *The Phantom Public Sphere.* Minneapolis: University of Minnesota Press, 1993.

Roberts, H. Edward and William Yates. "Altair 8800." *Popular Electronics.* January 1975.

Romm, Joseph J. *The Hype about Hydrogen: Fact and Fiction in the Race to Save the Climate.* New York: Island Press, 2004.

Rorty, Richard. *Achieving Our Country.* Cambridge, MA: Harvard University Press, 1999.

Rosemont, Franklin. "Edward Bellamy." In *Encyclopedia of the American Left*. Ed. Mari Jo Buhle, Paul Buhle, and Dan Georgakas. University of Illinois Press, 1990. 79–84.

Rosenberg, Donald. *Open Source: The Unauthorized White Papers*. Foster City, CA: IDG Books, 2000.

Rosetto, Louis. "Why Wired?" *Wired*. January 1993.

Ross, Andrew. *The Chicago Gangster Theory of Life*. London: Verso, 1995.

———. "The Mental Labor Problem." *Social Text* 63 (2000): 1–31.

———. *Strange Weather: Culture, Science and Technology in the Age of Limits*. New York: Verso, 1991.

Rothenbuhler, Eric W., and John Durham Peters. "Defining Phonography: An Experiment in Theory." *Musical Quarterly* 81.2 (Summer 1997): 242–264.

Russo, Vito. *The Celluloid Closet*. New York: Perennial, 1987.

Sackett, Susan. *The Hollywood Reporter Book of Box Office Hits*. New York: Billboard, 1990.

Safire, William. "Cyberlingo." *New York Times*. December 11, 1994.

———. "Virtual Reality." *New York Times*. September 13, 1992.

Salen, Katie, and Eric Zimmerman. *Rules of Play: Game Design Fundamentals*. Cambridge, MA: MIT Press, 2003.

Salsberg, Art. "The Home Computer Is Here!" *Popular Electronics*. January 1975.

———. "Jaded Memory," *InfoWorld*. November 12, 1984.

Schaffer, Simon. "Babbage's Intelligence: Calculating Engines and the Factory System." *Critical Inquiry* 21 (Autumn 1994): 203–227.

Scholder, Amy, and Eric Zimmerman. *Replay: Game Design and Game Culture*. New York: Peter Lang, 2003.

Schudson, Michael. *The Power of News*. Cambridge, MA: Harvard University Press, 1995.

Schwartz, Peter. "Long Live the Long Boom." *Wired*. September 1999.

———, and Peter Leyden "The Long Boom: A History of the Future, 1980–2020." *Wired*. July 1997.

Sculley, John. *Odyssey*. New York: Harper & Row, 1987.

Seagal, Howard. *Technological Utopianism in American Culture*. Chicago: University of Chicago Press, 1986.

sean. "Flash Mob in Central Park." *cheesebikini?* July 24, 2003. http://www.cheesebikini.com/archives/000300.html.

———. "Manhattan Flash Mob Photos." *cheesebikini?* June 17, 2003. http://www.cheesebikini.com/archives/000275.html.

———. "Phonecams: Beyond the Hype." *cheesebikini?* November 19, 2003. http://www.cheesebikini.com/archives/000901.html.

Segaller, Stephen. *Nerds 2.0.1: A Brief History of the Internet*. New York: TV Books, 1998.

Seldes, Gilbert. *The Seven Lively Arts*. New York: Sagmore Press, 1957.

Shapiro, Carl, and Hal R. Varian. *Information Rules*. Boston: Harvard Business School Press, 1999.

Shapiro, Robert. "Fantasy Economics." *Slate*. February 4, 2003. http://slate.msn.com/id/2078053.

Shapiro, Samantha. "The Dean Connection." *New York Times Magazine*. December 7, 2003.

Shelley, Bruce. *Sid Meier's Civilization Player's Manual*. Hunt Valley, MD: MicroProse Software, 1991.

Shimomura, Tsutomu, with John Markoff. *Takedown*. New York: Hyperion, 1996.

Shurkin, Joel. *Engines of the Mind: A History of the Computer*. New York: Norton, 1984.

Sichel, Daniel E. *The Computer Revolution: An Economic Perspective*. Washington, D.C.: Brookings Institution Press, 1997.

Sid Meier's Civilization. Designed by Sid Meier. MicroProse Software, 1991.

Silberman, Steve. "The Energy Web." *Wired*. July 2001.

Silverman, Ben. "Greene's Speech Misses the Mark and Why You Shouldn't Use KaZaa." *dMusic*. March 5, 2002. http://news.dmusic.com/article/4556.

SimCity. Designed by Will Wright. Maxis Software, 1987.

Sklar, Robert. *Subversive Pleasures: Bakhtin, Cultural Criticism, and Film*. Baltimore: Johns Hopkins University Press, 1992.

Slatalla, Michelle, and Joshua Quittner. *Masters of Deception: The Gang That Ruled Cyberspace*. New York: Harper Perennial, 1995.

Sloterkijk, Peter. *Critique of Cynical Reason*. Trans. Michael Eldred. London: Verso Books, 1988.

Slouka, Mark. *War of the Worlds*. New York: Basic, 1995.

Smith, Douglas K., and Robert C. Alexander. *Fumbling the Future: How Xerox Invented, Then Ignored, the First Personal Computer*. New York: William Morrow and Co., 1988.

Solomon, Les. "Solomon's Memory." In *Digital Deli*. Ed. Steve Ditlea. New York: Workman, 1984. 36–41.

Solow, Robert. "We'd Better Watch Out." *New York Times*. July 12, 1987.

"Solving the Paradox." *The Economist*. Sept 21, 2000.

Soni, Vivasvan. "The Promise: When Parallel Lines Touch." Unpublished paper.

Sonic Outlaws. Dir. by Craig Baldwin. Another Cinema, 1995.

Sorkin, Michael, ed. *Variations on a Theme Park*. New York: Noonday, 1992.

Spigel, Lynn. *Make Room for TV: Television and the Family Ideal in Postwar America*. Chicago: University of Chicago Press, 1992.

———. *Welcome to the Dreamhouse*. Durham, NC: Duke University Press, 2001.

Stallman, Richard M. "Byte Interview with Richard Stallman." July 1986. http://www.gnu.org/gnu/byte-interview.html.

———. "The GNU Manifesto." http://www.gnu.org/gnu/manifesto.html.

———. "Why Software Should Be Free." 1992. http://www.gnu.org/philosophy/shouldbefree.html.

Stanley, Autumn. *Mothers and Daughters of Invention: Notes for a Revised History of Technology.* Metuchen, NJ: Rutgers University Press, 1995.

Stephenson, Neal. *Snowcrash.* New York: Bantam, 1992.

Sterling, Bruce. *The Hacker Crackdown: Law and Disorder on the Electronic Frontier.* New York: Bantam, 1992.

Sterne, Jonathan. *The Audible Past: Cultural Origins of Sound Reproduction.* Durham, NC: Duke University Press, 2003.

Stevens, Tyler. "'Sinister Fruitiness': *Neuromancer,* Internet Sexuality and the Turing Test." *Studies in the Novel* 28.3 (Fall 1996): 414–433.

Stoll, Clifford. *Silicon Snake Oil: Second Thoughts on the Information Highway.* New York: Anchor, 1996.

Stone, Allucquère Rosanne. *The War of Desire and Technology at the Close of the Mechanical Age.* Cambridge, MA: MIT Press, 1995.

Stork, David G. "The Best Informed Dream: HAL and the Vision of *2001.*" In *HAL's Legacy: 2001's Computer in Dream and Reality.* Ed. David G. Stork. Cambridge, MA: MIT Press, 1997. 1–14.

Stowe, David W. "Just Do It: How to Beat the Copyright Racket." *Lingua Franca* 6.1 (November/December 1998): 32–42.

Summerhill, Craig A. "Top Ten Reasons Why 'Bunny Watson' Was Right about Computers in Libraries." http://web.archive.org/web/20010516211656/http://staff.cni.org/~craig/castalks/della/della-0a.html. Adapted from a talk given at the Delaware Library Association, Wilmington, DE. April 25, 1996.

Sussman, Herbert. "Cyberpunk Meets Charles Babbage: *The Difference Engine* as Alternative Victorian History." *Victorian Studies* 38.1 (Autumn 1994): 1–23.

Suvin, Darko. *Metamorphoses of Science Fiction.* New Haven, CT: Yale University Press, 1979.

Swade, Doron. *The Difference Engine.* New York: Penguin, 2002.

———. "Redeeming Charles Babbage's Mechanical Computer." *Scientific American.* February 1993.

"Tech History Series: Failed Products." *New Media News.* April 25, 1997. http://web.archive.org/web/19970707120153/http://www.newmedianews.com/tech_hist/failed.html.

Telotte, J. P. *Replications: A Robotic History of Science Fiction Film.* Urbana: University of Illinois Press, 1995.

Terranova, T. "Free Labor: Producing Culture for the Digital Economy." *Social Text* 63 (2000): 33–58.

Thompson, Clive. "Game Theories." *Walrus Magazine.* June 2004. http://www.walrusmagazine.com/article.pl?sid=04/05/06/1929205&mode=n ested&tid=1.

Thompson, E. P. *The Making of the English Working Class.* New York: Knopf, 1963.

Tomayko, Jay. "Electronic Computer for Home Operation. ECHO: The First Home Computer." *IEEE Annals of the History of Computing* 16.3 (1994): 59–61.

Triplett, Jack E. "The Solow Productivity Paradox: What Do Computers Do to Productivity?" *Canadian Journal of Economics* 32.2 (April 1999): 309–334.

Trippi, Joe. *The Revolution Will Not Be Televised: Democracy, the Internet, and the Overthrow of Everything.* New York: Regan Books, 2004.

Trudeau, Garry. "Doonesbury." September 9, 2003.

———. "Doonesbury." September 10, 2003.

Tumoi, Ikka. "The Lives and Death of Moore's Law." *First Monday* 7.11 (November 2002). http://www.firstmonday.org/issues/issue7_11/tuomi/index .html.

Turing, Alan. "Computing Machinery and Intelligence." *Mind* LIX.2236 (October 1950): 433–460.

Turkle, Sherry. *Life on the Screen: Identity in the Age of the Internet.* New York: Simon & Schuster, 1995.

Turner, Frederick C. "From Counterculture to Cyberculture." PhD dissertation, University of California, San Diego. 2002.

"20 Years of Macintosh 1984–2004." Apple.com. http://web.archive.org/web/ 20040109083640/www.apple.com/hardware/ads/1984/.

2001: A Space Odyssey. Dir. Stanley Kubrick. Screenplay by Arthur C. Clarke and Kubrick. MGM, 1968.

Tympas, Aristotle. "The Computor and the Analyst: Computing and Power, 1880s–1960s." PhD dissertation, Georgia Institute Technology. 2001.

———. "Essentialist Ideology and Technological Demarcation: Analog Computing as the Invention of Digital Computing." Presented at the Society for the History of Technology Conference. Pasadena, CA. October 17, 1997.

———. "From Digital to Analog and Back: The Ideology of Intelligent Machines in the History of the Electrical Analyzer, 1870s–1960s." *IEEE Annals of the History of Computing* 18.24 (1996): 42–48.

———. "Pepertually Laborious: Computing Electric Power Transmission Before the Electronic Computer." *International Review of Social History* 48 (2003): 73–95, supplement.

Ullman, Ellen. *Close to the Machine: Technophilia and Its Discontents.* San Francisco: City Lights, 1997.

Vaidhyanathan, Siva. *The Anarchist in the Library: How the Clash between*

Freedom and Control is Hacking the Real World and Crashing the System. New York: Basic Books, 2004.

——. *Copyrights and Copywrongs: The Rise of Intellectual Property and How It Threatens Creativity*. New York: New York University Press, 2001.

Valley, Jr., G. E. "How the SAGE Development Began." *Annals in the History of Computing* 7.3 (July 1985): 196–226.

Veit, Stan. *Stan Veit's History of the Personal Computer*. Asheville, NC: World-Comm, 1993.

Vicic, Shannon. "HAL, HAL: The Gang Was All Here—Cyber Success." *Inside Illinois*. March 20, 1997.

Vonnegut, Kurt. *Player Piano*. New York: Scribner's, 1952.

Wardrip-Fruin, Noah, and Pat Harrigan, eds. *First Person: New Media as Story, Performance, and Game*. Cambridge, MA: MIT Press, 2004.

Wardrip-Fruin, Noah, and Pat Harrigan. "Ludology." In *First Person: New Media as Story, Performance, and Game*. Eds. Wardrip-Fruin and Harrigan. Cambridge, MA: MIT Press, 2004: 35.

Wargames. Dir. by John Badham. Screenplay by Lawrence Lasker and Walter F. Parkes. MGM, 1983.

Warner, Michael. *The Letters of the Republic: Publication and the Public Sphere in Eighteenth-Century America*. Cambridge, MA: Harvard University Press, 1990.

Weinberger, David. "Is There an Echo in Here?" *Salon*. February 20, 2004. http://www.salon.com/tech/feature/2004/02/20/echo_chamber/print.html.

Weiner, Norbert. *The Human Use of Human Beings: Cybernetics and Society*. Boston: Houghton Mifflin, 1950.

Wilkes, Maurice V. "Babbage and the Colossus." *Annals of the History of Computing* 10.3. 1988: 218–219.

Williams, Raymond. *Television: Technology and Cultural Form*. Hanover, NH: Wesleyan University Press, 1974.

——. *Towards 2000*. London: Hogarth, 1983.

Wilson, Johnny. "A Brief History of Gaming, Part 1." *Computer Gaming World*. July 1992.

Winkless III, Nels. "Personal Technlogy: More Strength in a Free Society." *Computer Notes*. August 1976.

Winner, Langdon. "Silicon Valley Mystery House." In *Variations on a Theme Park*. Ed. Michael Sorkin. New York: Noonday, 1992. 31–60.

——. "Upon Opening the Black Box and Finding It Empty: Social Construction and the Philosophy of Technology." *Science, Technology & Human Values* 18.3 (Summer 1993): 362–378.

——. *The Whale and the Reactor: A Search for Limits in an Age of High Technology*. Chicago: University of Chicago Press, 1986.

Wolf, Mark J. P., ed. *The Medium of the Video Game.* Austin: University of Texas Press, 2001.

Wolf, Mark J. P., and Bernard Perron, eds. *The Video Game Theory Reader.* New York: Routledge, 2003.

"Women Get in the Game." *Microsoft Presspass.* January 8, 2004. http://www.microsoft.com/presspass/features/2004/Jan04/01-08WomenGamers.asp.

Wood, Denis. *The Power of Maps.* New York: Guilford, 1992.

Woolf, Virginia. *A Room of One's Own.* New York: Harvest Books, 1989.

Yang, D. J. "On Moore's Law and Fishing: Gordon Moore Speaks Out." *U.S. News Online.* October 7, 2000. http://www.usnews.com/usnews/transcripts/moore.htm.

Zadeh, L. A. "Fuzzy Sets." *Information and Control* 8 (1965): 338–353.

Žižek, Slavoj. *The Sublime Object of Ideology.* London: Verso Books, 1997.

Index

Aarseth, Espen, 154
Abbate, Janet, 231n. 3
ABC News, 211
Abercrombie & Fitch, 91
Academic discourse, 4–5, 203
Academic labor, 201–202
Adams, Ernest, 231n. 64
Adam's Rib, 51
Addiction, 169
Advanced Micro Devices, 90
Advanced Research Projects Agency
   (ARPA), 68, 162, 181
Adventure, 127, 129, 156
Advertising, 17, 42, 93–96, 102–120,
   152, 214. *See also* Apple computer,
   "1984" ad; Apple computer,
   "Lemmings" ad; IBM Charlie
   Chaplin ad campaign
Advertising Age, 110
Age, 4
Ahl, David, 91–92
Aiken, Howard, 26
Airy, George Biddell, 30
Akera, Atsushi, 224n. 2
Algorithms, 34, 36, 39, 69, 73, 136,
   155
Alienation, 2, 97, 139, 200–201
Allchin, Jim, 202
Alphaville Herald, The, 153
Altair 8800 minicomputer, 11, 82,
   91–103, 227n. 50

Alternate history, 28–31
Altruism, 205–206
America Online (AOL), 161–162, 201
American Film Institute, 68
American Heritage Dictionary, The,
   167
America's Army, 124
Amiga computer, 181
Analog computing: defined, 36–38;
   history of, 16, 35–46; ideological
   implications of, 38–46, 223n. 16,
   223n. 23, 224n. 26
Analytical engine, 15, 23–34
Andreessen, Marc, 161–162
Anestopoulou, Maria, 233n. 12
Anthropomorphism, 24, 64–68,
   72–75, 136, 174
Apple computer: Apple I, 102; Apple
   II, 95, 102–104, 106, 230n. 42;
   iPod, 115–116, 186, 193; iTunes,
   19, 188, 191–194; "Lemmings"
   ad, 116–117; Lisa, 108; Macintosh, 17, 102, 105, 108–121,
   185, 200; "1984" ad, 17,
   102–120
Appropriate technology movement,
   97, 171
Aramis, or the Love of Technology,
   136–137, 230n. 41
Arcade. *See* Games
Aristotle, 45–46

Armed forces: British, 36, 39, 223n.
  11; U.S., 36, 39, 49, 124
Aronowitz, Stanley, 58–59, 63
ARPANET. *See* Advanced Research
  Projects Agency (ARPA)
Artificial intelligence 16, 47–49,
  64–78, 136–137
Asimov, Isaac, 23, 66, 121, 207,
  228n. 2
Aspray, William, 12, 35, 106
Asteroid prospecting, 208
Asteroids, 127
Astral Weeks, 193
AT&T, 3, 109
Atanasoff, John V., 223n. 11
Atanasoff-Berry Computer, 223n. 11
Atari videogame system, 123,
  127–128
Atrios, 211
Audio Video Interiors, 84
Augarten, Stan, 26, 36, 92, 94
Austin Powers, 225n. 43
Authorship, 229n. 22
Automatic Sequence-Controlled Cal-
  culator (ASCC), 26
Automation, 50–54, 56–59, 63

Babbage, Charles, 15–16, 23–35, 62,
  64, 87
Babbage Institute, 26
Babbage's software chain, 26
Bakhtin, Mikhael, 49
Baldwin, Craig, 195
Balinese cockfight, 139–140
Ballmer, Steve, 202
Balsamo, Ann, 168
Barbie Liberation Organization, 195
Barbrook, Richard, 204–205
Bardini, Thierry, 228n. 19
Barlow, John Perry, 27, 176
BASIC programming language, 85, 95
Batch processing, 85

Batteries, 88
Baum, L. Frank, 154
Baym, Nancy, 13
BBD&O, 117
Bear, Greg, 166
Beastie Boys, 194
Beatles, 193
Being Digital. See Negroponte,
  Nicholas
Bell and Howell Schools, 97
Bellamy, Edward, 9, 23, 207–208
Beniger, James, 34
Benjamin, Walter, 224n. 26
Berners-Lee, Tim, 161–162
Bertlesmann AG, 188
Bérubé, Michael, 73–75
Berry, Clifford, 223n. 11
Bethke, Bruce, 166
Bible, 190
"Bicycle Built for Two," 78
Big Brother, 70, 109–120, 179
Bijker, Wiebe, 2, 81
Binary numbering system: defined, 38;
  ideological implications of, 16, 38,
  43–46; limitations in early home
  computer systems, 83, 95
Birkerts, Sven, 183
Bivalence, 44–46
Black & White, 133
Black box effect, 2
Black Entertainment Television (BET),
  212
Blade Runner, 3, 109
Bloatware, 89, 122
Bloch, Ernst, 6, 8
Blockbuster Video, 190
Blog for America, 212
Blogging, 19, 209–215
Blondell, Joan, 52
Boal, Iain A., 179, 183–184
Body. *See* Embodiment and disembod-
  iment

Bonfire of the Vanities, 45–46
Borders Books and Music, 100
Borg, 114–115
Bourdieu, Pierre, 4
Brand, Stuart, 97–98, 171 ,174, 176, 232n. 10
Braverman, Harry, 63
Bricklin, Dan, 103–104
British Broadcasting Corporation (BBC), 153
British, Lord, 128
British Register General, 30
British Royal Observatory, 30
Britney's Dance Beat, 169
Broadband internet access, 186, 194
Broderbund, 131
Bromley, Alan, 37–38
Brook, James, 179, 183–184
Bulletin board systems (BBSes), 161
Burawa, Alex, 100
Bureaucratization, 33–34, 47, 74, 126
Burkart, Patrick, 196–197
Bush, George W., 212–216
Bush, Vannevar, 35, 39–41
Bushnell, Nolan, 127
Business 2.0, 171
Butler, Judith, 76
Byron, 32
Byte, 11, 83, 100

Cable News Network (CNN), 153, 211
Caldera, 200
Calculator, 23–24, 35–36, 44, 90, 94, 96, 103–104
"California Ideology," 204
Cameron, Andy, 204
Campbell-Kelly, Martin, 12, 35, 106
Capek, Karel, 65
Card, Orson Scott, 124, 132, 166
Carey, James W., 8–10
Carpal tunnel syndrome, 1, 139, 168

Cash register, 35
Cassette recordings, 74, 189
Cassidy, John, 233n. 1
Cavett, Dick, 106
CD-ROM drives, 122, 183
Cell phones, 60, 218
Census Bureau, United States, 35
Ceruzzi, Paul, 12, 86
Chanan, Michael, 233n. 10
Chaplin, Charlie, 106–107
Chat programs, 163
cheesebikini?, 218–219
Chess, 127, 137
Chiat/Day, 106, 109–117
Ciment, Michel, 74
Circuit of culture, 11–15
City of Heroes, 153
Civilization series. See *Sid Meier's Civilization* series
Cixous, Hélène, 66
Clackers, 28
Clarke, Arthur C., 48, 69, 72, 225n. 39, 226n. 54
Class, 51, 62–64
Clinton, Bill, 216
Clocks, 36, 42, 90
Clones, of humans, 33. *See also* International Business Machines (IBM), clones
CNN. *See* Cable News Network
Cobb, Ty, 51
Co-Evolution Quarterly, 97
Cognitive mapping, 140–145
Cohen, I. Bernard, 26, 222n. 2
Colbek, Julian, 223n. 23
Collier, Bruce, 32
Colonialism, 141–147
Colonization. See Sid Meier's Colonization
Commodore computers, 119
Common Sense, 99
Communications Decency Act, 176

Communications Reform Act, 176
Communism, 202–205
Communitarianism, 99–100, 213–214, 218–219
Compact discs (CDs), 16, 19, 41–44
Compaq, 105, 180
CompuServe, 161
Computer: as commodity, 99, 102, 105; etymology of, 23–24; in home, 82–84; as information processor, 31–46, 108, 121, 169; in kitchen, 83; mainframe, 15–16; 21–78; as mechanical calculating device, 24, 26, 34–36, 90, 96, 103; minicomputer, 81, 85–86, 91, 94, 96, 126–127; as person who computes, 23, 30, 32, 34, 50; personal, 1–2, 11, 15, 17, 59–60, 81–157, 161; revolution, 98; in the workplace, 49–68. *See also* Apple computer; Apple computer, Lisa; Atanasoff-Berry Computer; Compaq; Digital Equipment Corporation; ENIAC mainframe computer; ENIGMA; International Business Machines (IBM); Internet; Mark IV mainframe computer; Mark–8 minicomputer; Radio Shack TRS–80; UNIVAC mainframe computer; Xerox Alto computer
Computer games. *See* Games
Computer Lib/Dream Machines, 97
Computer liberation, 97
Computer Notes newsletter, 97, 100
Conceiving Ada, 33
Conde Nast, 171
Congress, U.S., 196
Connectivity, 99
Consalvo, Mia, 230n. 52
Constitution, U.S., 196; First Amendment, 176
Consumer Reports, 11

Consumerism, 6, 12, 13, 17, 30, 99–100, 150–151, 186, 188, 197, 201
Consumption. *See* Consumerism
Consumption junction, 30
Contingency of history, 28–31
Control. *See* Power
Control revolution, 33–34
Convergence, 186
Conway, John, 127
Copyleft, 206
Copyright, 13, 19, 177, 195–197, 205
Costikyan, Greg, 231n. 64
Costner, Kevin, 106
Council of Conservative Citizens, 210–211
Cowan, Ruth Schwartz, 30, 226n. 6
Crawford, Chris, 141
Creative Computing, 11
Cringely, Robert X., 104
Crisis in the Kremlin, 133–134
Critical technocracy, 9–10
Croft, Lara, 149
Cronon, William, 144
Crowther, Bosley, 50–51
C-SPAN, 210
Cuisinart food processor, 108
Cultural discount, 201–202
Cultural studies, 6–15
Cut scenes, 129–130
Cybercafes, 100
Cyberfeminism. *See* Feminism
Cybernetics, 50, 126, 138–139, 164, 229n. 26
Cyberpunk, 10, 11, 28, 120, 166, 174, 179
Cyberspace, 18, 27, 161–170–209
Cybertopianism. *See* Technological utopianism
Cyborgs, 10, 17, 44, 113–115, 133, 135–140
Cynical reason, 8

Dada, 219
Daily Show, The, 153
Dance Dance Revolution (DDR), 169–170
Darth Vader, 114
David, Paul, 60
Davis, Jefferson, 211
Dawkins, Richard, 180
de Certeau, Michel, 142–144
de Sola Pool, Ithiel, 2–3
De Vries, Daniel, 74
Dean, Howard, 212–215, 219
Debs, Eugene, 9
Deep Blue, 137
Defamiliarization, 29
Dell, 105, 229n. 6
Delphi, 161
Democratic Party, 212–213
Demystification, 8
Dennett, Daniel, 75, 180
Department of Defense, U.S., 161, 181
Department of Labor, U.S., 6
Derrida, Jacques, 184
Descartes, René, 66
Desk Set, 14, 16, 47–78, 81, 105–106, 111
Deskilling, 16, 49–68
Desktop publishing, 103
Dialectic of technological determinism: and Babbage, 23–34; defined, 1–19, 27–28; and Moore's Law, 88–90
Dibbell, Julian, 153, 177
DiFazio, William, 58, 63
Difference engine: development abandoned by Babbage, 15–16, 23–34, 64, 87; completed development by Scheutz team, 29–30; "steampunk" alternate-history novel about, 28–31; successful recreation, 27–28

Difference Engine, The, 16, 28–29, 33
Differential analyzer, 35–41
Digital computing: defined, 36–38; history of, 16, 35–46; ideological implications of, 3, 38–46, 223n. 23, 224n. 26
Digital divide, 2, 162
Digital Equipment Corporation, 85–86, 91–92, 127; PDP–1 minicomputer, 85–86, 127; PDP–10 minicomputer, 86
Digitization of media, cultural implications of, 41–46, 186–197
Dion, Céline, 188
Disembodiment. *See* Embodiment and disembodiment
Dispossessed, The, 154
DNA, 178
Doom, 148
Doonesbury, 219
Dot-com boom, 18, 97, 171–185, 198, 209
Dot-com crash, 90, 119, 171, 185, 198, 213
doxa, 4–5
Dr. Dobb's Journal, 11
Dr. Strangelove, 74
Dracula's Daughter, 77
du Gay, Paul, 12–13
Duke University, Center for Advertising History, 11
Durham Peters, John, 43
DVDs, 187, 190
Dyer, Richard, 221n. 20
Dyer-Witherford, Nick, 34

eBay, 110, 153
ECHO home computer system, 81–84, 226n. 2
Eckert, J. Presper, 26, 39, 49, 64
Economist, 62–63
Edsall, Thomas, 211

Edwards, Paul, 39
18, 193–194
8-track cassettes, 189
Eisenstein, Sergei, 141
Eldred v. Ashcroft, 196
Electra.com, 57
Electric Dreams (the film), 84
Electrical analyzer, 40
Electricity, cultural history of, 8–9,
    11, 60
Electronic Arts, 148
"Electronic brain," as early term for
    computer, 16, 24, 47
Electronic folk culture, 19
Elecronic Frontier Foundation, 176
Electronic frontier thesis, 232n. 12
Electronic Home, 84, 232n. 12
Electronics hobbyists. *See* Hobbyists
Elitism, 97, 183
email, 60, 103, 162
Embodiment and disembodiment, 1,
    18, 43–44, 66–67, 113–115,
    138–139, 161–170
Employment. *See* Unemployment
Ender's Game, 124
Englebart, Douglas, 108
ENIAC mainframe computer, 26, 39,
    47, 49, 64, 66, 83, 181
ENIGMA, 223n11
Entertainment Software Ratings
    Board (ESRB), 151
Entrepreneurialism, 119–120,
    171–185
Environmentalism, 144–145,
    215–217
Ephron, Henry and Phoebe, 51
Escapism, 8
Escelinen, Markku, 231n. 64
Eschaton, 211
Essentialism, 27. *See also* Naturaliza-
    tion, of technology
Ethnocentrism, 146–147

Ethnography, 13, 43
Event marketing, 111
Everquest, 152–153, 155
Expansion cards, 95
Exploitation, 201
Extensive listening, 190–191, 197
Extrapolation, 48, 68, 86–90
Eye Toy, 169–170

Fair use, 195–196
Fairchild Semiconductor, 87, 90
False consciousness, 6
Fanning, Shawn, 186
Fantasy fiction, 154–155
Fast Company, 171
Federal Reserve, 4
Feedback loops. *See* Cybernetics
Femininity. *See* Gender
Feminism, 10, 13, 31–34, 51,
    112–113. *See also* Gender; Queer
    theory
Fetchmail, 203
Fetishization, 189
File sharing, 186–197
File swapping. *See* File sharing
File Transfer Protocol, 167
Final Fantasy, 129, 190
Final Fantasy Online, 153
First Amendment. *See* Constitution,
    U.S., First Amendment
Fischer, Claude, 231n. 7
Flamm, Kenneth, 64
Flash mobs, 217–220
Floppy drives, 122
Flow, 229n. 26
Folk culture. *See* Electronic folk cul-
    ture
Forrester, Jay, 131
Forrester Research, 233n. 4
Foundation series, 23
Frankenstein, 65
Franklin, Benjamin, 106

Frankston, Robert, 103
Frasca, Gonzalo, 231n. 63
Free Software Foundation, 206
Freeman, David, 229n. 12
Freeware. *See* Open source software
Freiberger, Paul, 45
Frontier myth, 232n. 12
FTP. *See* File Transfer Protocol
Full Spectrum Warrior, 124
Fuller, Buckminster, 97, 207
Fuller, Mary, 141–146
Futurism, 4–5, 8, 14, 44, 55, 68, 89
Fuzzy logic, 44–46
Fuzzy sets, 45

Gale, Wayne, 77
Game Boy videogame system. *See* Nintendo, Game Boy videogame system
Game Studies, 154
Games, 11, 14, 17–18, 104, 121–157, 167–170, 229n. 6, 231n. 62
Gardner, Martin, 127
Garfinkel, Simpson, 73
Garson, Barbara, 232n. 18
Gates, Bill, 84, 118–119, 180–182
Geertz, Clifford, 139–140
Gender, 4, 14, 16, 44, 48, 50–55, 75–78, 112–115, 148–152, 167, 176, 209, 225n. 43, 226n. 54, 230n. 48, 231n. 14. *See also* Feminism; Queer theory
General Electric Company, 34
General Motors, 217
General Public License. *See* GNU General Public License (GPL)
Gephardt, Richard, 212
"Giant brain," as early term for computer, 24, 47
Gibson, William, 16, 18, 28–29, 162–167, 174, 231n. 8
Gift economy, 205

Gilman, Charlotte Perkins, 9
Global warming, 216
Globalization, 140–141, 146, 167, 183, 202
GNU General Public License (GPL), 200–202
GNU operating system, 203, 206–207
Gödel, Kurt, 45
Godzilla, 131
Goldstine, Herman, 36–7
Good Morning America, 211
Goodell, Jeff, 232n6
Gourevich, Philip, 213–214
Gopher, 167
Grammy Awards, 187
Gramsci, Antonio, 203
Grand Canyon, 124
Grand Theft Auto, 129–130
Graphics cards, 155
Grateful Dead, 176
Great Wall of China, 146
Greece, 45, 85, 138
Greene, Michael, 187, 233n. 3
Griefers, 153
Groundhog Day, 229n. 11
Grove, Andy, 89

Habermas, Jürgen, 5–6
Hacker Crackdown, The, 163
Hacker Ethic, 174, 207, 232n. 11
Hackers, 18, 85–86, 127, 171–174, 204, 232n. 7
Hacking. *See* Hackers
Haddon, Leslie, 91, 96
Hafner, Kate, 231n. 3
HAL, 16, 47–49, 68–78, 84, 106, 111, 225n. 39, 226n. 54
HAL 2000 home automation system, 226n. 13
Hall, Stuart, 55–56
"Halloween Documents," 204
Hammacher Schlemmer, 91

Hammer, MC, 193
Haraway, Donna, 10, 17, 133, 139–140
Hard drives, 88
Harrigan, Pat, 231n62
Harvard University, 26, 180
Harvey, David, 140
Hawkins, Trip, 229n. 10
Hegemony, 8, 120
Heims, Steve J., 138
Heisenberg, Werner, 45
Henwood, Doug, 59–60, 62
Hepburn, Katharine, 16, 47–48, 51
Herstory of computing, 31–34
Heteronormativity. *See* Queer theory
Hewlett, Don, 180
Hewlett-Packard, 91, 180
Hidden Agenda, 133–134
Hip-hop, 16, 197
His Other Woman, 77
Hobbyists, 17, 91–102, 161, 227n. 50
Hochschild, Arlie Russell, 151–152
Hoff, Ted, 92
Hollerith, Herman, 35
Homebrew Computer Club, 97, 105
Homophobia. *See* Queer theory
Honeywell kitchen computer, 83
HotWired, 176
HTML (HyperText Markup Language), 161, 183
Hydrogen power, 19, 215–217, 234n. 14
Hyman, R. Anthony, 25
Hyperlinks, 126

Ian, Janic, 188
IBM. *See* International Business Machines
Identification, 129–130, 133–145, 151–152
Ideology, 1–22. *See also* Analog computing, ideological implications of;

Dialectic of technological determinism; Digital computing, ideological implications of; Gender; Power; Race; Utopian sphere
IMSAI 8080 minicomputer, 95
Individualism, 99–100, 144
Industrial Revolution, 24, 28, 33–34
Industry Standard, 171
Inside Politics, 211
Instapundit, 211
Intel, 89–92, 105, 109–110; 4004 microprocessor, 91; 8008 microprocessor, 94
Intellectual property, 186–208
Intensive listening, 190–191, 197
Interactive cinema. *See* Interactivity
Interactivity, 123–130
Interface. *See* Mouse interface; Whole-body interface
International Business Machines (IBM), 35, 49–50, 53–54, 63–64, 68–69, 85, 104–108, 111, 117–120, 126, 137, 161, 180, 202; Charlie Chaplin ad campaign, 106–107; clones, 104, 181; PC, 104–108, 121; System/360, 68
Internal Revenue Service (IRS), 179
International Correspondence Schools, 97
Internet, 15, 18, 68, 83, 99–100, 123, 126, 152–157, 159–234
iPod. *See* Apple computer, iPod
Iraq War (2003), 194, 211, 213
iTunes. *See* Apple computer, iTunes

Jackson, Thomas Penfield, 182
Jacquard loom, 24
Jameson, Fredric, 6–8, 17, 140–141, 154, 201
Java programming language, 123, 226n. 18
Jefferson, Thomas, 106

Jenkins, Henry, 7, 141–146, 153–154
Jobs, Steve, 102, 108–110, 118–119, 184–185
Johnson, Richard, 222n. 28
Juul, Jesper, 231n. 64

Kagan, Norman, 74
Kaplan, Philip J., 233n. 1
Karl, Jonathan, 211
Kasparov, Gary, 137
Kawasaki, Guy, 228n. 15
Kazaa, 187
Kellner, Douglas, 6
Kemeny, John, 85
Kerry, John, 212
Kestenbaum, David S., 226n. 54
Keyboard interface, 1, 82, 168
Kidder, Tracy, 43
Kilby, Jack, 87
Killer applications, 103, 106, 126
King, Martin Luther, 211
Kingdom of Loathing, 155–157
Kinsley, Michael, 212
Klein, Naomi, 232n. 14
Kolko, Beth, 230n. 45
Kosko, Bart, 45
Kravitz, Lenny, 194
Kubrick, Stanley, 48, 69, 72, 225n. 39
Kurtz, Howard, 211
Kurzweil, Ray, 73, 225n. 33

Labor. *See* Academic Labor; Deskilling; Organized Labor; Scientific Management; Unemployment
Labor Notes, 60
Laissez-faire economics, 18, 179
Lang, Fritz, 65
Lang, Walter, 51
Laptops, 88, 100, 115
Latour, Bruno, 2, 136–137, 230n. 41
Laurel, Brenda, 127

Lawnmower Man, The, 167
Lawnmower Man II, The, 167
Le Guin, Ursula, 154
Left Hand of Darkness, The, 154
Left-wing technotopianism, 97
Legion of Doom, 173–174
Lessig, Laurence, 13, 233n. 12
Levy, Steven, 85–86, 172, 232n. 11
Leyden, Peter, 234n. 14
Libertarianism, 17–18, 120, 203–208; corporate, 178–182, 204–206; left, 206–207
Librarians: in *Desk Set*, 16, 47–68, 77; and technological unemployment, 58–59
Liebling, A. J., 214
Life, 11, 47
LIFE (the artificial life simulation), 127
Light, Jennifer S., 222n. 2
Ligorio, Tatiana, 224n. 34
Lincoln, Abraham, 135
Linux, 14, 19, 182, 198–209
Literary theory, 12, 15, 120, 148, 154, 190
Littman, Jonathan, 232n. 6
Locke, John, 207
Logarithms, 37
Looking Backward, 9
Lord of the Rings, The, 190
Lorre, Peter, 77
Lott, Trent, 210–214
Lotus 1–2–3, 181
Lovelace, Ada, 31–34, 47, 112
Luddites, 28. *See also* Neo-Luddites
Ludlow, Peter, 153
Ludology, 154
Lyon, Matthew, 231n. 3

Macintosh. *See* Apple computer, Macintosh
MacKinnon, Catharine, 177

MacWorld, 11
MacWorld Expo, 118
Magnavox Odyssey videogame system, 127
Mainframe computer. *See* Computer, mainframe
Malone, John, 174
Malone, Michael S., 90, 92
MAME. *See* Multiple Arcade Machine Emulator
Manicheanism, 111
Manifest Destiny, 147
Manjoo, Farhad, 234n. 10, 234n. 12
Maps. *See* Cognitive mapping
Marchant, William, 51
Mark IV mainframe computer, 26
Mark–8 minicomputer, 94
Marshall, Ian, 45–46
Marshall, Joshua Micah, 211
Marvin, Carolyn, 231n. 7
Marx, Karl, 5, 141
Masculinity. *See* Gender
Massachusetts Institute of Technology, 3, 35, 39–41, 68, 70, 85–86, 127, 172–173, 206; Artificial Intelligence Lab, 206; Media Lab, 3; Tech Model Railroad Club, 127, 172–173
Massively Multiplayer Online Role Playing Games (MMORPGs), 152–153
Master narratives, 12
Matrix, The, 67, 164–167, 190
Matrix Online, The, 153
Mauchly, William, 26, 39, 49, 64
Maxis software, 131–132, 149, 153
McCaffery, Larry, 231n. 9, 231n. 10
McChesney, Robert, 221n. 5
McCloud, Scott, 155–156
McCourt, Tom, 196–197
McGovern, Gerry, 60, 62
McKenzie, Jon, 231n. 64

McKinsey Global Institute, 60
McLuhan, Marshall, 88
McNeill, Daniel, 45
"Mechanical brain," as early term for computer, 24
Meet the Press, 211
Meetup.com, 213
Meier, Sid, 135, 229n. 22. See also *Sid Meier's Civilization* series; *Sid Meier's Colonization*
Mellencamp, John, 194
Memento, 190
Metallica, 188
Methodology, 11–15
Metropolis, 65
Micro Instrumentation Telemetry Systems (MITS), 94–95, 227n. 50. *See also* Altair 8800 minicomputer
Microprocessor, 17, 32, 82, 86–101, 105, 123, 182, 217, 229n. 6
Microsoft, 19, 95, 104–105, 118–119, 180–182, 201–204; *Excel*, 181; Internet Explorer, 118, 182–183; *Office*, 192; Press, 97–98; Visual C++, 181; Windows operating system, 19, 57, 118, 122, 181, 198–200; *Word*, 181; X-Box videogame system, 124
Middle-Earth Online, 153
Military. *See* Armed forces
Mill, John Stuart, 176
Mims, Forest, 100
Miniaturization, 86–92
Minicomputer. *See* Computer, minicomputer
Minitel information network, 99
Mitnick, Kevin, 173
MITS. *See* Micro Instrumentation Telemetry Systems
MMORPGs. *See* Massively Multiplayer Online Role Playing Games
Mobile privatization, 115

Mobility, fantasy of, 113–115
Moby, 193–194
Model rocketry, 94
Modem, 99, 161, 194
Modern Times, 106–107
Monitor, 1, 155
Monopoly, 119–120
Monster.com, 110
Monty Python, 156
Moody, Fred, 224n. 27
Moore, Gordon, 86–90
Moore's Law, 14, 17, 81, 86–90,
    122–123, 125, 155, 180, 182, 198,
    229n. 6
Morgan Stanley, 60
Morpheus, 187
Morris, Meaghan, 6, 8
Morrison, Van, 193
Morse code, 38
Mosaic, 161
Mother Jones, 217
Mother Theresa, 206
Motion recognition, 169–170
Mount Rushmore, 124
Mouse interface, 1, 108, 137, 156
Movable Type, 210
MP3, 186–197
MS-DOS, 105
MUDs. *See* Multi-User Domains
Multinational corporations, 120, 174
Multiple Arcade Machine Emulator
    (MAME), 123
Multi-User Domains (MUDs), 152
Multi-User Dungeons (MUDs). *See*
    Multi-User Domains
Multivalence, 44–46
Museum of Broadcasting, 11
Music: as contract, 19, 187, 191–194;
    as folk culture, 19, 187–188,
    195–197; as tangible physical com-
    modity, 19, 187, 189–191, 197; as
    utility, 19, 187, 194–195

My Tiny Life, 177
Myers, David, 133, 141
Myst, 190

Nakamura, Lisa, 13, 230n. 45
Nancy, 155
Napster, 14, 18–19, 186–197, 207,
    209
Narrative, 134, 140–145, 153–157
NASA, 72, 74
NASDAQ, 119
National Academy of Recording Arts
    and Sciences, 187
National Security Council, United
    States, 74
Nationalism, 6, 145–148. *See also*
    Globalization
Naturalization, of technology, 2–3,
    27, 29, 44, 81, 88
Nautilus, 115
Navigation tables, 23
Nebula awards, 166
Negativland, 195
Negoita, Constantin, 224n. 34
Negroponte, Nicholas, 3, 27, 42–43,
    88
Neilsen, Jacob, 108
Nelson, Ted, 97–99, 105
Nelson, Thomas Allen, 74
Neo-Luddites, 44, 182–185
Netscape Navigator, 181, 204
Networks, 161–162, 173, 218
Neuromancer, 18, 139, 162–168,
    179, 231n. 8
New Hacker's Dictionary, 204
New Hollywood, 127–130
New Left, 98, 208
Newman, James, 231n. 62
New York Post, 212
New York Times, 50–51, 61, 88, 150,
    153, 212
New Yorker magazine, 213–214

Newsweek, 11, 131, 153
Nexis database, 167
Ninjas, 170; snowmen as, 156
Nintendo, 124, 141–144; Game Boy
   videogame system, 124; VR inter-
   faces, 167
Noble, David, 224n. 4
Norman, Donald, 43–44, 234n. 18
Northeastern University, 186
Nostalgia, 10, 16, 44, 123
Noyce, Robert, 87, 90
Nye, David, 11, 101

Odometers, 36
O'Keefe, Ed, 211
Olsen, Ken, 92
*On the Economy of Machinery and
   Manufactures*, 33
One Flew Over the Cuckoo's Nest,
   227n. 49
Online gaming. *See* Massively Multi-
   player Online Role Playing Games
   (MMORPGs)
Only the Paranoid Survive, 89
Open source software, 6, 14, 19,
   198–208
Opium, 31
O'Reilly & Associates, 204
Organized labor, 50, 58, 62–3, 120
Orwell, George, 84, 118, 120
Outsourcing, 60, 105
Owens, Larry, 37, 41
Oxford English Dictionary, 23, 167

Paine, Thomas, 98–99
PalmPilot, 123
Panopticon, 84, 218
Panship, Alexei and Cory, 227n. 56
Patel, Judge Marilyn Hall, 187
Patents, 177
Patriarchy, 54–55, 209. *See also* Femi-
   nism; Gender; Queer Theory

PDA (Personal Digital Assistant), 115,
   123
PDP–1. *See* Digital Equipment Corpo-
   ration, PDP–1 minicomputer
PDP–10 minicomputer. *See* Digital
   Equipment Corporation, PDP–10
   minicomputer
Peanuts, 155
Peer-to-peer technology, 186–197
Pencil, 1, 44
People's Computer Company, 17, 86
Perkins, Anthony, 77
Perlman, Marc, 223n. 21
Perron, Bernard, 231n. 62
Personal Computer (PC). *See* Com-
   puter, personal
Personal Digital Assistant. *See* PDA
Peters, John Durham, 43, 224n. 26
Petroski, Henry, 1
Pfaffenberger, Brian, 221n. 22
Phenomenology, 123
Phillips Electronics, 43
Pierce, Charles, 224n. 27
Pinch, Trevor, 2, 81
Pirates, 135
Planned obsolescence, 60, 89
Plant, Sadie, 13, 31–32
Play Money weblog, 153
Player Piano, 224n4
Playstation videogame system series.
   See Sony Electronics, Playstation
   videogame system series
Please Hammer Don't Hurt 'Em, 193
Podhoretz, John, 212
Poe, Edgar Allen, 75
Pogo, 155
Point-and-click interface. *See* Mouse
   interface
Pole Position, 124
Polyphony, 49
Pong, 127–128, 155
Popular Electronics, 92–101

Postmodernity, 44, 88–90, 122, 139–141, 190

Post-scarcity economy, 206–208

Power, 33–34, 62–64, 97, 99, 105. *See also* Class; Gender; Globalization; Race

PressPlay music service, 191–192

Privatization, 99–100, 115. *See also* Mobile privatization

Processed World, 232n. 18

Processor Technology, 95

Prodigy online service, 161

Productivity paradox, 30, 57–62

Progressivism, 9–10

Prospecting, asteroid, *see* Asteroid prospecting

Psycho, 77

Psychohistory, 23

P2P technology. *See* Peer-to-peer technology

Public sphere, 5–7, 47, 105, 163–167, 201, 209, 214

Punch cards, 25, 35, 85, 126

Punk rock, 166

QST, 94

Queer theory, 76–78, 151, 226n. 54. *See also* Feminism; Gender

Quirk, John J., 8

Quittner, Joshua, 232n5

R.E.M., 194

R.U.R., 65

Race, 4, 13, 146–147, 210, 212

Radio, 187, 190–191

Radio Shack TRS–80, 121, 228n. 2

Radio Userland, 210

Radio-Electronics, 94

Raid on Bungling Bay, 130

Railroad Tycoon, 135

Rain, Douglas, 77

Rape, 177–178

Raymond, Eric, 203–208

Reader response theory, 123, 126

Really Simply Syndication. *See* RSS

Recording Industry Association of America (RIAA), 187, 232n. 3

Red Hat Systems, 198, 200, 202

Red Herring magazine, 90

Reebok, 112

Reification, 201

Remington Rand, 49

Replicator, 5

Republican Party, 176

Resistance: in cultural studies theory, 8; futility of, 1

Retrogames, 122–123

Reuther, Walter, 50

Reynolds, Glenn, 211

Rhapsodic dystopianism, 231n. 8

Rhapsody music service, 19, 188, 194–195

Rheingold, Howard, 168, 171, 218–219

RIAA. *See* Recording Industry Association of America

Richards, Jay W., 225n. 33

Ripping, 187

Roach, Stephen, 60–61

Road Warrior, 174

Roberts, Ed, 94–95

Robots, 65–66, 208; as butlers, 226n. 4

Rockefeller Foundation, 40

Rodenberry, Gene, 23, 154

Rodman, Gilbert, 230n. 45

Roland MC–505 Groovebox, 43

Rolling Stone, 11, 166

ROM files, 203

Romm, Joseph, 216

Room of One's Own, A, 33

Rosemont, Franklin, 9

Rosen, Hilary, 232n3

Rosetto, Louis, 23, 171, 174

Ross, Andrew, 9–10, 201
Rothenbuhler, Eric, 43, 224n. 26
RSS (Really Simple Syndication), 210
Russert, Tim, 211

Safire, William, 167
SAGE computing system, 40
Salen, Katie, 231n. 62
Salsberg, Art, 95–96, 100
Sampling, 197
Sanders, George, 77
Scelbi 8-H minicomputer, 94
Scheutz, Georg and Edvard, 29–30
Schwartz, Peter, 234n14
Science fiction, 5–7, 10, 47–49,
    65–78, 84, 100–101, 106,
    154–155; 162–170, 226n. 4. *See
    also* Apple computer, "1984" ad;
    Asimov, Isaac; Bellamy, Edward;
    Bethke, Bruce; *Blade Runner*;
    Capek, Karel; Card, Orson Scott;
    Clarke, Arthur C.; Clones, of hu-
    mans; *Conceiving Ada*; Cyber-
    punk; Cyborgs; Defamiliarization;
    Difference Engine, The; Extrapola-
    tion; *Foundation* series; Gibson,
    William; Kubrick, Stanley; *Look-
    ing Backward*; Robots; Sense of
    wonder; *Star Trek*; *Star Wars*;
    Steampunk; Stephenson, Neal;
    Sterling, Bruce; Time travel; *2001:
    A Space Odyssey*; Varley, John
Science studies, 2
Scientific American, 127
Scientific Digests, 31
Scientific management, 33–34, 63
Scott, Ridley, 17, 109
Scratching, 16
Sculley, John, 109, 117
Sears, 161
Seattle Computer Products, 105
Second Life, 153

Second Life Herald, The, 153
Sega, 170
Seldes, Gilbert, 154
Selling out, 201
Semiconductors, 87–90
Semiotics, 14–15
Sense of wonder, 101, 227n. 56
"Sentimental education," 139–140
Seven Lively Arts, The, 154
Sex. *See* Feminism; Gender; Queer
    theory
*Sgt. Pepper's Lonely Hearts' Club
    Band*, 193
Shakespeare, William, 33
Shapiro, Robert, 230n. 56
Sharpton, Al, 219
Sheet music, 189
Shelley, Mary, 65
Sherman Antitrust Act, 182
Shimomura, Tsutomu, 173
Shurkin, Joel, 223n. 11
Sichel, Daniel, 59
Sid Meier's Civilization series, 17–18,
    122–123, 125, 135–148, 155,
    230n42
Sid Meier's Colonization, 147
Silence of the Lambs, 77–78
Silicon, 17, 92
SimAnt, 122
SimCity Classic Live, 132
SimCity series, 17–18, 122–123, 125,
    128, 130–136, 148, 155
SimCopter, 122
SimEarth, 122
SimFarm, 122
SimGolf, 122
SimHealth, 122
SimIsle, 122
SimLife, 122
Sims, The, series, 122, 126, 148–152,
    155
Sims Online, The, 122, 153

SimThemePark, 122
SimTown, 122
SimTune, 122
Simulation games, 17–18, 121–157
Sinatra, Frank, 193
Sinclair, Upton, 9
Six Million Dollar Man, 139
Skinner, David, 96
Sklar, Robert, 224n. 1
Slatalla, Michelle, 232n. 5
Slate, 88
Slide rule, 19, 36–37, 44
Sloterkijk, Peter, 221n. 19
Smart house, 84
Smart mobs, 11, 19, 217–220
Smithsonian Museum, 11
Snow White and the Seven Dwarfs, 117
Snowcrash, 179
Social Construction of Technological Systems (SCOT), 81
Social Darwinism, 180, 232n. 19
Socialism, 9–10
Socialist Review, 67
Software emulator, 123
Software evangelists, 228n. 15
SOL minicomputer, 95
Solomon, Les, 100
Solow productivity paradox. *See* Productivity paradox
Solow, Robert, 59
Songs for Swinging Lovers, 193
Soni, Vivasvan, 67
Sonic Outlaws, 195
Sonny Bono Copyright Terms Extension Act
Sony Electronics: 43; Playstation videogame system series, 153, 169, 229n. 6; Walkman, 115
Spacewar, 127
Speedometers, 36
Spatial stories, 142–144

Spigel, Lynn, 11
SPIN, 166
Spreadsheet software, 96, 102–104, 121, 230n. 42
Stairmaster, 115
Stallman, Richard, 203–208
Stanford University, 97, 127
Stanley, Autumn, 222n. 2
Stanton, Elizabeth Cady, 9
Star Trek, 5–6, 23, 100, 113–115, 221n. 9
Star Wars, 104, 113, 190
Star Wars Galaxies, 153
Starbucks, 100
"Steamboat Willie," 196
Steampunk, 28–31
Stephenson, Neal, 174, 179
Sterling, Bruce, 16, 28–29, 162–163, 174
Sterne, Jonathan, 44, 231n. 7
Stevens, Tyler, 75–76, 226n. 51
Stork, David G., 70
Streets of SimCity, 122
Suck, 77
Sullivan, Andrew, 211
Summerhill, Craig, A., 56–57
Sumner, Richard, 47–68, 75–78
Super Bowl, 17, 102, 109–117
Surveillance technology, 82–85, 218
Sussman, Herbert, 29
Sutherland, Jim, 82
Suvin, Darko, 227n. 56
SUVs (Sport Utility Vans), 215
Swade, Doron, 27–8, 31
Synthesizers, 42–43, 223n. 23

Talking Points Memo, 211
Taylor, Frederick, 33, 63
Taylorism. *See* Scientific management
TCI Cable, 174
Teachout, Zephyr, 213
Technical education, 96

Technocracy, 9–10
Technolibertarianism. *See* Libertarianism
Technological determinism. *See* Dialectic of technological determinism
Technological sublime, 101
Technological utopianism. *See* Utopian sphere
Technophilia, 10, 48–78, 84, 97, 209
Technophobia, 10, 14, 16, 48–78, 105, 209
Telephone, cultural history of, 2, 50, 55
Teletype, 82
Television, 2–3, 15, 83, 102–120, 139, 183, 210–212, 214
Terranova, Tatiana, 201
Tetris, 124–125, 151–151
Texas Instruments, 87, 94
Thermometers, 36
Thompson, E. P., 63
Thorburn, David, 7
3-D, 155–156, 164–165, 167
Thurmond, Strom, 210
Time, 133, 140–145, 150–151
Time, 11, 47, 50–51, 58–59, 63
Time bind, the, 151
Time sharing, 17, 81, 85–86, 96, 99
Time travel, 33
Time-sharing, 17, 81, 85–86, 99–100
Title IX, 113
Titus, Jonathan, 94
TiVo, 186
Tolkien, J. R. R., 153–154
Tomb Raider, 149
Tomayko, Jay, 226n. 2
Tommy, 193
Total Kitchen Information System, 83
Tracy, Spencer, 16, 47–48, 51
Transistor, 87
Treichler, Paula, 226n. 54

Trinary numbering system, 38
Trippi, Joe, 212
Trudeau, Garry, 219
Turing Test, 75–76
Turing, Alan, 75–76
Turkle, Sherry, 13
2001: A Space Odyssey, 14, 16, 47–49, 68–78, 81, 105–106, 111, 225n. 39, 226n. 54, 226n. 13
Tympas, Aristotle, 40, 65, 222n. 2, 223n. 16

Ubiquitous computing, 217–220
Ullman, Ellen, 224n. 27
Ultima, 128
Ultima Online, 152–153
Uncle Tom's Cabin, 9
Understanding Comics, 155–156
Unemployment, 4–5, 16, 49–68
Unions. *See* Organized labor
United Auto Workers, 50
UNIVAC mainframe computer, 26, 47, 49
University of Illinois, Urbana-Champaign, 70
University of Mississippi, 211
UNIX operating system, 206
Upside, 171
Utopian sphere, 4–9, 17–19, 48, 53–57, 68–72, 100–101, 105, 120–121, 163–167, 171, 182, 184–185, 198–220, 231n. 8, 232n. 12; defined, 4–8

Vacuum tubes, 87
Vaidhyanathan, Siva, 13, 196
Valley, George, 40
Varley, John, 166
VCR, 45, 83
Veit, Stan, 100, 103
Vicic, Shannon, 226n. 54
Videogames. *See* Games

Videotape, 186
Vietnam War, 68
Village Voice, 177
Vinyl recordings, 16, 42–44, 186, 189, 193
Vinylizer synthesizer feature, 43
Virtual reality, 18, 167–168, 183–184, 213
VisiCalc spreadsheet software, 102–105, 121
Vonnegut, Kurt, 224n. 4

Waldrip-Fruin, Noah, 231n. 62
Walkman. *See* Sony Electronics, Walkman
Walt Disney Corporation, 196
Wargames, 173
Washington Post, 211
Watson, Bunny, 47–68, 75–78, 224n. 7
Watson, Tom, 224n. 7
Wearable technology, 115
Weaver, Warren, 40–41
Webster's Dictionary, 167
Weinberger, David, 214
Weiner, Norbert, 50, 138
Well, The (bulletin board system), 161
Westinghouse, 82
Whig conception of history, 26, 29, 123
Who, The, 193
Whole Earth Catalog, The, 97, 171, 174
Whole Earth Review, The. See *Whole Earth Catalog, The*
Whole-body interface, 169–170
WiFi, 100
Wilkes, Maurice V., 25
Williams, Raymond, 2–3, 27, 115, 229n. 26
Williams, Robbie, 188

Winner, Langdon, 221n. 22
Wired, 10, 18, 23, 97, 171–185, 198–199, 215, 234n. 14
Wireless communication technologies, 115, 217–220
Wolf, Mark J. P., 231n. 62
Woman of the Year, 51
Wood, Denis, 145
Woolf, Virginia, 33
Word processing, 1–2, 89, 96, 103, 121, 126
WordPerfect, 181
Work. *See* Academic labor; Deskilling; Organized labor; Scientific management; Unemployment
World building, 121–122, 131–132, 141–145, 154–157
World News Tonight, 211
World reduction, 154–157
World Trace Organization, 219
World War I, 9
World War II, 36, 39, 41, 47, 50, 181, 223n. 11
WorldCom, 110
Wozniak, Steve, 97, 102
Wright, Will, 126, 128, 130–131, 148

X-Box videogame system. *See* Microsoft, X-Box videogame system
Xerox Alto computer, 108
Xerox Palo Alto Research Center (PARC), 108

Yin-yang symbol, 45–46

Zadeh, Lofti, 45
Zenith Corporation, 105
Zimmerman, Eric, 231n. 62
Žižek, Slavoj, 221n. 19
Zohar, Dana, 45–46
Zork, 129–130, 156

About the Author

Ted Friedman teaches classes on the politics of new media and popular culture in the Department of Communications and the Moving Image Studies Program at Georgia State University. He has contributed to *Spin, Vibe, Details, Critical Studies in Media Communication, Communication Research, Bad Subjects,* and other zines, magazines, and journals. His weblog can be found at http://www.tedfriedman.com.